Cleopatra's Nose, the Twinkie Defense, & 1500 Other Verbal Shortcuts in Popular Parlance

Jerome Agel and Walter D. Glanze

**PRENTICE
H A L L
PRESS**

Prentice Hall Press
New York   London   Toronto   Sydney   Tokyo   Singapore

First Edition

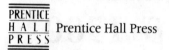

PRENTICE
H A L L Prentice Hall Press
P R E S S

Simon & Schuster, Inc.
15 Columbus Circle
New York, New York 10023

Colophons are registered trademarks
of Simon & Schuster, Inc.

Manufactured in the United States of America

1 2 3 4 5 6 7 8 9 10

Library of Congress Cataloging-in-Publication Data
Agel, Jerome.
    Cleopatra's nose, the twinkie defense & 1500 other verbal
    shortcuts in popular parlance / Jerome Agel and Walter D.
Glanze.—
    1st ed.
        p.   cm.
      ISBN 0-13-216797-2
      1. English language—Terms and phrases. I. Glanze, Walter D.
II. Title.
    PE1689.A38   1990   90-7547
      423'.1—dc20   CIP

About the Authors

JEROME AGEL is the author/producer of more than forty books, including collaborations with Marshall McLuhan, Richard B. Bernstein, Carl Sagan, Herman Kahn, Stanley Kubrick, R. Buckminster Fuller, Humphry Osmond, and Isaac Asimov. His works include *The Medium is the Massage, I Seem To Be a Verb, The Making of Kubrick's 2001, Predicting the Past, Herman Kahnsciousness, The Cosmic Connection, The U.S. Constitution for Everybody, Fasting: The Ultimate Diet, Understanding Understanding, Pearls of Wisdom, War and Peace in the Global Village*, and exclusive 200-year histories of *The Congress, The Presidency*, and *The Supreme Court* under the umbrella title *Into the Third Century*. He has coauthored with Eugene Boe two nonfiction novels, *Deliverance in Shanghai* and *22 Fires*. His new books are on geography, the 26 amendments and the 10,000 proposed amendments to the Constitution, English grammar and usage, and 100 fascinating Americans from Aaron to the Wrights.

WALTER D. GLANZE has written or edited over fifty reference works: dictionaries of science, music, law, psychology and psychiatry, geography, mass media and communications, poetry, medicine, and other fields, including *Art of Our Century* (Prentice Hall Press); reference works on the English language (dictionaries, thesauruses, crossword-puzzle dictionaries, and quotations books); and foreign-language dictionaries (French, Spanish, Italian, German, and Latin). He is also the editor of over 200 general books, from nonfiction to fiction. He has lectured widely and has chaired professional meetings on lexicography and linguistics.

Do You Know What They're Talking About?

THE ASWAN CONUNDRUM. THE NIXON IN CHINA SYN-
DROME. THE DORD EDITION. SOVIETNAM. THE ETERNAL
PREPPIE. HER DEEPNESS. THE NATIONAL RAZOR. THE
ONE-MAN PRISON. DH BURNOUT. THE EICHMANN EX-
PERIMENT. BEAUTIFUL PARRICIDE. THE ULTIMATE
HIGH. THE GANDHI SOLUTION. CLEOPATRA'S NOSE

All entries in this book are expressions that the authors have encountered in conversation and print in just the last two-and-a-half
years. All are familiar to people who use them—in the expectation
that the listeners and readers *do* KNOW WHAT THEY'RE TALK-
ING ABOUT, the way a William Buckley might use words like *vex-
illology* or *theriomorphic* or *eleemosynary* or *osculatory* or *dyslogistic*,
understood by many but perhaps not by most of his listeners or
readers, who if necessary can go to their dictionaries to expand
their verbal range. But there has been no dictionary for terms like
ANNA O and THE WOODEN O; THE BUTTERFLY BRIDGE and
THE BUTTERFLY EFFECT; WHISKEY VAN (President Van Buren)
and BRANDY NAN (Queen Anne); a SIX-HOUR RETARDED
CHILD and THREE FIFTHS OF A PERSON; THE DISHONEST
DECADE and THE DISMAL SCIENCE; THE DUMB OX, THE DOG,
and THE CROCODILE MAN; McLUHAN'S MESSAGE and A
MESSAGE TO GARCÍA, and nearly 1,500 more.

In our high-speed, fast-paced times, verbal shortcuts and shared
watchwords allow the cognoscenti rapid, intelligent, and *warm*
communication—allusions and metaphors as shared references
and signs of recognition among members of the same society, class,
or group.

"I see so many new folks nowadays who seem to have neither
past nor future," the American novelist Sarah Orne Jewett wrote.
"Conversations have got to have some root in the past, or else you

have got to explain every remark you make, and it wears a person out."

If you are looking for a particular term, consult the alphabetical index. The entries themselves are in chronological order (going back in time). This book is also meant for browsing—and to entertain.

Jerome Agel
Walter D. Glanze

The 1990s and Beyond

The Ohs. The Oughts.
The Naughts. The Zeros.
The Twenty Hundreds

All of these watchwords have been suggested as names for the first decade of the next millennium—2000–2009. The *New York Times*, for one, seems to prefer "the Ohs": "with a connotation of wonder, it would be fittingly optimistic for the start of a century." (Of course, there will be the quibble that 2000 is the last year of the old century and that the millennium does not begin till January 1, 2001, but that's not when all of humanity will celebrate.)

The Orphan Issue

In international negotiations, "the Orphan Issue" is the spread of The Bomb. Policymakers seem to be ignoring dramatically increased dangers of nuclear proliferation. In addition to the superpowers, South Africa, Pakistan, India, and Israel have nuclear capabilities. (An Israeli bombing strike took out Iraq's capability.) Among the nations with nuclear ambition is North Korea. The main and growing concern would seem to be the prospect of nuclear explosives in the hands of individuals—terrorist groups or the lone psychopath. A nuclear device can now be hidden in an attaché case; it could, for example, be left in a parked car in one of the largest cities and set off by remote control.

The 1980s

Rocky Mountain High.
The Broncs Zoo

The Denver Broncos gave a new meaning to "Rocky Mountain High" in 1987, 1988, and 1989. Players on the Mile High City's entry in the National Football League were involved in at least 17 clashes with the law. These incidents included charges of assault, kidnapping, rape, solicitation of prostitution, drug use, false imprisonment, officer impersonation, driving under the influence, speeding, alienation of affection, and driving without a license. Reporters dubbed the team "the Broncs Zoo," punning on a nickname of the raucous New York Yankees baseball team, "the Bronx Zoo." Denver coach Dan Reeves, who led the team into two straight Super Bowls, said, "Hopefully, the players will learn from their mistakes." Denver lost the Super Bowl game in 1990, 1989, and 1987.

The Last Word on Words. The OED

The revised 20-volume second edition of the *Oxford English Dictionary*, "the OED," is the repository of the Queen's English, comprising nearly 60 million words (1989). Coeditor John A. Simpson says he likes to think OED 2 is "the dictionary of record of every aspect of human emotions."

History's Most Peaceful Rebel. The Father of the Soviet H-Bomb

The physicist Andrei Dmitrievich Sakharov (1921–1989) helped the Soviet Union develop its first hydrogen bomb, in the 1950s, then became its leading dissident, the conscience of Soviet society. In midcentury, he vanished for a decade, working on the top-secret nuclear weapons project in remote Turkmenistan. In December 1979, he was stripped of his state honors and sent into internal exile in the city of Gorki, 250 miles east of Moscow, for denouncing the Kremlin's military intervention in Afghanistan. He was honored in 1975 with the Nobel Peace Prize for his human-rights campaigning. "History's most peaceful rebel," he was indefatigably and imperturbably active in struggles against oppression, censorship, and the threats to civilization from war and society's destruction of the environment.

November 9

The 44-year "cold war" between the Soviet Union and the "free world" ended on this day in 1989 with the cracking of the Berlin Wall—the cold-war symbol—and the free flow of peoples and goods between East and West Germany through Berlin for the first time in 28 years. (November 9 is also significant because it was on this day in 1923 that Hitler and storm troopers tried to overthrow Munich's republican government; 16 Nazis were killed, but Hitler emerged a national hero.) (*See also* 1938: Kristallnacht.)

The Pac Man Defense

The description "Pac Man Defense" refers to the video game Pac Man, in which small, snapping characters pursue other small, snapping characters, which suddenly turn on the hunter. When Paramount Communications made a bid to buy Time, Inc., in 1989, Wall Street traders said that if Time turned around and made a bid for Paramount, "it would be the first time in a long while that such a strategy, known as the Pac Man Defense, was raised in a takeover battle."

The Sinatra Doctrine

The Soviet Union in 1989 began employing what it called "the Sinatra Doctrine"—relaxing controls and letting its eastern European satellites "do it *their* way." Frank Sinatra's lyric "I did it my way" is well known even in the USSR.

V-A Day

The surprise announcement in 1989 that Japanese real-estate groups had purchased the controlling interest in Rockefeller Center—mid-Manhattan's most famous landmark—prompted coinage of "V-A Day" to mean, in some eyes, that the Japanese had won World War III (as "V-J Day" stands for the Allies' unconditional victory over Japan in 1945). Some New Yorkers griped that the traditional huge, ungraceful Christmas tree in Rockefeller Center would, of course, be replaced by a discreet bonsai tree. (Canada and Great Britain also have bought huge shares of the American dream.)

Pearl Mesta Bush.
The Eternal Preppie

President George Bush has been dubbed "Pearl Mesta Bush" because he's always ready to have a party or to have guests in the White House for the evening, often to Mrs. Bush's regret. (The US diplomat Pearl Mesta, 1889–1975, was known in Washington entertainment circles as the "hostess with the mostest." She was the subject of Irving Berlin's 1950 Broadway musical *Call Me Madam*.) Because the hyperactive Mr. Bush doesn't project substance, he's also been called "the Eternal Preppie."

The Yacht People

Twenty thousand well-off residents of Hong Kong, fearing the consequences of the takeover of the British crown colony by the People's Republic of China, near the end of the century, have fled to Vancouver, British Columbia. Because they have the wherewithal, buying up property and boosting rents, they have taken on the appellation "the Yacht People." (*See also* 1975: The Boat People.)

America's Troubadour

An immigrant from Russia, songsmith Irving Berlin (1888–1989) became "America's Troubadour." Many of his 3,000 tunes will be standards forever: *White Christmas, Alexander's Ragtime Band, Easter Parade, A Pretty Girl Is Like a Melody, Always, Blue Skies,* and *Oh, How I Hate to Get Up in the Morning.* There have been recently strengthened moves to have his *God Bless America* replace *The Star-Spangled Banner* as the national anthem of the United States.

Sovietnam

The Soviet Union admitted in 1989 that its 1979 invasion of Afghanistan had been a mistake and was morally wrong. More than one million Afghans were killed in the 10-year war, and another million fled before the Red Army. Moscow found itself in a quagmire there, much as the United States had in Vietnam in the preceding decade. Afghanistan, in other words, had become the Kremlin's "Sovietnam."

The First Lady of Letters

Norman Mailer called novelist-memoirist-journalist-critic Mary McCarthy (1912–1989) "the first lady of letters" and many other things: "our saint, our umpire, our lit arbiter, our broadsword, our Barrymore (Ethel), our Dame (dowager), our mistress (Head), our Joan of Arc." Ms. McCarthy, whose works include the popular books *The Groves of Academe* and *The Group,* seemed preoccupied throughout her career with two themes: what she called "the idea of justice" and the notion of self-reliance.

The Great One. No. 99

In only his 11th season, Wayne Gretzky (born 1961) became the greatest point scorer in the history of the National Hockey League. "No. 99" broke Gordie Howe's (born 1928) record of 1,850 points late in the third period of a Los Angeles Kings victory over "the Great One"'s former team, the Edmonton Oilers, in October 1989. (Howe had set the record, with 801 goals and 1,049 assists, in 26 seasons.) Gretzky's two goals in the game— one tied the score, the second won the game in overtime—gave him 642 career goals to go with his more than 1,000 assists. Edmonton had sold Gretzky to LA for $15 million in 1988. Gretzky's 10-year contract with the Kings is worth $31 million.

America's Conscience

Bird dog, maverick journalist, late-blooming Greek scholar, I. F. Stone (1907–1989) was "America's Conscience," burrowing into thick, unreadable documents to learn the truth of government action and to defend free speech everywhere in the world. "Izzy" 's suspicion of official wisdom led to scoop after scoop in his weekly newsletter, published from his garage in Washington, DC. He entered the hospital in Boston during the students' freedom campaign in China in 1989; coming out of anesthesia, he asked immediately, "What's happening in Beijing?"

The Rather Scale

The gravity of a situation can be determined on "the Rather Scale"—how CBS television-news anchor Dan Rather (born 1931) is dressed as he reports the event. For example, when he first covered the earthquake in northern California in October 1989, he was wearing a jacket. As the death toll mounted, he took off his jacket and his tie. At the scene itself, he rolled up his shirtsleeves. Viewers never saw him exiting the limo in which he had arrived at the camera position. (The *New York Times* has written, "Dan Rather's nervous, confrontational intensity is going to get us all into trouble someday.")

The Son of Heaven on the Chrysanthemum Throne. The God King. The Enlightened Peace

Showa—"the Enlightened Peace"—was the title chosen for the reign of Japanese Emperor Michinomiya Hirohito (1901–1989) when he succeeded his father in 1925. Hirohito had a tax-exempt annual salary of $1.6 million and a household staff numbering 5,000. Stunned commoners first heard his voice 19 years after he had become emperor, when he went on radio in mid-August 1945 to announce that Japan had surrendered unconditionally and that World War II was over. The God King was the first Japanese royal personage to leave the Floating Kingdom in more than 2,500 years.

Soft Society

Coined by fashion-media kingpin John Fairchild (born 1927), "Soft Society" reflects new attitudes among fashion-conscious couples. They no longer sport their jewelry and other finery when they go out at night in cities plagued with street problems. Many no longer go to big parties, instead hosting small ones in their homes.

Cultural Defense

Dong Lu Chen, a Chinese immigrant in New York, bludgeoned his unfaithful wife to death and later told the judge that he had merely expressed cultural identity. In China, Dong said, marriage is sacred, and a spouse could take appropriate action on discovering infidelity. Dong got off with five years' probation, and another quasi-legal term, "Cultural Defense," gained currency (1989).

The Van Buren Jinx

President George Bush broke "the Van Buren Jinx" in 1988 when he became the first sitting Vice President since Martin Van Buren, 152 years earlier, to be elected President. Nine Vice Presidents have become President following the death or resignation of the incumbent. Four others have won the presidency, but not immediately after serving as Vice President.

The Meal Ticket. King Carl

Southpaw Carl Hubbell (1903–1988) was one of major-league baseball's sterling pitchers for 16 years, with 253 wins, only 154 losses, and a .622 winning percentage. The New York Giants' "Meal Ticket" won a record 24 consecutive games over the 1936–37 seasons and 21 or more games five years in a row. "King Carl" led the National League in earned run average three times and earned the Most Valuable Player Award twice. In 1933 he twirled a record 46⅓ consecutive scoreless innings.

The Gray Market

"The Gray Market" is the importation into the United States of costly foreign-made goods. They can be sold by discount retailers at lower prices and over the objections of foreign companies and their authorized distributors. A Supreme Court decision (1988) upheld the most significant provisions of the 50-year-old customs-service regulation governing "the Gray Market," whose imports are profitable only when foreign businesses sell their products overseas for much less than they sell them for in the United States.

The Thin Blue Line.
The Thin Red Line

A US judge observed that only "the Thin Blue Line"—the police—stands between the citizenry and the tidal wave of encroaching barbarism (1988). The description was presaged by Sir William Howard's reference to British infantry—"the Thin Red Line"—at Balaclava in the Crimean War (1853–56). Rudyard Kipling was to write: "Then it's Tommy this, an' Tommy that, an' 'Tommy, 'ow's yer soul?' / But it's 'Thin red line of 'eroes' when the drums begin to roll."

Antarctic Donuts

Massive releases of chlorofluorocarbons from aerosol products form ozone "holes" over the South Pole. These "Antarctic Donuts" occur in the absence of sunlight, most particularly when winter darkness blankets the pole. The holes coincide with the location of polar stratospheric clouds, which also are thought to play a key role in the process by destroying the ozone.

DINKS. OTNM. WOOP. Nimby

In the 1980s' fondness for "alphabet labels," market researchers came up with the acronym "DINKS," for "double income, no kids" (about 7.4 million US households, or much of the "Yuppie" generation); the letterword "OTNM," for "over thirty, never married" (another marketing "target group"); and the acronym "WOOP," for "well-off older people" (a group singled out by "Snies": Special National Intelligence Estimates). More serious is the "Nimby" syndrome, namely, many individuals' and communities' acknowledgment of the need for finding locations for drug-rehabilitation centers, shelters for the homeless, garbage dumps, prisons, highways, and the like, as long as it's "Nimby"—"not in my backyard."

The Great Black-Dragon Fire

Fires swept the Hinggan forests of Manchuria and Siberia for a month in 1987, blackening an area about the size of New England. It destroyed about 18 million acres of timberland, including the world's largest stand of evergreens. The inferno was one of the worst environmental disasters ever. The Soviet Union has never revealed the full extent of "the Great Black-Dragon Fire."

The One-Man Prison

For a score of years, the only inmate in the West Berlin prison of Spandau was Rudolf Hess, once Hitler's loyal deputy Führer (his fellow Nazi inmates had all died). Hess had been sentenced to life behind bars by the International Tribunal at Nuremberg after World War II; he was spared the death sentence because his behavior both before and during the trial raised questions as to his sanity. The Spandau fortress on the Havel River was run at huge cost by British, Russian, French, and American authorities. The Russians didn't give an inch on releasing the octogenarian, who in 1987 finally took his own life. (*See also* 1941: The Hess Landing.)

The Last Refuge of the Insane

The British comedian Derek Nimmo (born 1932) has likened the British crown colony of Hong Kong to a psychiatrist: "It's the last refuge of the insane." The Chinese reckon it to be a three-legged stool, with one leg in London, the second in Beijing, and the third in Hong Kong itself. Britain's 99-year lease on the 399 square miles expires on June 30, 1997; the People's Republic of China will then march in.

Country 1, 2, 3, 4, 5

During the Iran-contra hearings in Washington, DC, in 1987, witnesses, lawyers, and legislators intentionally used a number of code names to confuse just about everyone, perhaps muddying the waters to escape closer scrutiny. It is believed that "Country 1" referred to Israel; "Country 2" to Saudi Arabia; "Country 3" to Taiwan; "Country 4" to China; and "Country 5" to South Korea.

Nosey Tongue

A person who ferrets out intimacies and other "good stuff" about celebrities, then gossips wildly about what he or she has learned, is known as a "nosey tongue." Such a person, for example, nosed about among friends of Truman Capote and then rushed around quoting the mighty mite about "Mr. Bidet, Mrs. Ronald Reagan's First-Lady-in-Waiting." A "nosey tongue" is also a person with a sense of rumor.

The Horizontal Telephone Booth. The Torture Chamber

Dick Rutan (born 1938) and Jeana Yeager (born 1952) became in 1986 the first to fly nonstop around the world without refueling. Their radical lightweight, nonmetal, 33-foot-long plane called *Voyager* was created from composite materials and "a lot of high-tech glue." The unpressurized cockpit—"the torture chamber" or "the horizontal telephone booth"—was seven feet long and three-and-a-half feet wide. The historic mission of 25,012 miles lasted nine days, three minutes, 44 seconds.

Glass Widows

Women who are forsaken by their alcoholic husbands are "glass widows," a description coined by the author Joyce K. Lubold (born 1924).

Water City

London's once-derelict East End docks, formerly the heart of the British Empire's mighty merchant fleet, have been transformed into an eight-square-mile "Water City." Docklands, a glass-and-metal metropolis, is the world's biggest property development and a symbol of England's yearning for economic respectability.

The Lily-White State.
The Green Mountain State

In 1986, Vermont's population of 541,000 was 99 percent white, making the Green Mountain state the most homogeneous in the Union. Only 1,135 residents were black, and only 3,304 were Hispanic. In 1989 *Forbes* magazine declared that Vermont was a "third-world state" and needed all the business help it could get.

The Father of Streamlining

The industrial designer Raymond Loewy (1893–1986) was "the Father of Streamlining." He applied to modern materials and methods of manufacture the ancient principle that form should follow function. Loewy put his streamlining hand to refrigerators, planes, trains, pens, soda bottles, and department-store interiors. His most famous design was the 1952 Studebaker automobile.

The Bitburg Blunder. The B.B.

After refusing time and again to make the obligatory visit to the site of a concentration camp on his trips to Europe, President Ronald W. Reagan, in May 1985, made a controversial visit to a cemetery in Bitburg, West Germany, whose many soldiers' graves include those of 48 SS men. His spokesperson said, "He meant no disrespect toward those who had died during the Holocaust. It was simply that if you had a choice of places to go, a concentration camp to him was too horrible even to be reminded of." Nancy Reagan said her husband decided to go to Bitburg in spite of the face-to-face, emotional, public protest in the White House by Holocaust survivor Elie Wiesel (born 1928, in Romania) because Mr. Reagan "didn't feel we could ask new generations of Germans to live with this guilt forever without any hope of redemption."

The Girl in the Black Helmet

Her face framed by her trademark pageboy bob, the movie actress Louise Brooks (1906–1985) was "the Girl in the Black Helmet"—a remarkable beauty with incendiary sensuality. She was touted as the quintessential flapper, a symbol of '20s licentiousness, the preeminent party-girl nihilist. She played Lulu in *Pandora's Box* and starred in *The Diary of a Lost Girl* for the German director G. W. Pabst, then made a half dozen films in Hollywood. Her career was over at age 33, and she lived the last three decades of her life alone in Rochester, New York, exuding, in the phrase of a movie biographer, "alleged integrity."

The Book of Life

Scientists call the 3-billion-letter genetic message that determines how human beings are made "the Book of Life." Strung along the 46 chromosomes of every human cell are about 100,000 genes, seven or eight of which can be lethal. Mapping a person's "Book of Life" will enable us to predict his or her future. To date, only a few sentences have been deciphered.

The Night Stalker

Richard Ramirez, "the Night Stalker," terrorized southern California in 1985, entering unlocked houses late at night, killing 13 people, and committing at least 30 other felonies, including rape, sodomy, and burglary. In 1989 he was sentenced to death in the state's gas chamber.

The Pitch of the 1980s

Introduced by former pitcher Roger Craig (born 1931), the current manager of the San Francisco Giants in the National League, the split-fingered fastball—"the pitch of the 1980s"—is really only a fast forkball. Because of the way it is gripped and thrown by the pitcher, the baseball sinks suddenly as it gets to the plate.

The Middle Parent.
The Sandwich Parent

An adult who cares for both his or her parent(s) and his or her own child(ren) is today popularly called "the middle parent" or "the sandwich parent."

Slasher Flicks

In "slasher flicks," such as the *Friday the 13th* series, blood and gore flow by the bucketful. A study of 474 victims in 56 such movies revealed that libidinous women and domineering men are the most likely to be slasher victims in these movies. The study director noted that "the message that the bad woman is sexual may be almost as pernicious as the message conveyed in pornography that violence can be fun for women."

Boomerang Kids

Offspring who return to their parents' homes to live—a more and more common occurrence in these days of tight, expensive housing in the United States—are known as "boomerang kids." Even some who have been "thrown out" so that they could "grow up" find themselves returning to the nest like a boomerang.

The Buckle of the Bible Belt

Nashville, the capital of Tennessee, is home to so many churches that their listings fill a dozen pages in the telephone directory. All but a few are Protestant, most of them Fundamentalist. The largest denomination is Southern Baptist, which has been described as "the religion of hellfire and damnation."

The Ultimate High

As more states opt for lethal injection as the preferred method of execution, the designation "the Ultimate High" for this perhaps euphoric kind of death gains currency beyond the language of death-row inmates, where the term seems to have originated.

The Amadeus Syndrome

Although this term was coined in the early 1980s by the German writer Wolfgang Hildesheimer (born 1916), it came into public focus with the release of the movie *Amadeus* in 1984. It refers to the apparent split between the shallowness of an individual and the profundity of his or her creation, as between the person and the music of Johannes Chrysostomus Wolfgangus Theophilus ("Amadeus") Mozart (1756–1791). (The Austrian writer Stefan Zweig suggested to Freud that he analyze Mozart's letters for their "infantilism and coprophilia.") But not all was shallowness outside Mozart's music; to his dying father he wrote that death is the "best and truest friend of mankind . . . the *key* that unlocks the door to our true happiness."

The De Facto Leader of the United States

Television in time of crisis becomes the de facto leader of the United States. Everyone, including government officials, now turns to the four networks—CNN, ABC, NBC, CBS—to find out what's going on. The medium first achieved this role when President John F. Kennedy was assassinated in Dallas in November 1963.

The Sharpeville Six

South Africa employed a prosecution for "common purpose" to convict, in 1984, six blacks, "the Sharpeville Six," for the murder of a township official in the Transvaal. An international outcry developed over the harshness of the original sentence—death by hanging—and the five men and one woman were reprieved by President P. W. Botha, who substituted long prison terms.

The DLE

The Great Salt Lake in Utah, lying between the Wasatch Range in the east and the Great Salt Lake Desert in the west, generates its own weather, called the Dreaded Lake Effect ("DLE"). In 1984 a meteorologist said, "If you compare it with earthquakes, it would be as if you had the Richter scale and the last two years were 15."

The Wheeze Kids

The Philadelphia Phillies baseball team that won the 1983 National League pennant included several relatively old players, "the Wheeze Kids." Among them were 42-year-old first baseman Pete Rose, 40-year-old infielder Joe Morgan, 38-year-old Cy Young-Award-winning pitcher Steve Carlton, and 39-year-old showboating relief pitcher Tug McGraw. But they bowed in the World Series, four games to one, to the Baltimore Orioles. Carlton was the first 300-game winner to pitch in a World Series in 55 years; he lost a 3–2 verdict. (*See also* 1950: The Whiz Kids.)

Mr. B.

George Balanchine (1904–1983), a Russian emigré, kept the dance world on its toes by choreographing classic after classic, principally for the New York City Ballet. He insisted on new rhythms for time-honored movements. Affectionately called "Mr. B." by his dancers, he once said in rehearsal, "First comes the sweat. Then comes the beauty—if you're vairy lucky and have said your prayers." Balanchine, who once noted that his muse "must come to me on union time," urged adoring balletomanes to "see the music" and "hear the dance."

The Comprehensivist of the Twentieth Century. The Comprehensivist

R. Buckminster Fuller (1895–1983), best known as the inventor of the geodesic dome, was also a mathematician, a philosopher, a cartographer of Spaceship Earth, a choreographer, a poet, and a tireless lecturer on nearly every subject. He once characterized himself in this way: "I live on Earth at present, and I don't know what I am. I know that I am not a category. I am not a thing—a noun. I seem to be a verb, an evolutionary process—an integral function of the universe."

The Zelig Syndrome

The hypothetical "Zelig syndrome" is exhibited by a protean person with the power, sometimes chameleonlike, sometimes schlemiellike, to change his personality to fit the situation: He can become a baseball player if he's in the on-deck circle at Yankee Stadium, a psychiatrist if he's near a couch, a Brownshirt if he's in Hitler's entourage, or a pilot if he's in the cockpit of a two-seater. The syndrome came to light in 1983 in Woody Allen's exclusive cinematic biography of the original Zelig.

Nuclear Winter.
The Burning-Cities Syndrome

It has been postulated by Carl Sagan (born 1934) and other prominent scientists that the fires and the overwhelming, dirty smoke caused by nuclear attacks on major cities would blot out the Sun and lead to arctic-level temperatures around the globe. Agriculture would be ruined, and mass starvation would result.

The Bradley Syndrome

The day before the California gubernatorial election in 1982, polls showed Mayor Tom Bradley (born 1917) of Los Angeles to be seven points in the lead, well on his way to becoming the nation's first black governor. He lost the election by a whisker to the white Republican candidate, George Deukmejian (born 1928). In the privacy of the voting booth, a substantial number of voters who had assured pollsters that they would be voting for the black candidate cast their ballots instead for the white aspirant. "The Bradley syndrome" was in evidence in the 1989 mayoral election in New York: According to exit-polled voters (who may not have wanted to appear to be racist when talking with the media), David Dinkins (born 1927) should have won by an immense margin. When the actual votes were counted, he barely squeezed through, to become the city's first black mayor; in fact, his victory by 47,080 votes was the smallest majority for a mayoral candidate in New York in more than eight decades. Mayor Dinkins's total of 917,544 votes was 48.3 percent of all votes cast.

Tchaikovsky's Skull

The Polish-born pianist André Tchaikovsky died in 1982 before his dream to be an actor could come true. But he upstaged many other would-be actors by willing his skull to London's Royal Shakespeare Company for use in the role of—who else?—the jester Yorick in productions of Shakespeare's *Hamlet*. Hamlet, holding Yorick's skull, says: "Alas, poor Yorick! I knew him, Horatio: a fellow of infinite jest, of most excellent fancy." Alas, poor Tchaikovsky: Real skulls are not used in *Hamlet*'s graveyard scene by the RSC because they can be easily broken by a blow or by being dropped;

only plastic reproductions get the part. But all was not for naught. Mr. Tchaikovsky's skull was the model for making the *Hamlet* poster in 1984, and it was used in rehearsals for the 1989 production.

Four Tigers. Little Dragons. NICs

"Four Tigers" refers to the rising economies of South Korea, Taiwan, Hong Kong, and Singapore. The countries themselves are called "Little Dragons" and are among a larger group of countries known as "NICs"—newly industrialized countries.

Bear

When he retired, Paul "Bear" Bryant (1913–1982) had coached footballers to 322 victories, more than any other coach in college football at the time. He had been at Maryland, Kentucky, and Texas A&M before a quarter-century stint at the University of Alabama. He died a few months after giving up his position with the Crimson Tide.

Human Resource

Isaac Asimov's calling card reads "Human Resource," which indeed he is, having composed nearly 400 books on you-name-it-he's-written-it subjects: mythology, science, history, dirty limericks, reference works, novels, science fiction. Born October 1919 or January 1920 (he's not positive), Asimov first made best-seller lists with his 262nd book, *Foundation's Edge*, published in 1982.

Boll Weevils

Renegade southern Democratic congressmen didn't cotton to some planks in their party's 1981 platform and chose to support Republican President Ronald W. Reagan's twin policies of cutting social programs and adding to the nation's defense budget. They were pejoratively labeled "Boll Weevils."

The Most Trusted Man in America. America's Uncle. Uncle Walter

The television newscaster Walter Cronkite (born 1916) gained the reputation of being "the Most Trusted Man in America" when he was the anchor of the CBS Evening News. His avuncular style gave Americans the confidence that he would never lie to them. Cronkite's was the voice that Americans wanted to hear if nuclear weapons assaulted the country—it would assure them that help was on the way. The government knew that the jig was up in Vietnam when "Uncle Walter" turned against American involvement in the war there. His nightly reminder of how long Americans had been held hostage in Teheran by Iranian Muslim radicals slimmed chances that President Jimmy Carter would win a second term in 1980 if the hostages weren't home by election day. The *New York Times* has editorialized: "The future felt safe until March 6, 1981, the night Walter Cronkite retired as anchorman of the CBS Evening News, leaving the nation floundering and leaderless." (Cronkite's mantle may have shifted to ABC's Ted Koppel in the wake of Koppel's confident live-television reportage on the night of the northern California earthquake in October 1989.)

The Toastmaster General of the United States

The premier toastmaster at banquets, "anywhere, anytime, anybody," was George Jessel (1898–1981), "the Toastmaster General of the United States." Every time he saw half a grapefruit, the comedian-yarnspinner automatically stood up and announced, "Ladies and gentlemen, we have here tonight . . ." He also did funerals. He gave the eulogy for a beloved cat of James Mason, who later said, "Jessel was quite moving. You know, I had that cat for 17 years but until the funeral I never realized how much she had done for Israel."

The Brown Bomber

From 1937 to 1949, Joe Louis (1914–1981)—"the Brown Bomber"—was the world's heavyweight boxing champion. He defended his crown successfully 25 times. In all, the son of black sharecroppers won 68 of his 71 professional bouts. Once, in the White House, President Franklin D. Roosevelt felt Louis's biceps and said admiringly, "These are the types of muscles needed to beat Germany with." In 1938 Louis dealt a KO blow to Hitler's thesis on the superiority of the Aryan race, blasting Germany's heavyweight champion and former world titlist, Max Schmeling, in the first round of their return bout.

Washington's Other Monument. Princess Alice

The 26th President, Theodore Roosevelt, once said, "I can do one of two things. I can be President of the United States, or I can control Alice. I cannot possibly do both." Alice Longworth Roosevelt (1884–1980) was his daughter, who became a popular society hostess in Washington, DC, feared for her biting wit.

Operation Blue Light. Desert One

The Carter administration's attempt at a military rescue of 52 Americans still being held hostage by Iranian Muslim extremists in Teheran in 1980 was code-named "Operation Blue Light." Unforeseen events and mechanical mishaps led to aborting the mission during a sandstorm at "Desert One" in Iran—the code word for the landing and rendezvous site for the assault force before its "invasion" of the Iranian capital. Eight US servicemen died at Desert One when their helicopters collided. Many Americans, if not most, believe it was a "suicide mission," though President Jimmy Carter still claims that with "one more helicopter" the raid (which violated the United Nations prohibition on the use of force) would have been successful—and presumably he would have been reelected.

The Hate Report

In 1980 the American author Shere Hite (born 1942) sent questionnaires to 100,000 women for a pseudoscientific study, which was eventually published under the title *Women and Love*. Because of its defective method of inquiry and the resulting distortions—reporting negative female–male sex and love relationships—this "Hite Report" (the third by the author) was soon referred to as "the Hate Report."

The 1970s

Hostage America

Iranian revolutionaries seized the US embassy in Teheran and confined 65 staff members (1979), creating a foreign-policy emergency for Washington, a political disaster for President Jimmy Carter, who was seeking a second term, and an opportunity for television to demonstrate its power. "Hostage America" ended on the 444th day of captivity, January 20, 1981, at the very moment that Mr. Carter left office and President-elect Ronald W. Reagan was sworn in. CBS television-news anchor Walter Cronkite could return to his familiar signoff, "and that's the way it is," without adding the number of days that Americans were being held against their will in Teheran.

ADA

The United States Department of Defense initiated, in 1979, a computer-programming language to end all programming languages and dubbed it "Ada," for Lady Ada Lovelace (1815–1852), Lord Byron's daughter, who had contributed to Charles Babbage's search for a mechanical calculating machine.

The Iron Lady. Attila the Hen

British Prime Minister Margaret Thatcher (born 1925), the first woman to lead a European democracy (1979), has been much admired and much despised, but she will certainly not be forgotten. Her nicknames run the gamut from "the Iron Lady" to "Attila the Hen." France's President François Mitterand remarked—gallantly?—that Mrs. Thatcher has the eyes of Caligula but the mouth of Marilyn Monroe.

Her Deepness

The marine biologist Sylvia Earle (born 1935) earned the sobriquet "Her Deepness" when she wore a diving system called a Jim suit to walk on Hawaii's ocean floor at 1,250 feet, in the deepest dive ever made without a tether to the surface (1979). Ms. Earle's dedication to the environment is particularly celebrated in the world of marine activities. She finds the world beneath the waters of the planet to be essentially a benign, and even wondrous, place.

The Suzy

The eight-sided silver coin worth one dollar and stamped with the image of the stout-hearted suffragette Susan B. Anthony (1820–1906) was naturally dubbed "the Suzy" (1979). It did not become popular, being often confused with the 25-cent piece, the quarter. The Suzies were removed from circulation in 1981 and now clutter government and Federal Reserve vaults.

The Hitler of Africa

Uganda's heavyweight boxing champion for nine years, Idi Amin Dada (born c. 1925) became president-dictator of the African country in 1971: "I am not an ambitious man; I am just a soldier with a concern for my country and its people." His eight-year reign was filled with terror and violence—he had about 300,000 Ugandans slaughtered—and with sudden and inexplicable changes and reversals in policy. "The Hitler of Africa" was ousted in 1979 by Tanzanian troops and Ugandan exiles.

The Twinkie Defense

The defense psychiatrist in former supervisor Dan White's 1979 murder trial (White had slain Mayor George R. Moscone and Supervisor Harvey Milk in San Francisco's city hall) argued that his client had overindulged in junk food, such as Twinkies, which led to bizarre, lethal behavior.

White served five years of his seven-year, eight-month sentence; 19 months after his release from prison, he committed suicide by carbon-monoxide poisoning in his garage.

The Éminence Blanche

In 1979, as the Republic of Zimbabwe was first experiencing independence, the last white prime minister, Ian D. Smith, was for a time retained as a behind-the-scenes adviser to his successor, Bishop Abel T. Muzorewa, the new nation's first black prime minister. Smith became known as "Éminence Blanche" (white eminence). The allusion is, of course, to Cardinal Richelieu's role as "Éminence Rouge" (red eminence) as a powerful adviser to the French throne, and to Richelieu's own adviser, the "Éminence Grise" (gray eminence), Father Joseph.

The Smoking Gun

Assassinologists who do not believe the government's conclusion that Lee Harvey Oswald alone gunned down President John F. Kennedy in Dallas on November 22, 1963, have never produced a "smoking gun" (conclusive evidence) leading to another killer or to a conspiracy. A source close to an official investigation, the House Select Committee on Assassinations, confessed, "There is no evidence of a meeting where the murder was planned, there is no account of the details of the plot," yet the committee declared in 1979 that a conspiracy, perhaps of organized crime, led to the murder. The term "smoking gun" gained additional currency when it was applied to the Nixon tapes in the Watergate scandal (1972–74).

Pistol-Packin' Mama

Minneapolis-born Golda Meir (1898–1978) was sometimes called "Pistol-Packin' Mama" when she was prime minister of Israel. The name was an affectionate nod to her readiness to grapple with Gamal Abdel Nasser (1918–1970), the tough-and-tumble president of Egypt, in the days before the two nations had made peace with each other.

The Jonestown Suicide

On November 18, 1978, only a few years after taking his followers from California to Guyana and building the agrarian-socialist "Jonestown" in the jungle interior, cult leader James Warren ("Jim") Jones (born 1931), "a madman with charisma" whose settlement had run afoul of the law, ordered his people to commit mass suicide: 913 of his followers, including 276 children, drank (a few were forced to drink) a grape-flavored punch laced with cyanide. "Take this potion," he said over the public-address system while his followers were drinking, "like they used to take in ancient Greece, and step over quietly because we are not committing suicide—it's a revolutionary act." Jones himself died of a bullet he put through his head, saying, "I curse the day I was born." Psychologists see this mass suicide as a classic example of "mass masochism," a term coined earlier by Theodore Reik to describe the willingness of a population to make sacrifices as demanded by a dictatorial leader to whom they have surrendered their own power.

The Fighting Marine

Joseph J. "Gene" Tunney (1897–1978) was a Marine in World War I and became known as "the Fighting Marine," as he won 82 of 83 bouts and the world's heavyweight boxing championship. His two most sensational triumphs, in 1926 and 1927, were with "the Manassa Mauler," Jack Dempsey (1895–1983). Tunney first knocked Dempsey's crown off; then, in the return match, the famous "long-count" slugfest, Dempsey didn't go immediately to a neutral corner after flooring Tunney, who thereby got extra seconds to get off the canvas, clear his brains, and catch his breath. The scholarly Tunney once lectured on Shakespeare at Yale University; *The Winter's Tale* was his favorite play.

Six-Hour Retarded Child

"Six-Hour Retarded Child" became a code term in the 1970s for a child who is judged, mistakenly, to be retarded or a slow learner because of poor performance in school (for about six hours a day) but who functions without any signs of retardation in a complex social world outside the classroom. This mistake, which often leads to lifelong programming for failure, is made by middle-class teachers and psychologists who fail to realize that the child simply may not have middle-class habits such as sitting still and following instructions.

The Dean of Hardwood Hyperbole

Sportscaster and former coach Dick Vitale (born 1939) earned the sobriquet "Dean of Hardwood Hyperbole" for his original language during televised reportage of college basketball games. A "trifecta" is a three-point shot. A "dipsy-doo-dunkeroo" is a flashy dunk. A "matador defense" is a player's mere waving of arms as the offensive player rushes by. "All-Windex" is a hoopster who's a great rebounder, cleaning the glass backboards of missed shots. Vitale, who once coached the University of Detroit quintet and, briefly, the Detroit Pistons of the National Basketball Association, was in 1989 voted Personality of the Year by the American Sportscasters Association.

The Transylvania Effect

The term "the Transylvania Effect" is sometimes applied to abnormal behavior that is related to the phases of the Moon—from Bram Stoker's wild tale, *Dracula* (1897), about Transylvanian vampires and werewolves that were affected by the different phases of Earth's only natural satellite. In *The Lunar Effect: Biological Tides and Human Emotions* (1978), American psychiatrist Arnold L. Lieber (born 1937) reports that police and fire departments are convinced of the relationship between the Moon and violence, but he adds that "Moon-driven acts of violence cannot be excused."

Mr. October

Because Reggie Jackson (born 1946) was twice voted Most Valuable Player in the World Series, he came to be known as "Mr. October." But stats indicate that he was at his pulverizing best before crowds of 10,000 to 20,000, which should have made him "Mr. Second Week in April" (the beginning of the baseball season). He was once voted Most Valuable Player in the American League and was four times its home-run leader. He also leads all major-league baseballers in strikeouts: a career total of 2,597.

Mommy Dearest

The appellation "Mommy Dearest," given to the movie actress Joan Crawford (1908–1977) in a biography by her adopted daughter, Christina, is now applied to any tyrannical mother, especially one who beats or abuses her child with a coat hanger. (Miss Crawford, once a blue-movie star— "she looked sexed to the gills," says the critic Pauline Kael—and Fred Astaire's first dancing partner in the movies, loved having admirers clutching at her coat and clamoring for autographs.)

The Brat

Tennis fans and tabloid-headline writers call American tennis ace John McEnroe (born 1959) "the Brat" because of his tempestuous, ungentlemanly on-court behavior. His mother once said, "I suppose I wanted a nice little Arthur Ashe, but we're happy with what we got." His deportment became only slightly more gentlemanly upon his marriage to the actress Tatum O'Neal. In January 1990, McEnroe became the first player in 27 years to be disqualified from a Grand Slam tournament for misconduct; his repeated boorishness led to his ouster from the Australian Open.

Jim

"Jim" looks like an astronaut's space suit but is a pressurized diving system often referred to as a Jim suit. It keeps the inside atmosphere normal while sealing out the threatening environment 1,000 feet under water.

Head and body are one piece, and the multijointed arms, or manipulators, have awesome-looking metal pincers as hands. The suit is named for Jim Jarratt, who wore extremely heavy metal diving suits a half century ago.

The Jackie Theory

Gun experts repeatedly testified before the Warren Commission investigating the assassination of President John F. Kennedy (Dallas, November 22, 1963) that they could not duplicate the alleged accuracy of the antiquated rifle used by accused killer Lee Harvey Oswald (born 1939). Bullets flew high and to the right of the aiming point. To hit the President, Oswald therefore had to aim at First Lady Jacqueline Kennedy (born 1929), who was sitting at her husband's left in the open limousine. There is no evidence that the incipient schizophrenic, lifelong-woman-hating Oswald knew that his rifle didn't shoot straight. "The Jackie Theory" holds that he was aiming intentionally at Mrs. Kennedy, because he wanted to slay *her*. During interrogations, Oswald—eager to be world-famous "for 10,000 years"—denied shooting at the President, whom he admired. On learning that shots had been fired at the presidential motorcade from her estranged husband's workplace, Marina Oswald (born 1941), who adored the First Lady, asked immediately (according to her autobiography), "Is Jackie all right?" The Jackie Theory is at the heart of the fact-based novel *22 Fires* (Bantam, 1977), by Jerome Agel and Eugene Boe.

The Skokie Dilemma

When American Nazis demonstrated in 1977 in Skokie, Illinois, a predominantly Jewish suburb of Chicago, the American Civil Liberties Union defended the demonstrators' First Amendment rights. Once again—as with the Ku Klux Klan—the ACLU defended *on principle* an organization whose tenets it abhors, with the result that many people refused to renew their ACLU membership. (ACLU membership increased dramatically after the organization was insulted by presidential candidate George W. Bush in 1988.)

The Steel Magnolia

Rosalynn Carter (born 1927), First Lady of the United States from 1977 to 1981, was a combination of the iron fist and the velvet glove. She sat in Carter Administration cabinet meetings in the White House and traveled the globe as an envoy for President Jimmy Carter. By her own account, Mrs. Carter was a tough, even a coldblooded, politician. The once-shy girl from Plains, Georgia, who became known as "the Steel Magnolia," was a determined campaigner and a ruthless strategist who had a close working relationship with her husband.

Mr. Cool. The Ice Man

Under pressure, the Swedish tennis star Bjorn Rune Borg (born 1956) had *is i magen*—ice in the stomach. He won the two-week Wimbledon Grand Slam tournament in England an unprecedented five straight years and the French Open Grand Slam six times, including four consecutive wins. It was said that "Mr. Cool" did more with the ball more often than anyone else in the game's history.

Bozo and the Pineapple

President Gerald R. Ford (born 1913) and Senator Robert Dole (born 1923) were the Republican party's presidential and vice-presidential candidates in the 1976 national election. President Lyndon B. Johnson once said of Ford, who had served as his party's leader in the House of Representatives, "He's a nice fellow, but he spent too much time playing football without a helmet." "Pineapple," of course, was an allusion to the giant fruit producer Dole.

The Great Tangshan Tragedy

The biggest earthquake in recent Chinese history occurred in the northern city of Tangshan in 1976. It killed 240,000, including many coal miners working underground. Word about the extent of the tragedy filtered out only gradually, over years.

10

A perfect score in gymnastics—the range is 0 to 10—is, of course, 10. (The first gymnast ever to be awarded 10.0 points was Nadia Comaneci of Romania, who, as a tiny 15-year-old, stole the Olympic spotlight in 1976.) "10" has come to mean any perfect situation or performance: The day's a 10, the wave's a 10, the trip's a 10.

Boat People

Since the North Vietnamese capture of Saigon in 1975, more than 100,000 Indochinese refugees who believed they were in danger of political persecution have sought havens by sailing throughout Southeast Asia and as far north as Japan. Everything that floats has been used to carry the terrified to safe shores. In December 1989, Hong Kong sent a group of 51 Vietnamese to Hanoi, the first repatriation of "Boat People" against their will. Nearly 44,000 of the Vietnamese held in camps and detention centers in Hong Kong were considered illegal immigrants.

Bo

By the age of eight, Vincent Jackson (born 1962) was "as tough as a wild boar," and he came to be called "Boar." When he got to high school, in a suburb of Birmingham, Alabama, his new friends shortened the nickname to "Bo." Today, Vincent "Bo" Jackson is simultaneously one of major-league baseball's (Kansas City Royals) and professional football's (Los Angeles Raiders) greatest stars. At Auburn, he won the Heisman Trophy in football. In the National Football League, he quickly became the first player ever to score two touchdown runs of 90 yards or more in a career.

The Living-Room War

The Vietnam War (which ended in 1975) became America's "Living-Room War" when pervasive coverage of front-line and aerial combat dominated network television's nightly newscasts in every home. Seeing firefights and defoliation raids and the futility of war firsthand turned many Americans to the antiwar movement.

The Lion of Judah.
The Black Napoleon

Supposedly the 111th descendant of King Solomon and the Queen of Sheba, Haile Selassie (1892–1975), born Tafari Makonnen, became emperor of Ethiopia in 1930 and attempted to modernize the African country. While he took great pride in the suppression of slavery, "the Black Napoleon" replaced it with his own brand of oppression. In 1935, he vainly appealed to the League of Nations for effective action against Italy's invading armies. After World War II, the "Lion of Judah" instituted social and political reforms before being stripped of powers and deposed.

Room 16

CREEP—the Committee to Re-elect the President, Richard M. Nixon—had its "plumbers" operating from Room 16 in the rococo Old Executive Office Building in Washington, DC. There is no longer a Room 16. Sealed during the Ford Administration, it was the symbol of the ultimate in media-leak plugging.

The China Syndrome Syndrome

"The China Syndrome syndrome" is a form of neurosis in which the victim is morbidly concerned about a possible catastrophic meltdown of a nuclear reactor core. The term was derived by psychologists from the folk fantasy in which the melting down of a runaway nuclear-reactor core would burn a hole all the way through the Earth, presumably to China on the other side, while producing a massive fallout of radioactive debris on the countryside.

D. H. Burnout

The designated-hitter (D.H.) rule in the American League allows a slugger to replace the (usually) weak-hitting pitcher in the baseball batting order. Because of the D.H. rule, American League pitchers have to make a larger number of high-level, high-strain pitches per game and are therefore suffering more pain and disabling arm injuries than National League moundsmen.

Clause 28

"Clause 28" is a shortened reference to a law tacked onto an English finance bill of the 1970s that would withhold funds from art created and promoted by homosexuals.

Snuff Movies

"Snuff movies" are porno flicks of the worst kind: Sexual excitement is linked intimately to torture, with the victim actually getting killed in front of a camera that records the agony in minute detail. Because a snuff movie can be made only with a person being murdered in reality ("snuffed out"), such movies are very expensive and are dangerous—and of course illegal—to buy.

YAVIS

The kind of people for whom psychoanalysis seems to work best are said to be those who are *y*oung, *a*daptable, *v*erbal, *i*ntelligent, and *s*uccessful—terms forming the acronym YAVIS.

The Rust Belt

America's smokestack industries and facilities have fallen apart, decayed, and gone out of business, particularly in the Midwest, which had generated the nation's industrial might. The transstate wipeout has taken on the description "Rust Belt."

The Cod War

Icelanders claimed that "Iceland is fish. No fish, no Iceland." And so the North Atlantic island forced—in the peaceful "Cod War"—establishment of a maritime economic zone that keeps trawlers of other nations more than 200 miles away and ensures a private and rich fishing ground.

The Flying Finn

irmi (1897–1973), "the Flying Finn," set 20 long-distance-run-
ld records and won nine Olympic gold medals, along with three
ds in team events.

The Boston Strangler. The Measuring Man. The Green Man

e was "the Measuring Man," claiming that he worked for a model
nd talking his way into the apartments of gullible women, getting
from touching them while he took their measurements. Wearing
rk pants, he was "the Green Man," who sexually assaulted about
men. Albert Henry DeSalvo (1931–1973), a semiskilled factory
d the father of two children, was being held in a Massachusetts
m-security asylum for another series of crimes when he confessed
"the Boston Strangler." Between 1962 and 1964, 13 women died
rangler's hands, most of them choked with a stocking.

The Munich Massacre

sraeli athletes were killed in events surrounding the invasion of
Olympic Village, in Munich, West Germany, by eight Palestinian
carrying machine guns and hand grenades in athletic-equipment
demanding the release of 200 Arab political prisoners held in
ve of the terrorists and one policeman were also slain. The Olym-
inued despite the massacre.

The Sunshine Boys

deville comedy team Smith and Dale was renamed Lewis and
d was brilliantly resurrected by Broadway playwright Neil Simon
27) as "the Sunshine Boys" in 1972. The vaudevillians were orig-
e Seltzer and Charlie Marks. They became Joe Smith and Charlie
en they needed business cards and the printer had extra "Smith
e" cards on hand. (The original Smith and Dale, whoever they
d decided to change their names to Moran and Mack and didn't
ith and Dale cards anymore.) The clowns became celebrated for
Kronkhite routines.

Mr. Aches and Pains

Pittsburgh Pirates outfielder and four-time National League bat-
mpion Roberto Clemente (1934–1972) was an unreconstructed
ndriac. After 18 storied seasons, "Mr. Aches and Pains" was bat-
, the highest average among active players, when he was killed in

The Sunshine Tree Girl

The singer and beauty queen Anita Jane Bryant (born 1940), once an outspoken critic of homosexuality, was "the Sunshine Tree Girl" for the Florida Citrus Commission. Florida Governor Reubin Askew quipped, "People
connect orange juice, Florida, and Anita Bryant so much that it becomes
difficult to decide which to visit, which to listen to, and which to squeeze."
President Lyndon B. Johnson said to her, "I want you to sing 'The Battle
Hymn of the Republic' when they lower me in the ground." She did.

The Russification of the US Armed Forces

With instant worldwide communications available, decisions are taken
out of the hands of military personnel on the spot and fingertip knowledge
is overridden by orders given by an individual or a committee far from the
action, usually in the capital. This is how the Soviet Union has run its wars.
Similar overcontrol by the White House is said to have been partially responsible for the failure of US operations in Vietnam and "Desert One" in
Iran. President Lyndon B. Johnson would spread maps of Vietnam on the
floor of the Oval Office, get down on his knees, peer closely, and pick the
next day's bombing targets.

The Stockholm Syndrome

"The Stockholm syndrome" is the bond that sometimes develops between
captor and captive, in particular, terrorist and hostage—as in the case of a
woman held hostage in Stockholm, Sweden. She eventually broke her en-
gagement to another man and married her former captor at the end of his
prison term. Another example of this syndrome is the case of newspaper
heiress Patty Hearst (born 1954). Kidnapped in 1974 by a revolutionary
group in California, she came to identify with its cause and participate in
its activities, including a bank heist, in which she was videotaped wielding
a machine gun.

The Goldwyn Touch

"The Goldwyn Touch"—what producer Sam Goldwyn (1879–1974)
brought to a movie—was "not brilliance or sensationalism." Instead, as
biographer Alva Johnson noted, it was "something that manifests itself
gradually in a picture; the characters are consistent; the workmanship is
honest; there are no tricks and shortcuts; the intelligence of the audience is
never insulted." Director William Wyler (1902–1981) once asked, only
half-jokingly, "Which pictures have the 'Goldwyn Touch' that I didn't direct?" Goldwyn films included *The Best Years of Our Lives* and *The Pride of
the Yankees*.

Goldwynisms

Colorful misuses of English were popularly referred to in Hollywood as "Goldwynisms," for Polish-born producer Sam Goldwyn. Many funny mistakes, mainly malapropisms, were created for Goldwyn as something like a hallmark by his press agent, Lynn Farnol, or worked up by gag writers and passed off as something Goldwyn had just said: "A verbal contract isn't worth the paper it's written on." "We've passed a lot of water since then." "I've been laid up with intentional flu." "I can answer you in two words. Im possible." Goldwyn, in a speech in 1945, remarked, "For years I have been known for saying 'Include me out.' "

The Crocodile Man

Psychiatrists have applied the term "Crocodile Man" to the forensically intriguing case of Charles Decker, whose sudden murderous assaults, in 1974, had no apparent reason and did not seem to be in keeping with his personality. The defense focused on brain chemistry, arguing that Decker suffered from a dysfunction or lesion of the limbic system in the brain that released primitive impulses that might be comparable to those of a crocodile.

The Cosmic Connection. Star-Stuff

The scientist Carl Sagan (born 1934) has observed that the great insights of modern astronomy have shown that humans are connected with the universe: "The matter out of which each of us is made is intimately tied to processes that occurred immense intervals of time and enormous distances in space away from us. All of the rocky and metallic material we stand on, the iron in our blood, the calcium in our teeth, the carbon in our genes were produced billions of years ago in the interior of a red giant star. We are made of star-stuff."

The Saturday-Night Massacre

Archibald Cox (born 1912), the special prosecutor in the Watergate scandal, argued that President Richard M. Nixon had to bow to the rule of law and turn over tape recordings secretly made in the Oval Office. Attorney General Elliot Richardson (born 1920) refused the President's order to fire Cox and resigned. Assistant Attorney General William Ruckelshaus (born 1934) also refused to fire Cox and was himself fired. The solicitor general, Robert H. Bork (born 1927), agreed to fire Cox, and he did. This "Saturday Night Massacre," in October 1973, outraged Congress and the nation; the firestorm of criticism prompted the President to reverse his course and begin to cooperate with investigators.

The House in th

The 80-ton, nine-story-tall space laboratory House in the Sky" for three different US astr of 171 days. It orbited Earth 34,981 times an sending data to Earth. In 1979 it reentered th hundreds of pieces, some weighing more tha

The Lip

The most outspoken baseball player and mar Leo "the Lip" Durocher (born 1906): "Sho sional sports and I'll show you an idiot. Sh show you a player I'm looking to trade." He "Nice guys finish last." Durocher's manage .546. He was bounced from baseball for a y Jackie Robinson's debut season with the Durocher was to manage), for associating wi

The Ice

Antarctica is called "the Ice" by its inhabitant ter and about 2,000 in summer. More people on a Saturday afternoon than have ever b nearly double the size of the United States; t dreds of feet thick, is equal in area to France. oratory for the joint United States–Soviet Uni has much in common with the fourth planet

Papillon

Henri Charrière (1906–1973) had been a safe demned in 1931 to hard labor for life for the claimed he had been framed. A butterfly tat nickname "Papillon." The popular book and story of Charrière's 14 years in penal colonies dramatic escape from Devil's Island, for good

Exhausted Volca

At the start of his second term (1973), Pres manded the resignation of top aides and offici try run by "Exhausted Volcanoes." The word metaphorical sense a century earlier by Benjar ish prime minister William Gladstone's ass Queen Victoria's prime minister himself.

Paavo
ning
more

At firs
agenc
his ki
green
1,000
hand
maxi
to bei
at the

Eleven
the 19
terror
bags a
Israel.
pics co

The v
Clark
(born
inally
Dale
and D
were,
need
their

All-sta
ting c
hypoc
ting .3

an airplane crash. Clemente was on board to take 26 tons of food and $150,000 in relief funds from Puerto Rico to earthquake victims in Managua, Nicaragua, where he had coached and played with Puerto Rican teams. In his very last time at bat in his last regular season, he had banged out his 3,000th hit.

Mrs. Winchell's Little Boy

The gossip "racketeur" Walter Winchell (1897–1972)—"Mrs. Winchell's Little Boy"—rat-a-tat-tattled his highly opinionated radio news of the week at 215 words a minute to "Mr. and Mrs. North and South America and all the ships at sea." "Other columnists may print it," Winchell boasted, "I make it public." His biggest scoop: Franklin D. Roosevelt would run for a third term. In addition to voicing his opinions, Winchell loved to coin words, including *terpsichorines, infanticipate, Renovated, phfft,* and *Ratzis.*

Hairs vs. Squares

Baseball's World Series in 1972 was given the sobriquet "Hairs vs. Squares" because of the physical appearance of the opposing teams: the Oakland Athletics, who were also referred to as the Mustache Gang for its many hirsute players, and the Cincinnati Reds, who were nearly all cleanshaven. The A's copped the Series by a hair, four games to three.

Woodstein

Carl Bernstein (born 1944) and Robert Woodward (born 1943), investigative reporters for the *Washington Post,* recognized that the June 1972 Watergate break-in at the Democratic party's headquarters in the Watergate complex in Washington, DC, was more than a "third-rate burglary attempt" (as it was described by a White House spokesperson). Their exclusive stories about the break-in and President Richard M. Nixon's resignation (August 1974) led to a Pulitzer Prize and to two best-selling books, *All the President's Men* and *The Final Days.* The duo has been thought of, and referred to publicly, as "Woodstein."

The Nixon in China Syndrome

The ability to effect change by those appearing to have the greatest stake in the status quo is saluted as "the Nixon in China Syndrome," for long-time anti-Communist Richard M. Nixon's presidential "journey for peace" to the blood-Red People's Republic of China in February 1972. At the time, the nations did not have formal diplomatic relations. In 1990, the term was applied to President F. W. de Klerk's decision to weigh integration of South African society and to the *Des Moines Register*'s series on rape revealing the victim's identity, which was reported and written by a woman and published in a newspaper edited by a woman—the most detailed account of the rape was finally considered the least offensive.

Deep Throat

To camouflage the source or sources of their inside information on the Nixon White House and its role in the break-in of Democratic party headquarters at the Watergate complex during the 1972 presidential campaign, *Washington Post* investigative reporters Bob Woodward and Carl Bernstein created the character "Deep Throat" for their book replaying the scandal, *All the President's Men*. "Deep Throat" knew all and told all—which led many to wonder whether it was President Nixon himself.

The 18½-Minute Gap

When they were turned over to investigators of the break-in of Democratic party headquarters in the Watergate complex in Washington, DC, tape recordings secretly made in the Oval Office by President Richard M. Nixon included a mysterious 18½-minute section that sound experts agreed had been erased deliberately. Mr. Nixon's secretary testified that she had erased the tape accidentally when she was transcribing it. The assumption is that the soon-famous gap was a "smoking gun"—evidence that Mr. Nixon knew more than he was revealing about the break-in, which had been masterminded by his 1972 reelection committee, known as CREEP.

Bloody Attica

In 1971, more than 1,200 inmates seized control of the maximum-security facility at Attica, near Batavia, New York. In what a state investigation described as the "bloodiest encounter between Americans since the Civil War," 29 inmates and 10 guards who were being held hostage were slain by police bullets when authorities suppressed the riot. Altogether, 43 men died. Governor Nelson A. Rockefeller (1908–1979) called the retaking of the prison "justifiable homicide."

The Lumber Company

The Pittsburgh Pirates were so awesome at the plate—their home-run and other extra-base smashes broke up wooden seats and walls around the National League—that in 1971 they came to be called "the Lumber Company." It was said that any tree in America would gladly have given its life for the glory of a day as a bat in the hands of a Pirate.

The Butterfly Effect

The possibility that large changes in the future state of a system will result from very small alterations of the present state is called "the Butterfly Effect," a term coined by Edward R. Lorenz in the wake of his 1971 paper "Can the Flaps of a Butterfly's Wings in Brazil Stir Up a Tornado in Texas?"

Doc. Dr. J

Basketballer Julius Erving (born 1950) came to his team's rescue so many times with last-shot winning hoops that he earned the sobriquets "Dr. J." and "Doc." His game-saving surgical strikes—half-court heaves and ballet flights to the basket—made the articulate college (University of Massachusetts) and professional (New York Nets and Philadelphia 76ers) sensation an enormously popular player, with both fans and other hoopsters.

The Pentagon Papers

More than 45,000 Americans had already been killed in the civil war in Vietnam when Defense Secretary Robert S. McNamara commissioned a top-secret study of the US role there. When the 47 volumes, "the Pentagon Papers," were leaked to the press (1971), the Supreme Court, by a 6–3 decision, ruled that newspapers could indeed publish articles on the history of the conflict. Neil Sheehan (born 1936), who coordinated publication of the history for the *New York Times* (and later wrote the Pulitzer Prize–winning book *A Bright Shining Lie: John Paul Vann and America in Vietnam* (1988), concluded that "the history as a whole demonstrates that . . . four [presidential] administrations progressively developed a sense of commitment to a non-Communist Vietnam, a readiness to fight the North to protect the South, and an ultimate frustration with this effort—to a much greater extent than their public statements acknowledged at the time."

Dollar Bill

Because he was parsimonious, basketball star (and, later, New Jersey senator) Bill Bradley (born 1943) was known as "Dollar Bill" to his teammates. The college (Princeton) All-American and Rhodes scholar played with the gold-medal US Olympic quintet in 1964 and with two championship New York Knickerbocker teams (1970, 1973) in the National Basketball Association. His principal goal as a senator is to restore integrity to the tax system "and, by so doing, to begin restoring confidence in government." His Princeton coach once noted, "I think Bradley's happiest whenever he can deny himself pleasure."

The Aswan Conundrum

The Aswan High Dam at the First Cataract of the Nile, completed in 1970, forms Lake Nasser, one of the world's largest artificial lakes. The dam backs up so much water—204 billion cubic yards—that if it were breached, just about every Egyptian (over 40 million people) would be drowned. The dam may be the true reason Egypt made a peace treaty with Israel, which now no longer has to worry about a second front in the south (and Egypt need no longer worry about an Israeli air strike against the dam).

The Great Uncompromiser

General Charles de Gaulle (1890–1970) was driven by one idea: France cannot be France without greatness. This led to his reputation as "the Great Uncompromiser." He was Joan of Arc one day, Georges Clemenceau the next. Winston Churchill bestowed grudging admiration: "A great man? Why, he's selfish, he's arrogant, he thinks he's the center of the universe. . . . He . . . Yes, you're right, he's a great man!" De Gaulle was the first president (1959–1969) of the Fifth Republic. No one was surprised to learn that when de Gaulle died of a heart attack he was playing solitaire.

The Huston Plan

With President Richard M. Nixon's approval, his aide Tom Charles Huston (born 1941) established the Interagency Group on Domestic Intelligence and Internal Security to conduct electronic monitoring, break-ins, and mail intercepts of foreign diplomats and suspected domestic radicals. The chief executive canceled "the Huston Plan" when the director of the Federal Bureau of Investigation, J. Edgar Hoover, objected strongly to the competition.

The 1960s

Nattering Nabobs of Negativism

Newsmen who are deemed negative, hostile to one's goals, are "nattering nabobs of negativism," per the coinage of William Safire (born 1929), first used in a 1969 speech by Vice President Spiro Agnew (born 1918). Safire also said (via Agnew) that opponents of the war in Vietnam were encouraged by "an effete corps of impudent snobs." And he used the phrase "hopeless, hysterical hypochondriacs of history," which Safire, again the author, saw as a nice updating of Adlai Stevenson's blast at pessimists as prophets of gloom and doom.

The Miracle Mets

The New York Mets baseball team won the World Series in 1969, only seven years after they had made their National League debut with a record of only 40 wins against 120 losses under managerial "genius" Casey Stengel (1891–1975) and after four years in tenth place. (The league champion in 1962, the San Francisco Giants, won 63 more games than the Mets did.) In 1969 the Mets won 109 of their 162 regular-season games, with pitcher Tom Seaver the stellar stalwart. (They were the first National League entry in New York since the Giants and the Dodgers had picked up stakes and moved to sunny California at the end of the 1957 season.)

The Spitter

Gaylord Jackson Perry (born 1938), the six-foot four-inch righthanded pitcher, was often accused of throwing a spitball—an illegal pitch because it does "funny" and "unnatural" things on its way to the plate. The strike-out artist (he notched 3,534 Ks) was also the subject of the most accurate prediction in the history of major-league baseball: Alvin Dark, manager of the San Francisco Giants, said a man would walk on the Moon before his light-hitting pitcher would ever hit a home run—neither expected either event to occur. Perry slammed the first homer of his eight-year career 34 minutes after Neil Armstrong took that historic giant step for mankind, on July 20, 1969. "The Spitter" then hit a homer in each of the next three seasons and surely was willing to be called "the Babe."

Enemies List

A first step in the Nixon administration's plan to "use the available federal machinery to screw our political enemies" was to draw up an "Enemies List" of businessmen, academics, leftists, show-biz personalities, politicians, and media personalities who were out to "get" the White House. The "Enemies List" included notes on the personal lives of the chosen "enemies" as well as official data; CBS newsman Daniel Schorr (born 1916) was described as "a real media enemy," and a black congressman was noted to have a "weakness for white females."

Juice

O. J. Simpson (born 1947) had rickets as a kid and wore braces. In 1973 he set the National Football League record as a ball carrier: He gained 2,002 yards on 332 carries. In 1975 he scored a league-record 23 touchdowns. He played for the Buffalo Bills and the San Francisco 49ers, always knowing when to turn on the juice, the backburners. His nickname, "Juice," comes from his love of orange juice and from his initials, O. J., which simply stand for Orenthal James.

The Greatest Week in the History of the World Since Creation

This was President Richard M. Nixon's (much-mocked) description of the first human landing on the Moon, "the noblest expression to date of the marriage of science and machine," in Norman Mailer's phrasing.

Tranquillity Base

The first humans on the Moon touched down in the dusty Sea of Tranquillity on July 20, 1969. Astronauts Neil A. Armstrong (born 1930), the civilian commander, and Colonel Edwin "Buzz" Aldrin, Jr. (born 1930), of the Air Force, found the surface at "Tranquillity Base" to be fine and powdery. Their first message back to Spaceship Earth was: "Houston, Tranquillity Base here. The Eagle has landed." Armstrong's spontaneous, historic words on first stepping on the Moon: "That's one small step for a man, one giant leap for mankind." After hopping around and collecting rocks, the astronauts blasted back to the command ship, *Apollo 11*, piloted by Michael Collins (born 1930), for the return flight home. (Twelve men, all Americans, have walked on the Moon, but no one has set foot there since 1972.)

The Brockton Bomber

When heavyweight boxing champion Rocky Marciano, born Rocco Francis Marchegiano (1923–1969), of Brockton, Massachusetts, hung up his gloves, he had roughed up 49 other boxers, winning every match. Forty-three of the triumphs were by knockout, 26 of them in three rounds or less. ("The Brockton Bomber" was killed in an airplane crash.)

Broadway Joe

"Broadway Joe," Joe Namath (born 1943), was never among professional football's passing leaders, but he had a flair, a savoir-faire, even sex appeal, that helped to make the sport more popular. He quarterbacked the New York Jets, of the American Football League, to a 16–7 upset victory over the heavily favored Baltimore Colts, of the National Football League, in the first official Super Bowl, in 1969. (His last pass was caught in late 1984 by Deborah Lynn Mays, age 22, who made the ultimate score: She married Broadway Joe.)

Ike. The Kansas Cyclone

Because he was born in Abilene and tore down the football field like a tornado, sweeping everything out of his path, West Point's Dwight D. Eisenhower (1890–1969) was known as "the Kansas Cyclone." Everyone, even newspaper-headline writers, called him "Ike." The five-star general was supreme Allied commander of the three-million-man force that invaded Hitler's Europe in 1944, and he became the 34th President of the United States in 1953. In his farewell address, he declared, "Every gun that is made, every warship launched, every rocket fired signifies in a final sense a theft from those who hunger and are not fed, those who are cold and not clothed." Supreme Court Associate Justice William O. Douglas described Ike as being "as American as apple pie."

Little Mo

Maureen Connolly (1934–1969)—"Little Mo"—was a one-woman tennis dynasty. In her teens she won the US tennis singles championship three consecutive times (1951–53), and she also won Wimbledon three consecutive times (1952–54). In the calendar year 1953, she won the Grand Slam—the four major tennis titles: the French Open, Wimbledon, the US Open, and the Australian Open. She was forced to quit tennis in 1955 after breaking a leg in a horseback-riding accident.

The Silent Majority

In his "us" against "them" speech on the Vietnam War, on November 3, 1969, President Richard M. Nixon asked for the support of "the great silent majority of my fellow Americans" to help "end the war in a way that we could win the peace . . . the more divided we are at home, the less likely the enemy is to negotiate at Paris." The term "Silent Majority" became a political buzzword for those supporting US foreign policy and was in use for at least half a decade.

The Secret War. The Sideshow

The United States' "Secret War" against Cambodia in 1969—a secret to the American taxpayer, well known to those being bombed—destroyed the Southeast Asian neutral country. It was regarded by Richard M. Nixon's White House and Henry Kissinger's State Department as "something of a sideshow" to the frustrating Vietnam War. This exercise of illegal force was unparalleled in American history.

The Evil Triad

During the Vietnam War, South Vietnam was infested with crime, drugs, and corruption. The last was the major element in "the Evil Triad" paralyzing the US war machine there.

The Rankin Brigade

At nearly 90 years of age, former Congresswoman Jeannette Rankin was still fighting for peace. The ardent Montana feminist and pacifist (1880–1973), the first woman member of the House of Representatives, was the only congressperson to vote against the entry of the United States into both world wars. In 1968 she led "the Rankin Brigade" of 5,000 women in a march on Capitol Hill, in Washington, DC, to protest the nation's involvement in the Vietnam War.

The Heidi Game

At 7 PM, EST, on November 7, 1968, the New York Jets were leading the Oakland Raiders, 32 to 29, in a National Football League game, with one minute, five seconds to go in the final period. NBC abruptly terminated its television coverage so that it could air the film *Heidi*, as previously scheduled. In the last 65 seconds of the game, the Raiders scored two touchdowns and won "the Heidi Game," 43 to 32.

Supertanker

When she was married in 1968 to shipping magnate Aristotle Onassis, Jacqueline Lee Bouvier Kennedy Onassis (born 1929) became known around Onassis's New York headquarters as "Supertanker," for her profligate spending practices and the amount it took to keep her in ballast.

The My Lai Massacre

When no enemy soldiers were found in the South Vietnamese hamlet of My Lai (1968), US Army First Lieutenant William Calley (born 1943) ordered his infantry platoon to round up the residents: men, women, and children. Calley began to shoot them, and he ordered his men to shoot them, too. The massacre of roughly 500 Vietnamese went on for several hours. In 1971 Calley was found guilty by court-martial of murdering 22 unarmed civilians and was sentenced to hard labor for life. Eleven other soldiers were acquitted, or the charges against them were dismissed. Calley was pardoned in 1975.

Cancer Ward

The *Cancer Ward* (1968), by Aleksandr Solzhenitsyn, provided a persuasive metaphor for life in the Soviet Union and led to his being seen as a dangerous and hostile critic of the regime and to his eventual expulsion. (*See also* 1946: Animal Farm.)

The King Revolts

Ghetto revolts erupted in 125 cities in 28 states around the United States in the wake of the murder of the Reverend Martin Luther King, Jr. (1929–1968). The nation's capital experienced the worst riots in its history; troops guarded the White House. In all, 46 persons, most of them blacks, died, 2,600 were injured, 21,270 were arrested, and there was an estimated $45 million of property damage.

HAL 9000

Stanley Kubrick (born 1928) and Arthur C. Clarke (born 1917) insist that it was merely a coincidence that the initials of the neurotic-fascistic computer, HAL, which controlled the spaceship *Discovery* in their 1968 motion picture *2001: A Space Odyssey*, were alphabetically one letter to the left of IBM. (HAL's original name was "Athena.")

The Pueblo Incident

The USS *Pueblo* was labeled an "environmental research ship" by the Pentagon, but it was armed with secret electronic gadgets so that the United States could spy on North Korean electronic devices. In 1968 it was seized by North Korea within its 12-mile limit in the Sea of Japan, and the two countries almost went to war. Eleven months later, Commander Lloyd M. Bucher (born 1927) and his 82-man crew were released by the North Koreans in exchange for an official American confession of espionage, an apology, and a promise that it would not happen again.

McLuhan's Message

Echoing the philosopher A. N. Whitehead's view that "the major advances in civilization are processes that all but wreck the societies in which they occur," the Canadian media observer Marshall McLuhan (1911–1980) said that the medium, or process, of our time—electric technology—is reshaping and restructuring patterns of social interdependence and every aspect of personal life. It was "McLuhan's Message," first stated in 1967, that electric technology is forcing everyone to reconsider and reevaluate practically every thought, action, and institution formerly taken for granted. "The medium is the message."

The Like Factor

Coined in 1967 by political media consultant Roger Eugene Ailes (born 1940), "the Like Factor" is the "magic bullet, because if your audience likes you they'll forgive you just about everything else you do wrong. If they don't like you, you can hit every rule right on target and it doesn't matter." Ailes also introduced the *Dislike* Factor when he created the

Willie Horton campaign for Republican presidential candidate George Bush in 1988.

Der Alte

"Der Alte" (literally "the old one," pronounced "dare ählta") was the affectionate name given to Konrad Adenauer (1876–1967). As the first chancellor (1949–65) of the German Federal Republic, he was probably the main factor in Germany's extraordinary economic and political recovery after World War II. Formerly mayor of Cologne, he was imprisoned several times by the Nazis.

The Worst Riot of the Century

Police raids set off rioting and looting in Detroit in 1967, and for the first time in 24 years US troopers were used to quell civil strife. Forty-three people were killed, 324 were injured, 7,200 were arrested, and 5,000 lost their homes in 1,500 separate fires. At one point, 15,000 armed men policed the black ghetto.

The Most Awesome Runner in History

Even the usually neutral Pro Football Hall of Fame hails Jim Brown (born 1936) as "the Most Awesome Runner in History." The Jim-dandy Cleveland Brown, an All-American at Syracuse University in 1956 (in one game, he scored 43 points), led the National Football League in rushing eight of his nine years, was all-NFL eight years, was named player of the year twice, and was also rookie of the year. Brown carried career marks of 12,312 yards rushing, 262 pass receptions, 15,459 combined net yards, and 756 points scored.

The Sick Comedian

Before a nightclub act or television personality could get away with using four-letter words, Lenny Bruce (1926–1966), "the Sick Comedian," was repeatedly busted for obscenity. Bruce has been regarded by many as a social satirist in the tradition of Swift, Rabelais, and Twain. He always claimed that he had "picked on the wrong god. If I had picked on the god whose replica is in the whoopee-cushion store . . . the Tiki god, the Hawaiian god, those idiots . . . but I picked on the Western god, the cute god, the IN-god, the Kennedy-god—and that's where I screwed up."

The First Lady of Contraception

Margaret Higgins Sanger (1883–1966), a birth-control movement pioneer, a trained maternity nurse, and the 10th child in a family of 11, was sentenced to a month in a workhouse for opening a birth-control clinic in Brooklyn, New York, in 1916. She was also arrested for sending birth-control information through the mail. She vowed that the "curse of Eve" must be lifted.

The Big Game

After both the 1966 and the 1967 seasons, there was a championship game between the best team in the National Football League and the best team in the American Football League—"the Big Game." Coach Vince Lombardi's Green Bay Packers of the NFL won both Big Games. The two leagues then merged, and the Super Bowl was established. In the first Super Bowl, quarterback "Broadway Joe" Namath led his American Football Conference New York Jets to an upset triumph over the Baltimore Colts of the National Football Conference.

The Third World

The Indian statesman Jawaharlal Nehru (1889–1964) is credited with coining the term "Third World," in 1965, to distinguish technologically less advanced nations of Asia, Africa, and Latin America from the technologically advanced nations influenced by the United States and by the Soviet Union. His daughter Indira Gandhi (1917–1984) became the nation's first woman prime minister; she ruled over 750 million Indians for 15 years until assassinated in 1984 by two Sikh members of her personal bodyguard. The murder was apparently motivated by religious hatred.

The Eighth Wonder of the World

When it was opened in 1965, the Houston Astrodome was the world's largest air-conditioned room—an 18-story building could fit inside it. It has the world's largest dugouts for baseball because everyone likes to say that he sat behind the dugout at a game. If the Astrodome is "the Eighth Wonder of the World," the rent is said to be the ninth.

The Watts Uprising

More than 12,000 National Guardsmen helped to end six days of anarchy, rioting, and interracial looting in the black ghetto of Watts, in Los Angeles, in the summer of 1965. Thirty-five persons (28 of them black) were killed, about 1,000 were injured, and at least 3,500 were arrested. Whole city blocks were destroyed.

The National Night Light.
The King of the Night

Johnny Carson (born 1925) has been called many things in the more than a quarter-century he's been the host of NBC television's late-night *Tonight* show, but affectionately he's been described as America's "National Night Light," the most important birth-control device since the invention of the headache. His jokes serve as an index of potential trouble for politicians. George Bush's rise to the presidency was probably aided by the fact that Carson wasn't on the air much during the election campaign of 1988. Carson may have destroyed Al Haig's candidacy for the Republican nomination with one monologue.

The Malta of the East

The island nation of Singapore is known as "the Malta of the East." Britain controlled the crown colony (about 60 islands) from 1824 until it was captured by a Japanese bicycle corps striking from the rear in 1942. The defending cannon were frozen in place, pointing out to sea. "The Malta of the East" has been an independent nation since 1965. The population is of extreme density: There are about 10,000 people per square mile.

Auto-Eichmannism.
America's Toughest Customer

When he published the best-selling book *Unsafe at Any Speed* (1965), consumer advocate Ralph Nader—"America's toughest customer"—told an interviewer that he had had an impossible time learning who makes the decisions in the design of automobiles; at least one had turned out to be lethal. Just about every executive in Detroit told him, "I merely follow orders," and passed the buck. Nader (born 1934) described the process as "Auto-Eichmannism."

The Cosmo Girl

The longtime editor-in-chief of *Cosmopolitan* (since 1965), Helen Gurley Brown (born 1922), pitches the monthly magazine at unmarried working women. One of her memorable tips to women on the make: Put perfume on the light bulbs around the house. Mrs. Brown has said that she really didn't "know how ladies raised in . . most provincial cities can wind up with any interest in sex. People do their very best to disinterest you."

The Great Society

President Lyndon B. Johnson (1908–1973) wanted to create for the United States the full enrichment of life, "the Great Society" (1964). His introduction of Medicare was the first step toward the goal. This, according to biographer Robert A. Caro, is the same politician whose path to power and means of ascent were marked by "utter ruthlessness . . . and a seemingly bottomless capacity for deceit, deception, and betrayal."

The Warren Report

At first, Chief Justice Earl Warren (1891–1974) did not want to preside over the commission investigating the assassination of President John F. Kennedy (November 22, 1963). He believed that the chief justice had a responsibility to the nation and to the Court that could not be put aside. But he gave in to President Lyndon B. Johnson, finally agreeing that the crisis was so special and the need to reassure the nation so great that he had to put aside his other obligations. The Warren Commission, after working for nearly a year, declared in 1964 that President Kennedy had been shot to death, for reasons unknown, by the *lumpen* Lee Harvey Oswald (born 1939) with his antiquated, misaligned rifle and that Oswald's murder was a bizarre crime by another loner. (A web of theories, including conspiracies, still surrounds Kennedy's murder.)

22 Fires

The Russian idiom "22 fires" was used by Marina Oswald, a key witness in 1964 before the Warren Commission investigating the assassination of President John F. Kennedy, to describe her mental state toward her overwrought, obsessive estranged husband, Lee Harvey Oswald, on the eve of Oswald's murder of JFK. She said she had felt volcanic fury, out-of-control anger, "22 fires," toward him. It has been suggested that the despondent Oswald himself was probably suffering "22 fires" that day—having just been kicked out of Marina's life—and must have seen in his deranged vision the chance to, at one stroke, avenge both his personal and the collective suffering of malekind and give the world proof of his own manhood. According to this theory, bullets aimed at First Lady Jacqueline Kennedy, Marina Oswald's idol, flew from Oswald's misaligned rifle inexorably to the right and struck down JFK by mistake. (*See also* 1977: The Jackie Theory.)

Blue Glow

An incident in which the victim knows that he or she will die is called a "blue glow," so named for the moment in 1964, at the secret laboratory near the main compound of the Los Alamos Scientific Laboratory in New Mexico, when a blue glow shrouded the room for an instant, then was gone. The glow was a lethal dose of radiation from the core of the plutonium bomb being tested. Several scientists were injured, and one died a week later. They had been part of the team that designed the atomic bombs that obliterated two Japanese cities in 1945.

The Four-Bar Coincidence

In 1948, songwriter Mack David (born 1912) composed a popular tune called "Sunflower." In 1964, songwriter Jerry Herman (born 1933) composed the title tune for his Broadway show *Hello, Dolly!* When David heard in *Dolly* four bars that he had written for "Sunflower," he sued Herman for copyright infringement. The out-of-court settlement was said to have been to the tune of a quarter of a million dollars.

Freedom Summer

During the civil-rights movement in Mississippi in 1964, later referred to as "Freedom Summer," three young men (two white New Yorkers, Michael Schwerner and Andrew Goodman, and a local black man, James Chaney) protesting racial discrimination vanished after being arrested and jailed on a traffic violation. Their bodies were found in an earthen dam six weeks later. No one was tried for murder, but eight men were convicted on federal charges of denying the three their civil rights, and each served a brief prison term.

The Birdman of Alcatraz

Robert Stroud (1890–1963) was a two-time murderer who became an authority on the care and breeding of canaries and other caged birds during his 54 years caged behind prison bars. He was in solitary confinement for 42 years. Parole boards found the ornithologist antisocial, uncooperative, a hard case. Rescuing baby sparrows in the prison yard nurtured his life's interest, and he was allowed to have scientific equipment in his cell. After "the Birdman" was transferred to Alcatraz (which in Spanish means "pelican"), in San Francisco Bay, he became fluent in French, Spanish, and Greek, and he wrote a book on American prisons.

The Eichmann Experiment

In Stanley Milgram's (1933–1984) psychological experiment, known as "the Eichmann Experiment," at Yale University, subjects were tricked into believing that they were participating in a study of the effect of punishment on learning and memory. In fact, what was being charted was their own capacity for cruelty under the pressure of authority. The subjects were ordered to apply an increasingly painful electric shock to a person giving wrong answers to test questions. Most of the subjects docilely continued to give shock after shock to the "victim," who was a trained actor. "The Eichmann Experiment" was named for the Gestapo's Jewish-section chief, Adolf Eichmann (1906–1962), who claimed he was only following orders in the extermination of millions.

The Galloping Ghost

All-American football sensation Harold Edward "Red" Grange (born 1903)—"the Galloping Ghost"—ran for glory for three years at the University of Illinois, then helped to put the National Football League on the map with his running and passing exploits with the Chicago Bears and the New York (football) Yankees. In a game against the University of Michigan in 1924, he ran for touchdowns the first four times he handled the ball and later scored a fifth TD and passed for a sixth. He was inducted into the College Football Hall of Fame in 1951 and was a charter enshrinee, in 1963, of the Pro Football Hall of Fame.

The Grassy Knoll

Some assassinologists believe to this day that President John F. Kennedy was fatally wounded by a gunman on "the grassy knoll" in Dealey Plaza, in Dallas. They claim that Abraham Zapruder's film, showing the President's head jerking backward, "proves" that he must have been shot from the front, from "the grassy knoll"—now a buzzword—instead of from the back by the accused Lee Harvey Oswald, as limned by the Warren Commission, which investigated the murder in 1964. Scientific evidence, which included pumping bullets into the back of 100 goats' heads, demonstrates that a head hit from behind *always* jerks backward, not forward.

The Zapruder Film

Dallas businessman Abraham Zapruder (1914–1970) was filming President John F. Kennedy's motorcade rolling through Dealey Plaza. He *alone* recorded the assassination, November 22, 1963, from the first 6.5mm bullet from Lee Harvey Oswald's rifle, nicking and traumatizing the President's spine and piercing his throat, to Jacqueline Kennedy's scramble across the trunk of the open convertible limousine to reach out and pull aboard an onrushing Secret Service agent. Zapruder sold the film to *Life* magazine, which sold the rights back to the Zapruder estate. The film has been scrutinized frame by frame by assassinologists to try to prove that the accused lone assassin couldn't have been the killer.

The Non-U-2 Mystery

Overflights of Cuba by American U-2 spy planes were continuing in late 1963, though President John F. Kennedy announced they'd been stopped in the wake of the Cuban missile crisis. On the morning of November 22, 1963, a U-2 fell into—or was shot down over—the Gulf of Mexico. There wasn't a ripple in the news about it. Later that day, President Kennedy was shot to death in Dallas; some assassinologists believe that the killer was in the hire of Cuban leader Fidel Castro, but the murder has never been linked with the renewed U-2 activity.

Charlie Hustle

Pete Rose (born 1941) has gotten more hits than any other major-league baseballer (4,256), he's hit in more consecutive games than any other National Leaguer (44), and he's the only player to play at least 500 games at each of five different positions: first base, second base, third base, left field, and right field. "Charlie Hustle" was banished from baseball in 1989 for gambling activities while he was manager of the Cincinnati Reds.

The Birmingham School Bombing

In 1963, the 21st unsolved bomb explosion in eight years killed four black girls (ages 11 to 14) and injured many other black children during a Baptist Church Bible class in Birmingham, Alabama. For half a decade, thousands of demonstrators carried signs with the four girls' names—or chanted their names—along with the names of other civil-rights martyrs. The four are Addie Collins, Denise McNair, Carol Robertson, and Cynthia Wesley.

The Other America

Thanks to a seminal study by the radical socialist Michael Harrington (1928–1989), the Kennedy administration (1961–63) discovered "the Other America"—its poverty-stricken citizens.

Honorary American

Only two foreigners have been voted honorary US citizenship by Congress: In 1963, British Prime Minister Winston Churchill (1874–1965), often celebrated as "the Man of the Century," and, in 1981, Raoul Wallenberg (1912–?), a Swedish banker who had served—at the behest of the US War Refugee Board and the World Jewish Congress—with the neutral Swedish delegation in Nazi-occupied Budapest, where he helped to save the lives of more than 100,000 Jews in the last year of World War II. He was taken into "protective custody" by liberating Russian troops in 1945, and the people of the West have not heard from him since.

The Black Pearl

Pelé, né Edson Arantes do Nascimento (born 1940) is celebrated as "the Black Pearl," soccer's all-time greatest player (1,281 goals) and once the world's highest-paid athlete. His outstanding ball control and tactical ability led Brazil to three World Cups.

The Cuban Missile Crisis

An American U-2 spy plane on routine reconnaissance over Cuba in 1962 discovered the construction of Russian missile bases capable of launching nuclear warheads. President John F. Kennedy ordered a naval quarantine to block the entry of additional offensive weapons, and the United States worked through the United Nations to get the bases dismantled. After 13 days, the cold-war confrontation ended as suddenly as it had begun.

The Big Dipper. The Stilt.
Wilt the Stilt

Seven-foot-one Wilton Norman ("Wilt") Chamberlain (born 1936) was the National Basketball Association's scoring champion for seven consecutive seasons. He made a 14-year career total of 31,419 points, including 100 in one game (in 1962), 78 in another game, and at least 50 in each of 118 other games. He played almost every minute of 1,045 games, which meant he ran up and down the 90-foot-long court for 797 hours. And he never fouled out of a game—another astonishing feat.

The Great White Mother.
The First Lady of the World

One hundred history professors voted Eleanor Roosevelt Roosevelt (1884–1962) the United States' most distinguished First Lady (1933–45). Her husband's successor as President, Harry S. Truman, was the first to call her "the First Lady of the World." In 1949, four years after FDR had died— he was elected chief executive a record-setting four times—Mrs. Roosevelt confessed that she selfishly would have preferred that he had not been President; she never mentioned those feelings to him. "The Great White Mother," as she was affectionately called, had enormous influence as First Lady and was always at the center of controversy because of her incessant support for human and civil rights. She represented the United States in the United Nations.

Our Antilles Heel

A sore spot with the United States has been its relationship with Cuba, popularly known as the Pearl of the Antilles. President Thomas Jefferson could have purchased the West Indies island for $3 million, but the United States didn't have the money after the Louisiana Purchase (1803). President Franklin Pierce (1804–1869) tried to persuade nearly-bankrupt Spain to sell Cuba to the United States. (It would have come into the Union as a slave state, and abolitionists were outraged.) The United States had troops in Cuba in 1898, it sponsored the "Bay of Pigs" invasion by Cuban exiles in 1961, and was embroiled in the Cuban missile crisis of 1962. Cuba—"Our Antilles Heel."

Vast Wasteland

Surely recalling that T. S. Eliot (1888–1965) had written in "The Wasteland," "I will show you fear in a handful of dust," Newton N. Minow (born 1926), the head of the Federal Communications Commission in the Kennedy administration, lambasted television as "a vast wasteland" (1962).

Broadway's Favorite Son. The King

Frank Fay (1894–1961) was the most popular master of ceremonies in vaudeville history, "Broadway's Favorite Son." One year he hosted shows at the famed Palace Theatre in New York for an unprecedented 26 weeks. An egomaniac and an alcoholic, "the Great Fay" was a skilled ad-libber. Heckled by Milton Berle, Fay retorted, "I never fight an unarmed man." He was also quick with his fists. He made headlines when he knocked out his wife, Barbara Stanwyck (1907–1990), with one punch.

Kennedy's Children

Volunteers in the Peace Corps (1961) have been called "Kennedy's Children." The Corps became in time, at least in the developing nations, the most stirring symbol of President John F. Kennedy's hope and promise. It worked to improve food production, health, education, and other basic needs. Liberals demeaned the Peace Corps as a gimmick; conservatives dismissed it as a nonsensical haven for beatniks and visionaries; Communist nations denounced it as an espionage front. (President Jimmy Carter's mother served as a Peace Corps volunteer in India.)

The Georgia Peach

Ty (Tyrus Raymond) Cobb (1886–1961), born in Narrows, Georgia, received the most votes in the very first balloting for the National Baseball Hall of Fame (1936), though he had once been banned from the national pastime for alleged misconduct. "The Georgia Peach" amassed many records in 24 seasons in the American League. He banged out 4,191 hits and was league batting-average champion 12 times. His career batting average of .367 is still the best ever—he hit .357 at age 40—and his hit total is second only to Pete Rose's 4,256. Cobb was also a terror on the base paths, stealing 892 bases with his spikes flying high.

The Bay of Pigs

Conceived by the Eisenhower administration and launched without air support shortly after John F. Kennedy became President, in 1961, the ill-starred invasion of Cuba by 1,500 CIA-trained exiles was aborted at Bahía de Cochinos, "the Bay of Pigs." Twenty months later, in December 1962, Cuban President Fidel Castro released 1,113 captured rebels in exchange for $53 million in food and medicine raised by private donations in the United States.

Catch-22. Catch-18

Novelist Joseph Heller's (born 1923) gift to the vernacular—"Catch-22"—describes the self-contradictory, endlessly circular, even insane snag that modern bureaucracy effortlessly produces. In Heller's book, titled *Catch-22*, a captain-bombardier of an American squadron in Italy in World War II seeks to be grounded for medical reasons. He suffers "Catch-22" when the Doc explains that he can ground anyone who is crazy—but anyone who wants to avoid combat duty must be sane. The officer was almost a victim of "Catch-18," which was Heller's original title, but Leon Uris (born 1924) published a novel about the World War II Warsaw-ghetto uprising with the title *Mila 18*, and Heller thought there would be confusion when his book came out in 1961.

The Missile Gap

During his campaign for the presidency against Richard Nixon, in 1960, Democratic standard-bearer John F. Kennedy insisted that the Eisenhower–Nixon administration (1953–61) had let the Soviet Union streak ahead in the missile race—the Soviets had far more missiles than the United States. It was a winning argument. However, after being elected, President Kennedy backtracked. There *was* a "Missile Gap," but it was the other way around: The United States had far more missiles than Moscow.

Two Cultures

C. P. (Charles Percy) Snow (1905–1980), who had a foot in both worlds as a physicist and a novelist, promulgated the notion, in 1960, that England's conservative upper-middle class, reared as it was on the classical and the literary, underrated the importance to the nation of the scientific, which was lower-middle class in origin—hence the phrase "Two Cultures."

The M&M Boys

The slugging baseball sensations Roger Maris (1934–1985) and Mickey Mantle (born 1931) paced the New York Yankees into the World Series for five straight years, 1960–64. Maris hit a record 61 home runs in 1961, and Mantle ("the Commerce Comet") blasted tape-measure jobs. "The M&M Boys" were a "murderers' row" of two.

The New Frontier

Accepting the Democratic party's nomination for President in 1960, John F. Kennedy declared, "We stand today on the edge of a New Frontier—the frontier of the 1960s—a frontier of unknown opportunities and perils—a frontier of unfulfilled hopes and threats." New Frontier aspirations were in part carried out by the Johnson administration, under the label of "the Great Society," following the assassination in 1963 of President Kennedy, who had described himself as an idealist without illusions. (*See also* 1964: The Great Society.)

Old Man River. Ol' Mongoose

Archie Moore (born Archibald Lee Wright in 1913) was at least 44 years old—the oldest man ever to hold a world boxing title—when he was stripped of his light heavyweight crown by the National Boxing Association in October 1960, because he had not defended it in ten months. Moore had copped the title in 1952 in a 15-round bout with Joey Maxim. He was elected to boxing's Hall of Fame in 1966.

The House on Garibaldi Street

Israeli agents staked out "the House on Garibaldi Street," in a suburb of Buenos Aires, Argentina, and in 1960 abducted Adolf Eichmann to Israel, where he was tried and hanged for crimes against the Jewish people and against humanity during World War II. Eichmann (1906–1962) had been chief of the Gestapo's Jewish section. He was arrested by Allied forces in 1945 but escaped and settled in South America.

The 1950s

The Ho Chi Minh Trail

In its successful war to defeat successive US-supported governments in Saigon, North Vietnam funneled materiel and its National Liberation Force (Vietcong) into South Vietnam along the jungle-protected "Ho Chi Minh Trail," named for North Vietnam's leader-president, Ho Chi Minh (1890–1969). Six years after Ho's death, the American army fled Saigon, the city was captured and renamed Ho Chi Minh City, and North and South Vietnam were united.

The Kitchen Debate

In a spontaneous verbal clash alongside a washing machine in a model American home in Moscow—the world-shaking "Kitchen Debate"—Soviet Premier Nikita Khrushchev boasted about Soviet rocketry, and US Vice President Richard M. Nixon retaliated with boasts about color television sets. The two leaders had been posing together in the model home at an exhibition in Moscow in 1959.

The Rock

"The Rock" is Alcatraz, a grim bastion of dungeons and doors when it was a 450-cell federal prison (1934–63): nine-by-five-foot steel-plated doors, "deep-six" solitary dark holes, 12 desolate acres on a craggy escarpment rising 135 feet out of the swirling currents of San Francisco Bay. Al Capone and "Machine-Gun" Kelly were locked up in the Rock, which became part of Golden Gate National Recreation Area in 1959.

Lady Day

The jazzy "Lady Day" was Billie Holiday (née Eleanora Fagan, 1915–1959). Why did she like being a jazz singer? "Nobody knows what you're going to sing before you get up there. Not even you."

Pumpsie

The Boston Red Sox were the last major-league baseball team to sign a black player—infielder Elijah "Pumpsie" Green (born 1933)—in 1959, a dozen years after the Brooklyn Dodgers had become the first club to break the color barrier. It had been thought that the St. Louis Cardinals or the St. Louis Browns would be the last team to integrate because they had not, until just before Pearl Harbor, even allowed black people to sit in the grandstands.

The Great Leap Forward

In 1958, Mao Tse-tung (1893–1976) set into motion "the Great Leap Forward" in an attempt both to break with the Soviet model of communism and to imbue the billion people in the People's Republic of China with renewed revolutionary vigor. The program was a failure economically; small labor-intensive industries, controlled by local peasant groups (Mao himself was of peasant stock), failed. Within a year, Mao was replaced as chairman of the Central Government Council, but he remained China's chief policymaker and chairman of its Communist party.

Father of the Blues

Blind by the age of 30, William Christopher Handy (1873–1958) was one of the most famous jazz composers and conductors in the United States. His "Memphis Blues" (1912), composed for the mayor of Memphis, and his "St. Louis Blues" (1914) earned him the sobriquet "Father of the Blues." "Most white people," Handy remarked, "think that the Negro is always cheerful and lively, but he isn't, though he may seem that way when he is most troubled. The Negro knows the Blues as a state of mind, and that's why his music has that name."

Mr. Cub

The Chicago Cubs' Ernie Banks (born 1931) was the best power hitter ever to play shortstop in baseball's major leagues. His 47 home runs in 1958 represent the most struck in a season by any shortstop. His 41 homers in 1960 were tops in the National League. In 19 seasons, the Hall of Famer played 2,528 games, banging out an average of more than a hit a game— 2,582 in all, including 512 home runs—and he knocked across 1,636 runs. He played in a record-setting 424 consecutive games at the start of his career, but as every Cub fan in the world knows, he never played in a World Series.

Loyalty Oaths

About a fifth of the work force of the United States underwent "loyalty oaths" and checks in the late 1950s as a condition of employment. In the cold-war era, the men and women whose political beliefs did not conform, especially schoolteachers, were fired. Civil libertarians aggressively challenged the government's loyalty–security program, contesting its scope, its denial of due process, and its restraint on freedom of speech and association.

The Shoe. Silent Shoe. Wee Willie

Willy (William) Lee Shoemaker (born 1931), who rode at just under 100 pounds, is horse racing's winningest jockey, with 8,833 first-place finishes and $118 million in prize money for his steeds. He won the Kentucky Derby on Swaps in 1955, on Tommy Lee in 1959, on Lucky Debonair in 1965, and on Ferdinand in 1986, but lost on Gallant Man in 1957 when he misjudged the finish line and stood up in the saddle too soon, holding back the three-year-old. "The Shoe" was inducted into racing's Hall of Fame in 1958—a long way from the first night of his life, when, as a premature baby, "Wee Willie" was not expected to live but was kept warm and alive by his grandmother in a shoe box.

Tail-Gunner Joe

Senator Joseph R. McCarthy (1908–1957), who attended high school at the age of 20 and completed four years of courses in nine months, was a dive-bomber's tail gunner during World War II. The Wisconsin legislator gained notoriety with his reckless anticommunism tactics and smears. After being censured by his peers in 1954, "Tail-Gunner Joe" retreated to his rooms, in Washington, DC, watched soap operas on television, stared into the fire, and eventually became an acute alcoholic.

Hammerin' Hank

Henry ("Hank") Aaron (born 1934) has hit more home runs than any of the more than 13,000 men who have played major-league baseball. In 23 seasons, he walloped 755 pitches out of the ballpark—at least 35 in each of 11 seasons. He holds other records as well: most runs batted in, most extra-base hits, and most total bases. Pitching a fastball past "Hammerin' Hank" was said to have been like trying to get the morning sun up past a rooster's crow. He is the only athlete who has ever been honored on the floor of the US House of Representatives.

Jack the Dripper

Jackson Pollock (1912–1956) was an "action painter." He nailed his canvas to the floor and charged over it with paint and brush. Out of the intricate net of drips, swirls, and spatters usually came a work pulsating with life and vigor: "I can do anything and call it art. Art can be anything I intend."

The Daughters of Bilitis

The first large-scale modern lesbian organization, founded in 1956, chose the name "the Daughters of Bilitis," from the lesbian poet in the *Chansons de Bilitis* by the French writer Pierre Louÿs, who successfully passed off the work as a "translation from the Greek" when he published it in 1894. Bilitis was a Greek courtesan to whom Sappho, the sixth-century-BC Greek lyric poet, wrote love songs.

Phanerothyme

The English writer Aldous Huxley (1894–1963) proposed the term "phanerothyme" for drugs that are capable of producing altered states of consciousness, which may include an unstable flow of ideas and emotions, distorted perception, and hallucinations. Huxley's proposal stimulated his friend, the English psychiatrist Humphry Osmond (born 1917), to coin a word of his own, "psychedelics," which stuck. Osmond introduced his term in this rhyme, in a 1956 letter to Huxley: "To fall in hell or soar angelic / You'll need a pinch of psychedelic."

Baseball's "est" Pitcher

Denton True "Cy" Young (1867–1955) has been both the winning*est* pitcher and the losing*est* pitcher in the major leagues. The Boston Red Sox lefthander, for whom baseball's annual pitching award in each league is named, scored 511 victories in 828 decisions, for a .617 winning percentage. He hurled a no-hitter in 1908, when he was 41, and he holds the record for consecutive hitless innings pitched: 24. The Cy Young Award was inaugurated in 1956 to focus more attention on moundsmen.

The Suez Crisis

When Egyptian President Gamal Abdel Nasser (1918–1970) nationalized the Suez Canal, in 1956, Great Britain, France, and Israel tried to take it over to keep it open. A cease-fire was called after an atomic threat from the Soviet Union and US pressure through the United Nations.

Babe

Mildred Ella Didrikson (1914–1956) picked up her nickname because she could throw and hit a baseball like "Babe" Ruth. She wanted to be the greatest athlete in the world; she was certainly the greatest woman athlete in running, throwing, swimming, jumping, boxing, bowling, fencing, skating, golfing, shooting, cycling, baseball, football, tennis, lacrosse, handball, and billiards. It was said that the five-foot-four, 105-pound Texan was capable of winning everything except the Kentucky Derby. She was a one-woman team, who lost only to cancer.

Brinkmanship

President Dwight D. Eisenhower's secretary of state, John Foster Dulles (1888–1959), declared, in 1956, "You have to take chances for peace, just as you must take chances in war. The ability to get to the verge without getting into the war is the necessary art. If you try to run away from it, if you are scared to go to the brink, you are lost." The secretary practiced "Brinkmanship," often taking the United States to the edge of the atomic abyss.

The Brain. The Smartest Man in the World

Albert Einstein! (The genius [1879–1955] once made a telephone call to the comedian Sid Caesar [born 1922], suggesting they meet to discuss the human condition.)

The DEW Line. Sentry of the Far North

The Distant Early Warning system—the DEW line—was built by the United States and Canada above the Arctic Circle in the western hemisphere to warn of trans–North Pole missile or aircraft attacks on North America. Igloo- or dymaxion-shaped radar stations have dotted the landscape since 1956.

The Miracle Maker

Jonas Salk (born 1914), as a microbiologist at the University of Pittsburgh School of Medicine, developed a vaccine that helped eradicate poliomyelitis. Going against medical orthodoxy, "the Miracle Maker" produced a dead-virus vaccine (1952–55) after cultivating the polio virus in the kidney tissue of monkeys. He has also produced a flu vaccine and is working on a vaccine for AIDS.

Big Blue

IBM, the International Business Machines corporation, has been known for years as "Big Blue." The company has a work force of nearly 400,000 worldwide. IBM cannot, or would not, say (in 1990) when exactly or under what circumstances it was first referred to as "Big Blue."

The Black Cabinet

Mary McLeod Bethune (1875–1955), the first black woman to head a federal agency of the United States (the Division of Negro Affairs of the National Youth Administration), founded "the Black Cabinet," namely, officials in President Franklin D. Roosevelt's New Deal administration who strove to enlist government concern in the interests of blacks.

Skinner Box

The laboratory animal in operant-conditioning experiments must learn to operate the bar or lever at one end of a "Skinner box" in order to receive rewards or to avoid punishments. The device was created by the psychologist B. F. Skinner (born 1904), who is known chiefly for studies of operant conditioning and its application to language learning, educational methods, psychotherapy, and cultural analysis. (A conditioning experiment, according to the *Psych-Illogical Dictionary* by Ickes, Wegner, and Vallacher, is "a negotiated contract between an experimenter and a rat, wherein the rat, in exchange for temporary attenuation of its misery, refrains from violating the experimenter's faith in determinism.") Skinner wrote, "I treat myself exactly the way I treat my rats." This treatment may have extended to his daughter, for whom he created a "Skinner box" that he maintained was healthier than a crib or playpen. Skinner defines "reality" as "a practical matter of dealing with behavior traceable to two or more conflicting sets of variables."

Vatican Roulette

The rhythm method of birth control, which depends on calculating the period of ovulation and avoiding sexual intercourse around that time, became known as "Vatican Roulette" because this hit-or-miss method is the only type of birth control that the Roman Catholic Church permits. James A. Reynolds III remarked that "it's an odd and hypocritical attitude that allows for mathematics in birth control but prohibits chemistry and physics."

Open Skies

President Dwight D. Eisenhower proposed in 1955 that the United States and the Soviet Union enter into an agreement permitting surveillance by aircraft of each other's territory, particularly with an eye on intercontinental-missile-launching pads: the "Open Skies" proposal. The suggestion was made obsolete when spy-in-the-sky satellites began to clutter the heavens.

The Silent Generation

Because college students and graduates in the 1950s held opinions close to the chest, rarely getting involved in national politics or social and public-interest issues, they became known as "the Silent Generation."

Ghoti

For much of this century, "ghoti" has been a code word for the erratic and illogical nature of English spelling. It was George Bernard Shaw (1856–1950) who demonstrated that "fish" can be spelled "ghoti" by following the rules—namely, the sound /f/ as in "enou*gh*," /i/ as in "w*o*men," and /sh/ as in "na*ti*on."

The Sunday Ghetto

In the early days of network television in the United States, quality programming was cast into the Sunday afternoon schedule—"the Sunday Ghetto"—on the theory that few people were watching the new medium in those hours: It was a time for family dinners, and the "Sunday driver" was on the road. When the networks discovered that there would be a huge audience for telecasts of the Sabbath's professional football games, prize-winning programs like *Omnibus, Adventure, Odyssey,* and *The Last Word* were unceremoniously kicked off the air. (Football's Super Bowl coverage has pulled some of TV's largest audiences.)

The Little Miracle of Coogan's Bluff

The New York Giants baseballers surprised just about everyone by winning the National League pennant in 1954 by a five-game margin over the favored Brooklyn Dodgers and then going on to sweep the American League champion Cleveland Indians in four straight games in the World Series. It was in the first game of the Series that Giants centerfielder Willie Mays made the still-talked-about catch, with his back to the plate, of Vic Wertz's 440-foot drive with two Indians on base; the Giants won that game with a three-run pinch homer in the tenth inning. (*See also* 1951: The Miracle of Coogan's Bluff.)

The Genius

Alan Mathison Turing (1912–1954), who helped to break the Nazis' most secret code, was a pioneer of the modern computer and was nicknamed "the Genius." His eccentricities helped to cultivate his reputation as "the Genius": At night he would listen to a children's play on the BBC about Larry the Lamb; he arrived at conferences in London having run 40 miles in old flannels and a vest and with an alarm clock tied with binder twine around his waist, and he was given to long, disturbing silences punctuated by a cackle, which wracked the nerves of even his closest friends.

Eight Millionaires and a Plumber

With one exception, President Dwight D. Eisenhower's first cabinet was comprised of business people. The exception was Labor Secretary Martin Durkin (1894–1955), head of the Journeymen Plumbers and Steamfitters Union. It didn't take the media long to dub the cabinet "Eight Millionaires and a Plumber." Durkin was also the first Eisenhower-cabinet appointee to toss in his wrench.

The Athlete of the Century

James Francis ("Jim") Thorpe (1888–1953), who attended the government-operated Carlisle Indian School, in Pennsylvania, excelled in football, baseball, track and field, hockey, tennis, and boxing. At the 1912 Olympics, in Stockholm, he was called "the greatest athlete in the world" by King Gustavus. Thorpe played major-league baseball for six seasons, and his football exploits put the Canton (Ohio) Bulldogs on the map. He was the first president of the association that became the National Football League. He was active in the fight for Indian rights, and lectured widely. (His Indian name was "Bright Path.") Thorpe's father was half Indian and half Irish; his mother was three-fourths Indian and one-fourth French.

The Man of Steel. Stalin

The revolutionist Joseph Vissarionovich Dzhugashvili (1879–1953), who had taken on the more formidable name "Stalin," "the Man of Steel," was exiled to Siberia for life in 1913, but "life" turned out to be the amnesty after the February revolution of 1917. In 1928 he became the Soviet dictator. Stalin believed that you cannot make a revolution with silk gloves, and that the dictatorship of the Communist party is maintained by recourse to every form of violence. Tens of millions of his political prisoners were killed in the Gulag. A recorded performance of a Mozart concerto by the pianist Mariya Yudina was on a turntable in Stalin's room when he was found dead.

Big Bill

Bill Tilden (1893–1953) won seven US Open tennis titles—six in a row—and three Wimbledons. He hung out with President Harry S. Truman, played bridge with financier Bernard Baruch, ran around Hollywood with the stars—and died alone, penniless and scorned. He twice served time in jail, in 1946 and again in 1949, for homosexual activity, in particular for his advances to young boys.

The Rosenberg Case

The only American civilians to be executed for espionage were Julius and Ethel Rosenberg. The couple had been indicted for conspiracy to transmit classified military information to the Soviet Union. The prosecution's chief witnesses were David Greenglass, who was Mrs. Rosenberg's brother, and his wife, Ruth. Many court appeals and pleas for executive clemency delayed the controversial electrocution until June 19, 1953. It is generally believed that Mrs. Rosenberg (born 1915) was merely a messenger for her husband (born 1918), who had been an electrical engineer with the US Army Signal Corps.

The Doctors' Plot

To curtail what he saw as growing Jewish cosmopolitan influence, Stalin, in 1953, made the baseless allegation that nine physicians, mainly Jewish, were trying to poison the Soviet leaders in their care. The dictator had the nine arrested; two were beaten to death. Stalin himself died, in 1953, before he could carry out his plan to have all Jews in Russia deported to Siberia. Some sources say that the dictator died of rage when he was rebuked by a close associate, Marshal Kliment Voroshilov (1881–1969), for this absurd act of "revenge." (The marshal became president of the USSR on Stalin's demise.)

The Checkers Speech

When Senator Richard M. Nixon was the Republican vice-presidential candidate in 1952, he had to defend himself against charges of corruption. In a TV speech, he tugged heartstrings by referring to his wife's simple cloth coat, to demonstrate that he was poor, and by admitting that his family had in fact accepted a present, a cocker spaniel named Checkers. Nixon reasoned that "the kids, like all kids, loved the dog, and . . . we are going to keep it." The phrase "Checkers Speech" now means any emotionally charged and sympathy-seeking political speech.

The Queen of Burlesque.
The Nation's No. 1 Exotic Dancer

Blaze Starr (née Fannie Belle Fleming, born 1932) was for years the flamboyant red-haired "Queen of Burlesque," "the Nation's No. 1 Exotic Dancer." She bumped and grinded to fame in a Baltimore strip-joint, the 2 O'Clock Club, and had a celebrated romance with Governor Earl Kemp Long (1895–1960), of Louisiana, who raved, "There's nothing I'd rather do in the whole world than roll in the hay with Blaze." She was "at ease being a stripper. I kept my head held high, and if there is such a thing as getting nude with class, I did it."

The Miracle of Coogan's Bluff

The New York Giants lost 11 games in a row at the start of the 1951 baseball season and were 13½ games behind the pacesetting Brooklyn Dodgers in August. Then, miraculously, they drew even with the Dodgers by winning 39 of their last 47 games, including 16 in a row. The Giants went on to win the third and final game in a playoff—and the National League pennant—when Bobby Thomson fired the "shot heard round the world": a last-of-the-ninth-inning pop-fly three-run homer off Dodger relief pitcher Ralph Branca, which barely made it into the left-field seats in New York's Polo Grounds, for a 5–4 victory. (Coogan's Bluff overlooked the Polo Grounds, now the site of a housing project.) The Giants lost the "Subway

World Series" to the New York Yankees in six games. (*See also* 1954: The Little Miracle of Coogan's Bluff.)

True Believer

The San Francisco longshoreman-philosopher Eric Hoffer (1902–1983) used the phrase "True Believer" (in his book with this title, 1951) to describe Hitler's otherwise nondescript followers: the physical, moral, and spiritual cripples and perverts who aspired to the healing purity of the Nazi racial concept of the "pure" Aryan. "True Believer" has been inaccurately used to mean true blue or some other statement of loyalty to a just cause.

The Munchausen Syndrome

The repeated invention of symptoms and a false medical history that are usually quite convincing to the physician is known as "the Münchausen syndrome." It was named, in 1951 (by R. Asher), after Baron Karl Friedrich Hieronymus von Münchhausen (1720–1797), a German soldier-adventurer who was known for his tall tales (later published in many editions), and whose name became a byword for any wild and improbable story.

The UFO Myth

The psychiatrist and philosopher Carl Gustav Jung (1875–1961) saw UFOs as "a living myth . . . a product of the unconscious archetype . . . involuntary, automatic projections based on instinct . . . whose simple, round form portrays the archetype of the self . . . and is therefore best suited to compensate the split-mindedness of our age" (1951). He added that should an unknown physical phenomenon be the outward cause of the myth, this would not detract from the myth.

The Baseball Midget

Eddie Gaedel (1925–1961), wearing No. 1/8 on the back of his St. Louis Browns uniform, went to bat exactly once in his major-league baseball career; two days later, his contract was voided "in the best interests of baseball." Gaedel was a three-foot seven-inch tall midget, and Browns owner Bill Veeck (1914–1986) inserted him into a game against the Detroit Tigers as a stunt to promote slumping interest in his team. Without advance announcement, Gaedel stepped up to the plate, was walked on four laughable pitches, and was immediately replaced by a pinch-runner. It made page one everywhere.

The Wake Island Principle

The United Nations supreme commander in South Korea in the Korean Civil War, Douglas MacArthur (1880–1964), wanted to wipe out North Korea and bomb China, which supported the North Koreans. His letter urging a full-scale attack on communism and publicly criticizing President Harry S. Truman was read in the US Congress and eventually led to his removal from command by commander in chief President Truman after a meeting on Wake Island in the Pacific Ocean in 1951. Truman reaffirmed the principle of the subordination of the military to civilian officials and the theory of limited power.

Sun Belt. Frost Belt

According to the 1951 standard Census Bureau regional breakdown, the "Sun Belt" is 15 southern states, from California to the Carolinas. The "Frost Belt" is the northeast and north-central sections of the nation. Because the population of the United States has been shifting from the Frost Belt to the Sun Belt—millions of retirees seek the warmer climes—the Sun Belt has overtaken and outstripped the Frost Belt in the number of electoral votes it has in national elections.

The Whiz Kids

In the 1950 baseball season, the Philadelphia Phillies had a starting lineup of players who were all under 30 years of age—"the Whiz Kids." They won the National League pennant by two games over the Brooklyn Dodgers. Del Ennis was the league runs-batted-in champ with 126; Richie Ashburn led the league with the most triples, 14; and Jim Konstanty pitched in 74 games. They lost four straight games to the New York Yankees in the World Series. (*See also* 1983: The Wheeze Kids.)

GBS

The Irishman George Bernard Shaw (1856–1950) was perhaps the greatest English-writing playwright since Shakespeare. His stature was such that he came to be referred to by his initials, "GBS," and dictionaries list the special adjective derived from his name, "Shavian." Shaw was a master of prose, both on the stage and in his music and theater criticism. He always had a lot to say: "How can what an Englishman believes be heresy? It is a contradiction in terms." "A lifetime of happiness? No man alive could bear it: it would be hell on earth." "I liked sexual intercourse because of its amazing power of producing a celestial flood of emotion and exaltation of existence which, however momentary, gave me a sample of what one day may be the normal state of being for mankind in intellectual ecstasy." "I often quote myself. It adds spice to my conversation." The Welsh poet Dylan Thomas quipped, "George Too Shaw To Be Good."

The Say-Hey Kid

Baseball Hall of Famer Willie Mays (born 1931) has trouble remembering names, so he always gets another person's attention by calling out "Say Hey." His biggest moment in baseball occurred when he signed his first contract, in 1950, with the New York Giants. It was for $15,000, enabling "the Say-Hey Kid" to buy his family a house, clothes, and an automobile. Baseball was a "fun game" for him: "I played baseball to do everything good, not to beat any records." He slammed 660 home runs and was twice the National League's most valuable player, in 1954 and in 1965.

The Forgotten War

When President Harry S. Truman decided to "draw the line" against communism in South Korea, US armies fought for 37 months in the Korean Civil War (1950–53), nearly three times as long as they had fought in World War I and almost as long as they had fought in World War II. Total American casualties in Korea were 33,629 killed on the battlefield, 20,617 military dead from other causes, and 103,284 wounded. Military casualties on both sides came close to 2.4 million. About six million men and women served in the US armed forces during the war. The United Nations also supplied troops. Yet the fighting in Korea (*Cho-son* or *Chyosyon* in Korean, *Chosen* or *Tyosen* in Japanese, *Kao-li* in Chinese—whence our *Korea* or *Corea* and the French *Corée*) is still referred to as "the Forgotten War."

The Mackmen

For a half century, from 1901 to 1950, the Philadelphia Athletics baseball team of the American League was in the hands of manager and part-owner Connie Mack (Cornelius Alexander McGillicuddy), and the team became known as "the Mackmen." Mack (1862–1956), "the Tall Tactician," led the A's into eight World Series, and he was voted into the Baseball Hall of Fame in 1937 when he was still very active. He retired at the age of 80, with an overall record of 4,025 losses and "only" 3,776 wins.

The 1940s

Minnie

Saturnino Orestes Arrieta Armas "Minnie" Minoso (born 1922) broke into major-league baseball in 1949 and played in the 50s, 60s, 70s (three games, in 1967, lining out one hit in eight at bats), and 80s (he pinch-hit twice in 1980). He hopes to play in at least one game in the 1990s. His career batting average, to April 1, 1990, was .298.

Axis Sally

Mildred E. Gillars (born 1900) broadcast Nazi propaganda under the nickname "Axis Sally" during World War II. In 1949 she was sentenced for treason; in 1961 she was released.

Tokyo Rose

Iva Toguri d'Aquino (born 1916), an American citizen and a graduate of the University of California, was in Tokyo at the time of Pearl Harbor (1941) and became a propaganda broadcaster for the Japanese during World War II, first under the name "Ann," short for Announcer, then as "Tokyo Rose." In 1949 she was imprisoned for treason; she was paroled in 1956, and pardoned, by President Gerald Ford, in 1977.

Barefoot Doctors

The description "Barefoot Doctors" has been applied to the thousands of medical paraprofessionals in the People's Republic of China who have been trained to provide health care for remote populations. In a general sense, any medically trained personnel giving health care in areas that are not served by modern hospitals may be referred to as "Barefoot Doctors."

Black Jack

Strong-willed, 200-percent American, General John Joseph Pershing (1860–1948), pejoratively called "Black Jack" by West Point cadets for his devoted service with the black Tenth Cavalry in Montana, was the country's most famous general and the commander in chief of the American Expeditionary Forces in World War I. In 1921 he became Army chief of staff. His memoirs, *My Experiences in the World War*, received the Pulitzer Prize in history in 1932. (*See also* 1886: Black Jack.)

Babe Ruth. Bambino. The Sultan of Swat

When George Herman Ruth (1895–1948) retired in 1935, he held more than 50 baseball records for both hitting and pitching. He called baseball "the only real game in the world," and was voted into the Baseball Hall of Fame in the very first year of balloting (1936). His most popular nickname goes back to 1914, when a teammate on the Baltimore Orioles minor-league club, on meeting him, remarked, "Well, here's Jack's newest babe now." ("Jack" was the manager, Jack Dunn.) When he hit 59 home runs in 1921, Ruth passed the previous career home-run record by a player since 1900, Gavvy Cravath's (1881–1963) 119. Ruth held the career-homer record for 54 years, until Hank Aaron dislodged him with his home run No. 715 in April 1974.

The Veep

President Harry S. Truman's Vice President, Alben W. Barkley (1877–1956), of Kentucky, was the first to be nicknamed "the Veep," a title bestowed affectionately. An informal man, who had been majority leader of the US Senate, Barkley appropriated "the Veep" for his television series, "Meet the Veep." (Almost every Vice President has loathed the position. One described himself as being "like a man in a cataleptic state: he cannot speak; he cannot move; he suffers no pain, and yet he is perfectly conscious of everything that is going on around him.")

The Missouri Mule

Harry S. Truman (1884–1972) became the 33rd President of the United States when he succeeded the late Franklin D. Roosevelt in April 1945; he was elected to a full four-year term in 1948. He made the decision to drop the atom bombs on Japan, embraced the doctrine of containment of communism, and took the country to war against Korea over this principle. "The buck stops here," said a sign on his Oval Office desk. Truman's earthiness was proverbial. In a speech before the Senate (on July 5, 1941) he declared, "If we see that Germany is winning, we ought to help Russia, and if we see Russia is winning, we ought to help Germany, and that way let them kill as many as possible." After his confrontation with General Douglas MacArthur on Wake Island in 1951, he remarked, "I didn't fire him because he was a dumb son of a bitch, although he was, but that's not against the law for generals. If it was, half to three quarters of them would be in jail." He was as stubborn as a Missouri mule. But his daughter, Margaret, said, to understand her father "you must grasp the importance of humility in his thinking."

The "Give 'em Hell" Campaign

During his 1948 drive for the presidency—30,000 miles whistlestopping, 300 speeches—Harry S. Truman denounced the "do-nothing" Republican-dominated Congress for blocking his programs. His supporters dubbed the "Missouri Mule"'s campaign "the 'Give 'em Hell' campaign." Truman said that he was "not giving them hell. I'm telling the truth, and they think it's hell." Truman won the election, edging the overconfident Thomas E. Dewey narrowly in the popular vote and decisively in the electoral college.

Black Betsy

Babe Ruth (1895–1948), and then others, called his 44-ounce bat "Black Betsy." In one 12-year stretch, he blasted an average of 46.8 home runs each year, with a career slugging average of a fantastic .690. He single-handedly made baseball the national pastime, expunging from fans' minds the Black Sox scandal of 1919.

Orwellian. 1984

By reversing the last two digits in the year in which he wrote the book, George Orwell (1903–1950), in critic George Steiner's words, "put his signature and claim on a piece of time." *1984* is celebrated for preempting a calendar year in human history. The thinly veiled allegory of Stalinism—every one of its major themes, and most of the actual narrative situations—was inspired by Eugene Zamiatin's *We*, which in itself is an "Orwellian" gesture by the author.

The Pumpkin Papers

Whittaker Chambers (1901–1961), a *Time* magazine senior editor, revealed to the House Committee on Un-American Activities in 1948 that he had served as a courier for the Soviet Union, and he fingered Alger Hiss (born 1904) as a principal contact in Washington, DC. Hiss, once a key US official and diplomat and the temporary secretary-general of the embryonic United Nations, sued for slander. Chambers produced from pumpkins on his Maryland farm a cache of microfilms containing State Department documents typed on what the Federal Bureau of Investigation claimed to have been Hiss's typewriter. Hiss was twice tried for perjury, and he served nearly five years in prison.

The Little Flower

Fiorello H. La Guardia (1882–1947)—the petty, petulant "Little Flower" (*fiorello* in Italian)—has come to be regarded as New York City's greatest mayor. His core constituency was the middle- and working-class ethnics, and in his three four-year terms he married political skill with conviction, style, and genuine ability. He once said to an aide, "I can outdemagogue the best of demagogues." He believed that "on Judgment Day we'll be judged by what we didn't do rather than by what we did." He was director-general of the United Nations Relief and Rehabilitation Agency (UNRRA) after leaving the mayoralty.

The Hollywood Ten.
The Unfriendly Ten

"The Hollywood Ten" were motion-picture directors, producers, and writers who refused (1947) to answer questions from the House Committee on Un-American Activities about membership in the Communist party. They essentially based their position on the First Amendment's guarantee against incursions on free speech rather than on the Fifth Amendment's protection against self-incrimination. They were imprisoned for short terms. (An eleventh, German playwright Bertolt Brecht [1898–1956], was called. He answered the questions: "No, no, no, no, no, never," then skipped the country.)

The Agency. The Company.
Langley

The supersleuths who work for the US Central Intelligence Agency refer to it as "the Agency" or as "the Company" or as "Langley," for the town in Virginia, near Washington, DC, in which CIA headquarters is said to be situated.

Scarface. Big Al

Chicago's crime-syndicate boss Al Capone (1899–1947) tried to conceal with talcum powder the scar on his left check. Windy City police said he was responsible for 25 murders, including the rubout of seven Bugs Moran associates in a warehouse on St. Valentine's Day 1929. When Capone learned that lieutenants were conspiring to dethrone him, he first treated them to a party, then beat them to death with a baseball bat. The Feds got him on 22 counts of income-tax evasion. "Big Al" once said, "Public service is my motto."

Mr. X

Ambassador George F. Kennan's anonymously signed 1947 article in *Foreign Affairs* magazine—by "Mr. X"—warned of Moscow's expansionist tendencies and encouraged the United States to seize the initiative in the cold war with a policy of "firm and vigilant" containment. "Containment" became the term that characterized US foreign policy in the post-World War II era. In 1989, there was a call for an article by another Mr. X, this time with suggestions on how best to deal with the turmoil that the Soviet Union's reforms were provoking as the cold war ended: What should the United States do about the new realities in Europe? In 1990, in *Daedalus* magazine, a mysterious "Mr. Z" argued—to the satisfaction of conservative hard-liners—that if Soviet President Gorbachev's goal was to strengthen the Communist system through reform, he could not succeed:

the "system cannot be restructured or reformed . . . On this score, Mr. Gorbachev is beyond our help." "Mr. Z"'s position was that Gorbachev has no intention of liquidating Communist party rule, and therefore merits no help in maintaining it.

The Lubitsch Touch

Sophisticated movie comedies of manners characterized by wit, frivolity, piquancy, and subtle innuendo were said to have "the Lubitsch Touch," for the German-born film director Ernst Lubitsch (1892–1947). His films included *Ninotchka, To Be or Not to Be, Trouble in Paradise,* and *Design for Living.*

The Freedom Train

In 1947 a three-car train, or mobile museum, decked out in red, white, and blue, began toting to nearly 350 cities around the United States a collection of about 130 basic documents relating to the establishment and preservation of American liberties and the federal government. The "sacred texts" on "the Freedom Train" included the Bill of Rights, the Mayflower Compact, and President George Washington's farewell address. In its year-and-a-half tour, amid considerable fanfare, the train bypassed segregated cities such as Memphis and Birmingham; some cities lifted Jim Crow laws so that the train could stop there.

Tenno

The brilliant Japanese motion-picture director Akira Kurosawa (born 1910)—*Rashomon, Seven Samurai, Throne of Blood, Ran, The Lower Depths, Kagemusha*—is a legendary tyrant, dubbed "Tenno" (emperor) by the Japanese press. Most Kurosawa films portray people overcoming their weakness by force of will.

The Marshall Plan

General George C. Marshall (1880–1959), one of the greatest military geniuses in the history of the United States, won universal praise for a postwar program he put forward as President Harry S. Truman's secretary of state. In 1947, in a commencement address at Harvard University, he proposed a $13.3 billion plan—"the Marshall Plan"—to help 15 devastated European countries in the wake of World War II: "Whether we like it or not, we find ourselves, our Nation, in a world position of vast responsibility. We can act for our own good by acting for the world's good." He was honored with the Nobel Peace Prize in 1953. (Formulation and promotion of the Marshall Plan initiative was conceived by Will Clayton, the assistant secretary of state for economic affairs, and drafted on a flight from Europe to the United States.)

Leftover Americans

Thousands of illiterate black farm workers who were driven off the land in the South by the mechanization of agriculture couldn't find even unskilled work in major cities; many became disoriented and redundant in the cities' hard and dirty backwaters. "Leftover Americans" are said to be economically superfluous.

Animal Farm

Subtitled "A Fairy Tale," George Orwell's *Animal Farm,* a searing 1946 satire on dictatorship, became a sobriquet referring to the contemporary, Stalinist Soviet Union and to the fate of communism. The farm's pigs, leaders of the animals' revolution against the humans, make the famous declaration, "All animals are equal, but some animals are more equal than others." (*See also* 1968: Cancer Ward.)

Vinegar Joe

Joseph Warren Stilwell (1883–1946) saw more frontline combat than any US four-star general in World War II, as commander in the India-Burma-China area. A key figure in the long Sino-American relationship, impatient, acid, impolitic "Vinegar Joe" was involved with China from the year of the Revolution (1911) to the decisive year in the decline of the Nationalist government (1944). He was recalled to the United States because of friction with China's Nationalist leader, Chiang Kai-shek, who had powerful friends in Congress.

The Old Redhead

For many years, the literate Walter "Red" Barber (born 1908)—"the Old Redhead"—was the broadcast voice of major-league baseball's Brooklyn Dodgers. When he learned from Dodger boss Branch Rickey, in 1946, that the club was signing a black player (Jackie Robinson), the southern-born Barber thought seriously about quitting. He had never worked or traveled with blacks. When he got home that night and told his wife both the news and his plans, she suggested, "Let's have a martini and talk about it." Barber stayed with the Dodgers. When Giants' announcer Russ Hodges screamed "THE GIANTS WIN THE PENNANT! THE GIANTS WIN THE PENNANT!!!" in the 1951 playoff with the Dodgers, decided by Bobby Thomson's dramatic ninth-inning homer, Barber was quietly saying, "It's in there—for the pennant."

27 Rue de Fleurus

The Paris address of Gertrude Stein (1874–1946), "27 rue de Fleurus," was for many years a magnet for artists, writers, philosophers, and critics of the "lost generation." Stein said, "I am an American and I have lived half my life in Paris, not the half that made me but the half in which I made what I made." A literary cubist, she felt that in poetry "you can love a name and if you love a name then saying that name any number of times only makes you love it more." She also did advanced work in brain anatomy at Johns Hopkins University, in Baltimore, received the highest grade in William James's philosophy course at Radcliffe College, and bought early Picassos.

The Nazi Ideologist

Alfred Rosenberg, born in Estonia in 1893, educated in Russia, hanged as a war criminal in Germany in 1946, was one of Hitler's earliest, most devoted, and most prominent followers. He was editor of *Der Völkische Beobachter,* the official paper of the Nazi party, as of 1922; he was director of the party's foreign policy; he was founder and leader of the *Kampfbund* for German culture; he was generally in charge of the education of party members, until 1941, when Hitler made him minister for the occupied eastern territories (it was mainly for this last role, with responsibility for the terror of slave labor and the murder of millions of Jews, that he was given the death sentence at the Nuremberg Tribunal). However, he was primarily "the Nazi Ideologist," the Nazis' chief racial theorist, the author of the theoretical underpinnings of the entire Nazi *Weltanschauung,* as published in his 1930 book, *Der Mythos des 20. Jahrhunderts* (The Myth of the Twentieth Century). Names like Göring, Himmler, Goebbels are often associated with Hitler, but less often recalled is the at least equally important name Rosenberg, the name of the man who wrote, "The idea of National Socialism is an accomplishment of the human soul that ranks with the Parthenon, the Sistine Madonna, and the Ninth Symphony of Beethoven."

The Big Train

Walter Johnson (1887–1946) was an express train on the pitcher's mound. The National Baseball Hall of Fame sidearmer roared the ball past batters for a strikeout total of 3,508. Though he pitched for the lowly Washington nine in the American League, the six-foot-one "Big Train" was always on the right track: His 413 triumphs included 110 shutouts in a 21-year career. His career strikeout record, 3,508, was unsurpassed in 56 seasons, until 1983.

Old Blood and Guts

American General George S. Patton (1885–1945) claimed he would even go through hell to destroy enemy forces. On November 11, 1944, he "celebrated" his birthday "by getting up where the dead were still warm" on the western front. Patton's Third Army relieved Bastogne in the Battle of the Bulge, leaped the Rhine, then dashed across southern Germany into Czechoslovakia after he was ordered to let the Russians capture Berlin. "To be a successful soldier," he said, "what you must know is how man reacts. Weapons change but man who uses them changes not at all. To win battles you do not beat weapons—you beat the soul of man, of the enemy man." During the Sicilian campaign, in 1943, he slapped a hospitalized soldier whom he suspected of malingering; "Old Blood and Guts" was sharply reprimanded by his superiors and criticized publicly. With his trademark ivory-handled revolvers in his holster, he castigated postwar denazification of Germany. It is believed that it was no accident that he was killed in an automobile crash in Germany, just before Christmas 1945.

V-J Day

On August 6, 1945, a US Superfortress dropped an atomic bomb on the Japanese city of Hiroshima. (A seminal question is only now being raised: Was it the hope of the United States and Great Britain that Japan would surrender immediately, before the Soviet Union, in accordance with the Yalta agreement, joined the war in the Pacific—thus keeping the Soviet Union out of the peace treaty in the East?) On August 8, the Soviet Union kept its word to the day—exactly three months after V-E Day—and attacked Japanese forces in Manchukuo. The next day, a second US atomic bomb destroyed Nagasaki. On August 15, remembered as "V-J Day" for victory over Japan, Emperor Hirohito surrendered unconditionally. The "Son of Heaven" told his people, in his first-ever radio message, that "the war situation has developed not necessarily to our advantage," and he called on the Japanese to "endure the unendurable." Five months later, Hirohito again took to the radio to say that the people were sovereign and that the emperor was not divine.

The Air-Conditioned Nightmare

This name for the United States became popular after Henry Miller (1891–1980) published his book with this title in 1945. Its subject is the horrifying impression of a trip over much of America, pointing out its failings, in landscape and in matters of the spirit, including the industrial desolation of steel towns.

The First Nuclear War

Nine days after it started, "the first nuclear war" was over. The United States used the last two atomic bombs in its arsenal to all but wipe the Japanese cities of Hiroshima and Nagasaki off the face of the Earth and to bring a quicker end to World War II.

Little Boy. Fat Man

"Little Boy" was the name of the US uranium bomb that obliterated Hiroshima, Japan, on August 6, 1945. "Fat Man" was the plutonium bomb that devastated Nagasaki three days later. The original target for the second atomic attack was Kokura, on the northern coast of the Japanese island of Kyushu, but smoke and haze obscured the city when the B-29 Superfortress *Bock's Car* flew over it not once but three times, before going on to its secondary target, Nagasaki, where a hole was found in the cloud cover.

Enola Gay. Bock's Car

The *Enola Gay* was the US B-29 Superfortress bomber that dropped an atomic bomb on Hiroshima; *Bock's Car* was the B-29 that A-bombed Nagasaki, southwest of Hiroshima, in early August 1945, bringing an end to World War II. Colonel Paul Tibbets, Jr., had named the *Enola Gay* in honor of his mother. *Bock's Car* was named for the bomber's regular pilot, Captain Frederick Bock, but it was flown on the Nagasaki mission by Major Charles Sweeney, whose plane, the *Great Artiste,* armed with scientific instruments, had accompanied the *Enola Gay* on the Hiroshima mission and would observe the Nagasaki raid as well.

The Gadget

The first atomic bomb, tested in the desert at Trinity Site, near Alamogordo, New Mexico, on July 16, 1945, was called simply "the Gadget." Scientists believed that there was one chance in 30 that when "the Gadget" exploded the entire state would be destroyed. There was even the possibility that the whole world would catch on fire.

The Father of Space Travel

In 1926, Robert H. Goddard (1882–1945) correctly predicted that humans would one day escape Earth's gravity and fly to the Moon. A professor of physics, "the Father of Space Travel" spent decades experimenting with jet propulsion and progressively-more-sophisticated rockets. He invented, built, and launched the first liquid-fuel rocket to fly under its own power. He was the first to suggest a staging concept, a two-step rocket. The Nazis incorporated many of his discoveries into their manless, jet-propelled V-1 (buzzbomb) and V-2 (robot bomb) rockets, which terrorized England.

The Empire State Building Crash

A twin-engine US B-25 bomber, *Old Feather Merchant,* was flying through the soupy overcast shrouding the skyline spires of Manhattan in July 1945. The pilot became lost over Rockefeller Center and flew south—

downtown—at too low an altitude. He flew right into the 78th and 79th floors of the 102-story Empire State Building, at 34th Street and Fifth Avenue. Fourteen people were killed, 25 injured.

The Hongkew Catastrophe

About 20,000 European Jews fled Hitler's lethal grasp and found a haven in Hirohito's Shanghai. In mid-1943, they were shunted into a mile-square ghetto in the Chinese "suburb" of Hongkew. On July 19, 1945, American B-24 Liberators, intending to raid Japanese fuel storage tanks in Hongkew Park and airplane repair shops in the West District, miles away, accidentally unleashed their bombs on Hongkew, killing 280 people, including 31 Jewish refugees, and wounding almost 1,000 others.

The Big White Jail. The Palace. The President's House

The first President who referred publicly to the White House as "the Big White Jail" was Harry S. Truman, but other Presidents have used similar descriptions to confer a sense of imprisonment. Reservations were also expressed in comments like Theodore Roosevelt's "You don't live there, you're only Exhibit A to the country" and Calvin Coolidge's "Nobody [lives there]. They just come and go."

"The Palace" is what the White House was designated in the original plans, drawn by James Hoban (c. 1762–1831) for the site chosen by President George Washington himself. It is the oldest public building in the nation's capital, its cornerstone having been laid by Washington in 1792. In 1818 President James Monroe had the executive mansion restored after its torching by British troops during the War of 1812. Scorch marks on the smoke-stained gray walls were painted white, but sometime between excavation and restoration the cognomen "White House" had already superseded "the Palace" and "the President's House." "White House" became the official name when President Teddy Roosevelt engraved it on his stationery.

V-E Day

German General Alfred Jodl, Admiral Hans von Friedeburg, and Admiral (and briefly Hitler's successor) Karl Dönitz surrendered the Fatherland unconditionally to the Allies on May 8, 1945, called "V-E Day," for victory in Europe. The Third Reich that was to have been the glory of the world for a thousand years had collapsed after only 12 years, and Germany was free of its tyranny.

Il Duce

Italy's Fascist dictator Benito Mussolini (1883–1945)—"Il Duce," Italian for "the leader"—declared that Rome's "universal mission" was the defense of Western civilization against the "colored races." He also said: "We have buried the putrid corpse of liberty . . . War alone brings up to its highest tension all human energy and puts the stamp of nobility upon the peoples who have the courage to face it . . . To make a people great, it is necessary to send them to battle even if you have to kick them in the pants." At the end of World War II he was captured and shot by Italian partisans, and his corpse was hanged in a public square of Milan.

The Führerbunker

At the turn of the year in 1945, Führer Adolf Hitler (born 1889) moved into the 18 rooms of the submarinelike bunker under the Reich Chancellery in battered Berlin and perhaps never saw the light of day again. He despised Berlin, but he would stay in the German capital until the end. He wished to share his fate "with the millions of others who have chosen to remain inside the heartbeat of our beloved Reich." He said he chose death willingly, joyously, knowing of the immeasurable deeds and achievements carried out in his name by the peasants, the workers, and the youth. On April 29, 1945, he married his secret companion of many years, Eva Braun (born 1912), and both committed suicide the following day.

The Four-Term President. That Man in the White House

Franklin D. Roosevelt (1882–1945) was, and probably will be, the only President of the United States ever elected to a third, and then a fourth, term. Republicans, incensed at FDR's repeated Democratic successes, pressed for restricted presidential tenure. The Twenty-second Amendment to the Constitution (1951) prohibits election to the office more than twice. The only amendment to be secured by conservative political forces, it took the longest of all 26 amendments to be ratified—almost four years. All living former Presidents, except Ronald W. Reagan, favor a one-time six-year term.

The Yalta Conference

At Yalta, in the Crimea region of the Soviet Union, the Big Three—Russian dictator Joseph Stalin, British Prime Minister Winston Churchill, and US President Franklin D. Roosevelt—met for the last time, in February 1945, to demand Germany's unconditional surrender in World War II and to plan Europe's geographical and political future. Germany would be divided into four zones of occupation, and there would be war-crimes trials. The Soviet Union agreed to enter the war against Japan within three months of V-E Day—and it did, precisely to the day, just over a week before the Sons of the Rising Sun also raised the white flag.

The Spirit of '45

The Pulitzer Prize-winning Joe Rosenthal–Associated Press photograph of five US marines and a sailor planting the Stars and Stripes on rocky, volcanic Mount Suribachi on Iwo Jima in the western Pacific, in 1945, has been titled "The Spirit of '45." Capturing the jagged eight-square-mile island cost the lives of 4,189 US servicemen. Three of the marines in the historic picture died later in the bloody clash with Japanese defenders.

The Doorstep of Japan

Eight-square-mile, volcanic Iwo Jima—"the Doorstep of Japan"—was needed as a base for US fighter planes, a haven for crippled aircraft, and a refueling depot for B-29 Superfortresses returning to bases in the Mariana Islands after raids on Japanese cities in the last year of World War II. Seventy-four consecutive days of pounding by air and sea preceded the Marines' bloody invasion of Iwo Jima in February 1945. More than 21,000 Japanese soldiers were killed in interlocking underground strongholds, in thousands of blockhouses, pillboxes, and fortified caves; only 200 were taken prisoner.

The Battle of the Bulge

One of the surprising maneuvers in World War II was German General Karl von Rundstedt's (1875–1953) last-ditch Ardennes Offensive in December 1944. His troops created a large salient, or "bulge," in the Allied front line, a tactical victory (at the cost of 100,000 dead and wounded) that stalled, until March 7, 1945, the Allied crossing of the Rhine and the invasion of the Fatherland itself.

The Man on the Wedding Cake

Thomas E. Dewey (1902–1971) was cruelly described as "the Man on the Wedding Cake" when he was the Republican presidential candidate against fourth-term-seeking Franklin D. Roosevelt in the 1944 election. Dewey, a multiterm governor of New York and a racketbusting New York County district attorney, is said to have evoked the inspired characterization because he was short, formal-looking, and mustachioed. He ran again in the 1948 election, losing to the incumbent Harry S. Truman in a cliffhanger. "DEWEY DEFEATS TRUMAN" was the screaming front-page banner headline on an early edition of the *Chicago Tribune*—but then the final results were posted: Truman, 303 electoral votes; Dewey, 189.

The Morgenthau Plan

So that Germany would not rise from the ashes of World War II and become a military threat to the world for a third time, US Secretary of the Treasury Henry Morgenthau (1891–1967) proposed in 1944 that the defeated nation could be controlled by transforming it from an industrial economy to an agricultural economy. The idea was discussed but never effected.

The Port Chicago Mutiny

The worst disaster on the home front in the United States during World War II occurred in 1944 at the northern California town of Port Chicago. Two military cargo ships being loaded with bombs exploded. The ships were vaporized, the town and its waterfront virtually erased, and 320 stevedores were killed. Of the dead, 202 were black Navy enlistees. Because no white men toted bombs at Port Chicago, 258 surviving blacks refused to return to their hazardous work, declaring that they were merely munitions fodder. Fifty were tried, convicted of mutiny, and sentenced to 15 years in prison. The 208 others were court-martialed and dishonorably discharged.

Tom, Dick, and Harry. The Great Escape

"Tom," "Dick," and "Harry" were the names of the tunnels that 76 Allied soldiers who were prisoners of war dug and escaped through—"the Great Escape" from the Nazis' Stalag Luft III, 60 miles northeast of Berlin, in 1944. Fifty of the 73 recaptured POWs were executed by the Gestapo.

The July Plot

Conspiratorial German generals and civil officials executed a long-fomented plot against Hitler on July 20, 1944. Realizing that there was no way to stem the onrushing Russian armies in the east and the Allied armies streaming across the English Channel and into France and the Low Countries in the west, the conspirators planted a bomb in a briefcase at the Führer's feet during a staff meeting. Instead of being blown apart, Hitler was only slightly injured, which he interpreted as a further sign that he was carrying out God's work. He promptly instigated a bloody purge.

The Karl

The most powerful single artillery piece in World War II was a tractor-mounted 600-millimeter mortar that could lob more than three miles a two-and-a-half-ton German shell two feet thick. "The Karl" was used to batter Brest-Litovsk and Sebastopol. It was not used to batter Paris and stall the advancing Allied armies in the summer of 1944 because Hitler's Paris commander did not want to go down in history as the man who blew out "the city of light."

The $50 Million Game

In baseball's most unusual game, in 1944, the New York Yankees played the New York Giants played the Brooklyn Dodgers played the New York Yankees in a mathematically conceived exhibition in New York's Polo Grounds to support the US effort in World War II. Admission was the purchase of a US Savings Bond; $50 million was raised. Each team was at bat six times and in the field six times, and no team was at bat for more than six successive outs or in the field for more than six successive outs. The capacity crowd saw the Dodgers score five runs (three in the first against the Yankees) and the Yankees one. The Giants didn't score, and the Dodgers weren't scored on.

The Desert Fox

German Field Marshal Erwin "the Desert Fox" Rommel's Afrika Corps rolled to within 30 miles of the Suez Canal in the summer of 1942. The British stalled the clever Rommel for four months, then began a counterattack that was the turning point in the North African campaign. After being driven out of Africa, Rommel (1891–1944) commanded Hitler's army at the Atlantic Wall. He was forced to commit suicide, by poison, for having supported the July 20 assassination plot against Hitler. (*See also* 1944: The July Plot.)

The Smokeless City

Almost every building in Reykjavik, Iceland's capital (the world's northernmost capital), is heated by waters channeled from subterranean thermal springs. Iceland—first reached by Norwegian settlers in 874 AD, independent since 1944—is a world unto itself: No tree may be cut on the island, *everyone* learns to read and write, and there are no prisons.

The Longest Day

"The Longest Day" was D-Day, the invasion of Hitler's Europe by Allied forces on June 6, 1944. "Believe me, Lang," German Field Marshal Erwin Rommel had said to an aide two months earlier, "the first 24 hours of the invasion will be decisive . . . the fate of Germany depends on the outcome . . . for the Allies, as well as Germany, it will be the longest day."

The Zoot-Suit Riot

Favored by "hep cats" and used pejoratively as a synonym for "Mexican," the zoot suit has a very long jacket, flared at the bottom, with exaggeratedly padded, boxy shoulders, and pegged sleeves. The trousers are pleated at the waistline, cut very wide over the hips, and taper to such narrow bottoms that men with big feet have trouble slipping the pants on. During World War II, its manufacture was seen as a glaring example of waste. After a riot in Los Angeles in 1943, in which Mexicans and blacks were dragged into streets by soldiers and civilians, stripped, and beaten, the city council, in a blatant antiminority action, made wearing the zoot suit a misdemeanor.

The Sword of My Emperor

Japanese Admiral Isoruku Yamamoto (1883–1943)—"the Sword of My Emperor"—was the principal plotter of the devastating surprise attack on US military forces at Pearl Harbor, Hawaii (December 1941). He was also the commander of the Japanese fleet (8 aircraft carriers, 11 battleships, 18 cruisers, 65 destroyers) that was routed by a rejuvenated US Navy at Midway Island in the mid-Pacific in June 1942. This was an early turning point of World War II in the East, and Japan's first naval setback since 1592 (when Koreans whipped the Japanese). Yamamoto was shot down by US P-38 twin-tailed fighter planes over the Solomon Islands in the South Pacific after the United States had learned of his whereabouts by breaking the Japanese code; President Franklin D. Roosevelt gave the final authorization for the attack on Yamamoto's plane. The admiral was given a hero's funeral, only the second state funeral for a commoner in the history of Japan.

Flag Idolatry

The Supreme Court of the United States ruled in 1943 that free exercise of religion gives schoolchildren the right to refuse to salute the flag, reversing the earlier decision (involving Jehovah's Witnesses) that a school board could constitutionally require pupils in school to pledge allegiance and salute the flag. (Jehovah's Witnesses believe that saluting the American flag is tantamount to worshiping an idol, which the Bible commands against.) The justices said that they were upholding the freedom of conscience of the individual. Forcing everyone to agree on an idea, even one as noble as patriotism, achieved only "the unanimity of the graveyard."

The Hinge of Fate

Under Field Marshal Friedrich Paulus (1890-1957), Hitler's Sixth Army flashed southward toward Stalingrad and the prodigious power plant there on the eastern terminus of the Volga–Don Canal in the Soviet Union.

The region was a prime target of Germany's '42 Russian campaign. If Stalingrad fell, European Russia would be the Third Reich's. One million Russians perished there, but the 353-year-old city held. Every man was a fortress. Stalingrad was "the Hinge of Fate," the turning point of World War II in eastern Europe. (With Stalin in disfavor, Stalingrad—formerly Tsaritsyn—is now known as Volgograd.)

The Rocket

Maurice "the Rocket" Richard (born 1921) joined the Montreal Canadiens in the 1942–43 season, and in 1945 he became the National Hockey League's first goal-a-game scorer. He was an All-Star 14 times in his 18-year career, scoring 544 goals in 978 league games, including 83 winning goals and 28 tying goals. In 133 playoff games, he scored 82 goals and notched 44 assists—126 points. The president of the NHL once said about "the Rocket," "Never . . . have I met a man with such singleness of purpose and so completely devoted to his profession."

The Big Three

The Allies' "Big Three" leaders, President Franklin D. Roosevelt (1882–1945), of the United States, Prime Minister Winston Churchill (1874–1965), of Great Britain, and Premier Joseph Stalin (1879–1953), of the Soviet Union, were in frequent contact during World War II, and they met in conference at Teheran (1943) and at Yalta (1945). Their goal was the unconditional surrender of the Axis powers: Germany, Italy, and Japan. At the Potsdam conference (July 1945) after V-E Day, there was a new "Big Three." Harry S. Truman (1884–1972) had succeeded the late President Roosevelt, and Clement Attlee (1883–1967) replaced Churchill after the first day of the conference, when Churchill was voted out of office. Only Stalin was still in power.

Associated Powers

"Associated Powers" was the name first proposed for what became the United Nations in 1942 when 26 countries made the pledge to continue their joint war efforts against the Axis powers and not to make peace separately. President Franklin D. Roosevelt is often credited with having coined "United Nations," but British Prime Minister Winston Churchill seems to have quoted to Roosevelt—urging a move away from the term "United Powers"—these lines by Lord Byron: "Millions of tongues record thee, and anew / Their children's lips shall echo them, and say— / 'Here, where the sword united nations drew, / Our countrymen were warring on that day!' / And this is much, and all which will not pass away."

Yankee Doodle Dandy

The exuberant song-and-dance patriot George Michael Cohan (1878–1942)—"Yankee Doodle Dandy" himself—claimed to have been born on the Fourth of July, but actually it was a day earlier. He was the ultimate American morale booster in both world wars. He was awarded a special Medal of Honor by Congress in 1940 for having composed the popular rallying tunes "Over There" and "You're a Grand Old Flag."

The Manhattan Project

The ultrasecret $2.2 billion investment that was a gamble on the theoretical calculations of US scientists brought forth the decisive atomic bomb during World War II. "The Manhattan Project"—begun in 1942, with 37 installations in 19 states and in Canada, with tens of thousands of contract employees—consumed slightly more of the gross national product than did the Apollo project, which put 12 humans on the Moon. The A-bomb project proceeded on the possibility that false information had been planted in Allied ears by the German Nobel Prize-winning physicist Werner Heisenberg (1901–1976) when he secretly divulged that German scientists would not be cooperative with the Nazis in developing nuclear devices.

The Chairman of the Board. Ol' Blue Eyes. The Bony Baritone. The Crooner.

Frank Sinatra (born 1917), enormously popular with both the bobbysox and the gray-haired sets, once said, "If I've had all the affairs I'm given credit for, I'd be in a jar at Harvard Medical School." The blue-eyed singer is "Chairman of the Board" of fellow entertainers, a much publicized "rat-pack."

The Divine Wind

Kamikaze in Japanese means "divine wind." The Japanese *kamikaze* pilots in World War II flew suicide missions, crashing their explosive-laden planes into enemy targets, particularly warships.

The Doolittle Raid. 30 Seconds Over Tokyo

Four months after Japan's attack on Pearl Harbor, General Jimmy Doolittle (born 1896) led 16 B-25 Army Air Force two-engine bombers in a surprise raid on several major Japanese cities, including Tokyo. Armed with one-ton bombs, they took off from the aircraft carrier *Hornet* pitching about in heavy seas 650 miles east of Japan. They left a battleship in flames, smashed an airplane factory, and set fire to oil tanks, boosting the morale of all Americans. A few of the fliers who crashed in China after the raid and were captured by the Japanese military were beheaded at the Bridge House prison in Shanghai.

Shangri-La

President Franklin D. Roosevelt called his simple, secret retreat in Maryland's Catoctin Hills, a couple of hours by automobile from the White House, "Shangri-La," for the mythical Tibetan land of eternal youth and safety in James Hilton's popular novel *Lost Horizon* (1933). "Shangri-La" expressed FDR's appreciation of the few hours he spent there on weekends during the war years, beginning in 1942. Today it is called Camp David, having been renamed by President Dwight D. Eisenhower for his grandson.

The Bataan Death March

Tens of thousands of American and Filipino soldiers captured by the Japanese in the Bataan Peninsula in the Philippines were forced, in 1942, to march 65 miles to an internment camp near Cabanatuan. Already crippled by starvation and disease, nearly 25,000 died along the route, and another 22,000 died in the first two months of captivity. Bataan Day has been a national holiday in the Philippines, and soldiers have solemnly rewalked a part of the death route.

The Longest Night

The Holocaust in World War II.

Executive Order #9066

In the year after Pearl Harbor, 112,000 Japanese-Americans were forced from their homes on the west coast of the United States and relocated, through the provisions of "Executive Order #9066," to a series of inland concentration camps. Two thirds of the internees were citizens. The American Civil Liberties Union branded Washington's directive as "the worst single wholesale violation of civil rights of American citizens in our history." Lawsuits over 40 years overturned the Supreme Court's decision that the evacuation and internment had been valid wartime acts of the federal government. Survivors received monetary awards.

The Death Railway

The Burma–Thailand "Death Railway" was built by European prisoners of war for the Japanese in 1942. It took 331,000 men to build the 250-mile road, which included the celebrated bridge over the River Kwai in Thailand.

Mae West

Life jackets used by Allied pilots downed over water were nicknamed "Mae West," for the pulchritudinous, buxom actress Mae West (1892–1980), the unparalleled mistress of the double entendre. Among her most-quoted remarks are "It's not the men in my life, it's the life in my men" and "It's better to be looked over than overlooked."

The Wannsee Conference

About a half-million Jews had already been murdered by the time ranking SS and other Nazi officials met in 1942 in the Wannsee section of Berlin to discuss "the final solution of the Jewish question." The conference had been requested by Gestapo chief Reinhold Heydrich (1904–1942) to obtain the moral support of the propaganda ministry, the party chancellery, and other government departments and individuals.

PAF

A number of Americans who had fought for the Loyalists against Francisco Franco's Fascists in the Spanish Civil War (1936–39) joined the US armed forces in World War II but were not trusted. They were considered to be "PAF," or "premature Anti-Fascists."

The Paradise Camp

The Nazi concentration camp at Theresienstadt, an old fortress town in Bohemia, was set up, in 1941, as a ghetto for aged Jews. Purporting to be an autonomous community, it was the only camp in which foreign observers were allowed. "The Paradise Camp" was in reality a sham, merely a way station on the road to the Auschwitz killing facilities.

The Splendid Splinter.
The Thumper

The last major-league baseballer to hit .400 was Ted Williams—"the Splendid Splinter," "the Thumper"—with .406 in 1941, on 185 hits in 456 ABs. The six-foot-three Boston Redsoxer (born 1918) also hit .400 in 1952 and .407 in 1953 but hadn't been at bat enough in those seasons to qualify for the record book (only 10 times in 1952 and 91 times in 1953); he also served both of those years as a Marine pilot in the Korean war. In 420 at bats in 1957, he swatted .388; he was 39 years old at season's end. In 113 games in 1960, he batted .316.

Date of Infamy

President Franklin D. Roosevelt, in a six-minute speech before a joint session of Congress on December 8, 1941, described as "a date which will live in infamy" Japan's wildly successful December 7 sneak attack on US naval and air bases in Hawaii while peace negotiations were being held in Washington, DC. Congress then all but unanimously voted to declare that a state of war existed between the United States and Japan.

The Blue Division

Spain's dictator, Francisco Franco, repaid Germany for its aid in his successful civil war in Spain, in the late 1930s, by sending the "Blue Division" to reinforce the Nazis' siege of Leningrad in 1941. The force was made up of volunteer Spanish soldiers and mercenaries.

Rosebud

The story is that "Rosebud" was newspaper magnate William Randolph Hearst's (1863–1951) pet name for his great and good friend Marion Davies' (1900–1961) genitalia—a fact said to be known to his friends Orson Welles (1915–1985) and Herman Mankiewicz (1897–1953) as they plotted their film classic, *Citizen Kane*. *Kane* (1941) was modeled on Hearst's exuberant career, and the moviemakers mischievously used the name for young Charles Kane's sled—"Rosebud"—as the film's leitmotif.

The Streak

Major-league baseball's most awesome record is Joe DiMaggio's 56-consecutive game hitting streak in 1941. "The Streak" constituted 56 games, 223 official at bats, 56 runs, 91 hits, 16 doubles, 4 triples, 15 home runs, and a .408 batting average. After being shut down in a night game in Cleveland, before 67,468 roaring fans, on July 17, the Yankee Clipper then hit safely in 16 more consecutive games! He never once bunted to reach first base safely during the Streak.

The Hess Landing

Hitler's chief deputy, Rudolf Hess (1894–1987), felt confident that he could negotiate a peace agreement with Great Britain. On May 10, 1941, Hess, acting alone and clandestinely, took off in a small plane and parachuted into Scotland. He told British authorities that he was on a mission of humanity: The Führer did not want to defeat England, and Hess wished to stop the fighting. "The Hess Landing" hit Hitler "as though a bomb had struck the Berghof." Hess never got to carry off his stroke of statesmanship; he was imprisoned in the Tower of London, later put away for life. (*See also* 1987: The One-Man Prison.)

The Iron Horse.
The Pride of the Yankees

New York Yankee first baseman Henry (Lou) Gehrig (1903–1941)—the "Pride of the Yankees"—played in 2,130 consecutive games, from June 1, 1925, to May 2, 1939, a baseball record some deem even greater than Joe DiMaggio's 56-consecutive-game hitting streak in 1941. "The Iron Horse" hit 493 homers and knocked in 1,990 runs in 17 glorious seasons with the Bronx Bombers, and he was the American League's most valuable player four times. (Cal Ripkin, Jr., born 1960, the Baltimore Orioles shortstop, had played in more than 1,000 consecutive games through the end of the 1989 season; he would have to take the field in every Oriole game well into the 1996 campaign to break Gehrig's super feat.)

Lou Gehrig's Disease

Amyotrophic lateral sclerosis (ALS) is a motor-neuron disease with muscle wasting and other problems as a result of defects in the nervous system; the disease progresses rapidly, causing death in two to five years. It is also known as progressive muscular atrophy and as anterior-horn-cell disease. But its most popular name is "Lou Gehrig's disease," for slugging Henry (Lou) Gehrig (1903–1941), whose illness did much to promote interest in its cause and treatment.

The Unknown War

At noon on June 22, 1941, Soviet Foreign Minister Vyacheslav Molotov (1890–1986) announced through loudspeakers on the principal streets of Moscow: "Men and women, citizens of the Soviet Union, the Soviet Government and its head, Comrade Stalin, have instructed me to make the following announcement: At 4:00 AM, without declaration of war and without any claims being made on the Soviet Union, German troops attacked our country, attacked our frontier in many places and bombed from the air Zhitomir, Kiev, Sevastopol, Kaunas, and other cities . . . Our cause is just. The enemy will be crushed. Victory will be ours." "The Unknown War" was underway: 4,200,000 Nazi troops were smashing across the 1,800-mile-long Russian frontier. By war's end, in 1945, the toll on the eastern front would be 30 million lives.

Barbarossa

The code name for Hitler's surprise invasion of the Soviet Union along a 3,000-mile front in June 1941 was "Barbarossa." From the Finnish border to Byelorussia, the Nazis crushed the Russian bear. Stalin was shattered by the attack. The Soviet dictator could not believe that his 1939 pact with Hitler would literally go up in smoke. "The Man of Steel" suffered a breakdown and disappeared for a time, leaving his Red Army in chaos and letting the invaders have their way. The code name evokes Holy Roman Emperor Frederick I (c.1123–1190), called "Barbarossa"—"Redbeard"— who drowned in a river in Asia Minor while leading the Third Crusade. One of the greatest rulers in Europe's history, he had become a major symbol to German nationalist movements. According to tradition, he sits sleeping at a marble table at Kyffhäuser Castle in central Germany, his red beard having grown so long that it encircles the table; he dreams of Germany's fate, and will wake and save the nation at some critical juncture.

The Fateful Months

Until the invasion of Poland (1939), Nazi Germany exerted pressure on its Jewish citizens to emigrate. Hitler then (into early 1941) considered shipping Europe's Jews to the French-controlled African island of Madagascar. But there followed, in historian Christopher Browning's description, "the fateful months"—the jelling of "the Final Solution," the program to exterminate the Jews, the Holocaust, "the longest night."

Four Freedoms

The United States was still almost a full year away from actively entering World War II when President Franklin D. Roosevelt declared in a 1941 message to Congress that "Four Freedoms" should prevail everywhere in the world: freedom of speech and expression, freedom of worship, freedom from want, and freedom from fear.

The Flying Tigers

In 1941, an American general, Claire Lee Chennault (1890–1958), organized an air corps for China's General Chiang Kai-shek. The pilots and technicians of this American Volunteer Group, most of whom had been released from the US Army and Navy for service in China, became known as "the Flying Tigers," for the large sharks' teeth painted on the noses of their obsolete Curtis P-40B fighter planes. They achieved remarkable successes with hit-and-run tactics against heavy Japanese odds.

A Shrine of Democracy

Five-story-tall busts, carved out of a granite cliff, of Presidents George Washington, Thomas Jefferson, Theodore Roosevelt (bespectacled), and Abraham Lincoln create "a Shrine of Democracy" in the Black Hills of southwest South Dakota, 25 miles from Rapid City. The Presidents represent the founding, the expansion, the preservation, and the unification of the United States. The Mount Rushmore memorial group was designed and begun by the American sculptor and painter John Gutzon de la Mothe Borglum (1867–1941).

The Injustice Collector

The Irish novelist James Joyce (1882–1941) had a need to feel deceived, and he saw treachery everywhere, which is why critic Leon Edel dubbed him "the Injustice Collector," a name that caught on. A Joyce biographer noted that the glaring truth in a shady episode about who had had his way with Joyce's common-law, then legal, wife, Nora Barnacle (1884–1951), is that Joyce could not have written *Ulysses* "without the surge of fear and relief that he derived from it." Not all of the great in literature saw Joyce as their equal. Thus H. G. Wells (1866–1946) wrote in a letter to Joyce: "You have in your composition a mighty genius for expression which has escaped discipline. . . . So I ask: Who the hell is this Joyce who demands so many waking hours of the few thousands I have still to live for a proper appreciation of his quirks and fancies?" And D. H. Lawrence (1885–1930): "My God, what a clumsy olla putrida James Joyce is! Nothing but old fags and cabbage-stumps of quotations from the Bible and the rest, stewed in the justice of deliberate, journalistic dirty-mindedness." And, to add an American voice, Clifton Fadiman (born 1904): "You pays your money and you takes your Joyce."

The Butterfly Bridge

Architect Frank Lloyd Wright's Imperial Hotel in Tokyo "floated" safely through the earthquake of 1923 that killed 143,000 Japanese and leveled the capital and Yokohama. The maverick architect (1867–1959) planned to use the same design principles to build an earthquake-safe, reinforced concrete bridge—a "Butterfly Bridge"—over Southern Bay in San Francisco, but lobbyists for the steel industry in the United States were able to turn back the scheme.

Stan the Man. No. 6

Stan Musial (born 1920) was the star-spangled St. Louis Cardinal baseballer for 22 years. His 3,630 hits, in 10,972 official times at bat, included 1,377 extra-base wallops (475 home runs). "No. 6" won the National League batting title seven times and the Most Valuable Player honor three times. He played in four World Series and in 1969 was elected to the National Baseball Hall of Fame.

The Arsenal of Democracy

Before declarations of war in both 1917 and 1941, the United States was the chief armaments supplier to Allied powers. In a "fireside chat" on radio on December 29, 1940, a year before Pearl Harbor, President Franklin D. Roosevelt declared that America "must be the arsenal of democracy."

No. 158

A person who is the first to be selected by a mass lottery is referred to as a "No. 158," for the first draft number selected in the very first US peacetime selective-service draft, on October 29, 1940. Over 6,000 American men held the number—every community that had at least 158 eligible men had a No. 158. (They were scheduled to put in a year of army training; many were in the service for at least five years.)

Operation Sea Lion

Hitler couldn't gain control of the air—he had lost the aerial Battle of Britain in 1940—so he turned away from a cold-water invasion of England toward the east and an attack on the Russians, with whom he had in 1939 signed a "Pact of Steel." His military code name for the planned invasion of England had been "Operation Sea Lion."

The Surrender Car

Hitler forced France to capitulate in 1940 at the same little clearing in the woods at Compiègne, France, where the German Empire had capitulated to the Allies on November 11, 1918—and in the same *wagon-lit* (railroad sleeping car). At the Führer's order, a three-foot-high granite block at the site of "the Surrender Car" was destroyed. The script on the block had read: "Here on the eleventh of November 1918 succumbed the criminal pride of the German empire—vanquished by the free peoples which it tried to enslave."

The Battle of Britain. Their Finest Hour

From July 10 to October 31, 1940, the German Luftwaffe tried to destroy the British Royal Air Force so that an invasion of the British Isles could proceed without British aerial resistance. The RAF lost more than a quarter of its pilots (415) but hung on—Britain's finest hour. Thwarted, Hitler turned away from "Operation Sea Lion," his plan to cross the Channel, and turned his sights on the invasion (June 1941) of his "Pact-of-Steel" partner, the Soviet Union. British Prime Minister Winston S. Churchill, on the eve of "the Battle of Britain," had said in the House of Commons: "Upon this battle depends the survival of Christian civilization. Upon it depends our own British life, and the long continuity of our institutions and our Empire. The whole fury and might of the enemy must very soon be turned on us. . . . Let us therefore brace ourselves to our duties, and so bear ourselves that, if the British Empire and its Commonwealth last for a thousand years, men will still say: 'This was their finest hour.' "

Lord Haw-Haw

The sobriquet for the Brooklyn-born Nazi propagandist William Joyce (1906–1946) was coined by a British professor who taught pronunciation to BBC announcers. Joyce was a Fascist, and he traveled on an improperly issued British passport, broadcasting in English for Berlin throughout World War II. He was adjudged subject to British jurisdiction and was hanged for treason.

Operation Dynamo

"Dunkirk" has come to stand for the greatest military evacuation in history, one of the epic actions of naval history in the midst of defeat. When German armies broke through to the French ports on the English Channel in 1940, more than 300,000 Allied troops were cut off at Dunkirk, in northern France, on the North Sea. In week-long "Operation Dynamo," 1,200 naval and civilian crafts removed 338,226 military personnel from the Dunkirk beaches. Hitler could almost easily have prevented the escape, but he chose not to do so for private reasons, which he kept from even his closest military leaders. (His secret admiration for anything British, psychologists say.)

Old Duckboards. Gimlet Eye. The Fighting Quaker

Brigadier General Smedley D. Darlington (1881–1940), a two-time Medal of Honor winner, was one of the most picturesque military men in US history. He was scarred with wounds, and he wore on his breast rows of medals that he had won protecting American interests in China, the Philippines, and Central America. He told Congress, "I feel I might have given Al Capone a few hints. The best he could do was to operate his racket in three city districts. We Marines operated on three continents." As director of public safety for Philadelphia, he said that cleaning up the city's vice "is worse than any battle I was ever in."

The 1930s

The Katyn Forest Denial

The NKVD (the Soviet secret police, replaced by the KGB) massacred thousands of Polish officers in 1940, in the first year of World War II, after Stalin and Hitler had divided Poland between themselves: 4,254 were shot at Katyn; 3,841 others were killed at Dergachi; 6,376 from the camp at Ostaszkowo were murdered at Bologoye. Until recently, Moscow had always claimed that the German army had carried out the butchery. The grisly event occurred more than a year before the Nazis invaded the region in their march on Moscow.

Molotov Cocktail

First used by Finns against the invading Russian army in 1939, a "Molotov Cocktail" is a homemade incendiary bomb—an alcohol- or gasoline-filled bottle that is hurled at the target. The explosive was named for the Soviet diplomatic representative Vyacheslav Molotov (1890–1986), who had a reputation for personal inflexibility and unswerving adherence to Soviet policies. (His original surname was Skriabin; he adopted Molotov, which means "hammer.") During the Nazis' 900-day siege of Leningrad, distilleries cut production of vodka and turned out "Molotov cocktails."

Ultra. Enigma

The Nazis' ultrasecret coding machine during World War II, called "Enigma," had been created in 1919 by a Dutchman, Hugo Koch, for business use. The British computer genius Alan Turing broke the Enigma code in 1939—the intercepts were in turn code-named "Ultra"—allowing the Allies to decipher messages between Hitler and his field commanders. Hitler did not use Enigma to prepare for the "Battle of the Bulge," in late 1944, catching the Allies by surprise.

The Voyage of the Damned

German Jews seeking a haven in the United States fled Nazi Germany on the ocean liner *St. Louis* in 1939. Because the German immigration quota was filled, the refugees planned to lay over in Cuba to await their visas. But Cuba allowed only 22 of the 1,128 refugees to land. The *St. Louis* sailed north along the east coast of the United States, hoping for intervention, but was denied permission to dock. "The Voyage of the Damned," as it became known, returned to Europe, where France, Great Britain, Belgium, and the Netherlands provided sanctuary. Most of the emigrees were eventually captured by the Nazis after their invasion of the Low Countries in the spring of 1940 and were shipped to death camps.

September 1

World War II started on September 1, 1939, when Hitler's armies rolled eastward into Poland, "counterattacking" with tanks and Stukas. Under a treaty, Britain and France came to Poland's defense by declaring war on Germany, but both countries more or less went about their business without sending in troops. (The war lasted six years and consumed close to 60 million lives.)

The Long Weekend

The 21-year lull between the two world wars—November 11, 1918, to September 1, 1939—is "the Long Weekend" in Robert Graves and Alan Hodge's 1940 work, *The Long Weekend: A Social History of Britain 1918–1939.*

The Bloomsburys.
The Bloomsbury Group

For a quarter-century (to 1939), Bertrand Russell, Rupert Brooke, John Maynard Keynes, E.M. Forster, Clive Bell, Lytton Strachey, and Leonard and Virginia Woolf were among the group of English writers and artists who met regularly in the Bloomsbury section of London. "The Bloomsburys" were the British intelligentsia, pacesetters of their generation. More than a half-century later, their unconventional lifestyle, socialist views, and esthetic sensibility continue to be examined.

El Caudillo

General Francisco Franco (1892–1975) adopted the title "El Caudillo"— army chieftain—when he ruled Spain, assuming for himself the mantle and the reputation of earlier *caudillos*, whose personal magnetism commanded the blind allegiance of their constituencies. The power of an "army chieftain" is uncontested; the people usually suffer because their constitutional rights are not being protected. In his 36-year reign, Franco was a typical *caudillo*.

The Good Doctor

The sobriquet "the Good Doctor" was conferred upon Sigmund Freud (1856–1939), the Austrian neurologist and psychiatrist who cofounded psychoanalysis. The American psychiatrist W. Bertram Wolfe (1896–1977) wrote: "Freud found sex an outcast in the outhouse, and left it in the living room as an honored guest." *Freud* literally means "joy" or "pleasure." (A *Freudenhaus* is a brothel; a *Freudenmädchen* is a prostitute. But, then, there is Friedrich Schiller's *Ode to Joy*, which makes a surprise appearance in Ludwig van Beethoven's *Ninth Symphony:* "Freude, schöner Götterfunken . . ."—joy, you beautiful spark from the gods. . . .)

Daring Dickie

World traveler and author Richard Halliburton (1900–1939) went where angels feared to tread. He climbed many of the most challenging mountains around the world, swam dangerous waters, flew where no one had dared fly before—and wrote about it in many books. Swimming the Panama Canal, he paid at the regular tonnage rate—for him, it was less than a dollar each way.

Typhoid Mary

Because it was impossible to divest "Typhoid Mary"—Mary Mallon (c. 1870–1938)—of the bug she was carrying, which was causing infection and death in at least seven epidemics in New York, she was quarantined for the last 26 years of her life. She had worked as a cook in many homes and was herself immune from the carrier-borne disease.

Crystal Night. Kristallnacht. Walpurgisnacht

The murder of a German official in Paris by a Jewish art student angered by the abuse that the Nazis were heaping on his parents led to a night of incalculable savagery against Jews in Germany. On November 9, 1938, the glass fronts of 10,000 shop windows were smashed (thus *Kristallnacht*, "Crystal Night"), hundreds of synagogues were torched, and innocent thousands were routed from their homes and businesses. More than 1,000 were killed, and 30,000 were arrested and hauled off to concentration camps—a tenth of all German Jews. The mayhem was engineered by the German minister of propaganda, Dr. Joseph Goebbels (1897–1945).

The Invasion from Mars. The Martian Landing

Orson Welles (1915–1985) scared the pants off America with his Halloween-eve radio-broadcast drama based on H. G. Wells's (1866–1946) 1898 sci-fi book *The War of the Worlds*. Hundreds of thousands of terrified Americans ran into the streets believing Welles's reports that Earth had been invaded by Martians. A Nazi party newspaper blamed the panic on the Jews; the columnist Dorothy Thompson wrote that Welles had proved how easy it could be to ignite panic in time of war. (The New Jersey town in which the Martians landed, Grovers Mills, celebrated the 50th anniversary of the broadcast with all kinds of "Martian" tricks and treats.)

The Gandhi Solution

Mohandas Karamchand ("Mahatma") Gandhi (1869–1948), deploring violence as the resolution of *any* problem, made the proposal that German Jews, all half-million of them, should commit collective suicide, thereby dramatizing the horror of burgeoning Nazism and making the world arise in righteous wrath. (Later, the German author Arno Schmidt [1914–1979] wrote: "Mankind, in protest against God's cruelties, should decide to commit collective suicide, on, say, November 15 . . . [in 5 seconds . . . at the sound of the gong . . .]. Then God will see if He can do His own dirty work.")

Disney's Folly

Even Walt Disney's wife was dubious about his plan to make an animated movie involving dwarfs. Her immediate reaction was one of repulsion: "There's something so nasty about them." But Disney (1901–1966) went back to his looking glass and asked, "Looking glass, looking glass, on the wall, who in this land is the fairest of all?" And the looking glass responded, "Thou, O Walt, *art* the fairest of all." Such was Disney's art that "Disney's Folly," *Snow White and the Seven Dwarfs*, was hailed as the "ten best" pictures of 1938.

The Cop-out Conference

In the wake of Hitler's absorption of Austria, President Franklin D. Roosevelt called an international conference on refugees, with the stipulation that "no state would be expected to receive greater numbers of emigrants than is permitted by existing legislation." Delegates to the 1938 conference, at France's deluxe resort of Évian-les-Bains, heard the host country complain that it was "saturated" with exiles. Canada urged tightening quotas to force Nazi Germany to solve the "Jewish problem" internally. Four months later, more than 1,000 of Germany's 300,000 Jews were dead and more than 30,000 arrested in the *Kristallnacht*.

MacGuffin

A "MacGuffin" is described by director Alfred Hitchcock (1899–1980) as the thing his movies' plots spun about: a secret formula, a spy code, a piece of loot gone astray, anything that caused the characters to run, jump, suffer, love, or die in its pursuit.

China's Sorrow

The Yellow River, or Huang Ho, is China's second-longest river (nearly 3,000 miles); since time immemorial, its floods have been killers—hence its name "China's Sorrow." In 1938, nearly a million northern Chinese were drowned—sacrificed when General Chiang Kai-shek's retreating army dynamited dikes along the Yellow, flooding 20,000 square miles and hundreds of cities and villages and damming the onrushing Japanese military tide.

The Grand Slam

The four major titles in the world of tennis are the French Open, Wimbledon in England, the US Open, and the Australian Open—"the Grand Slam." The Australian Rod Laver (born 1938), who won twice, and the American Don Budge (born 1915), who won once, are the only men to win the Grand Slam, and the German Steffi Graf (born 1969) and the Americans Margaret Court Smith (born 1942) and the late Maureen "Little Mo" Connolly (1934–1969) are the only women to win it. (The Czech-American Martina Navratilova, born 1956, won the four titles consecutively but not in the same calendar year.)

Wrong-Way Corrigan

A person who does something backward or takes the wrong course (legally or illegally) is a "Wrong-Way Corrigan," for the pilot-mechanic Douglas Corrigan (born 1907), who in 1938 took off in his Curtis Robin monoplane from New York's Floyd Bennett Field supposedly for the return flight to Long Beach, California, and 24 hours later—when he emerged from a pea-soup fog—found himself over Ireland, where he had really wanted to go in the first place. (In 1900, George Moore had said, "The wrong way always seems the more reasonable.") Corrigan was an "embarrassed" hero when he returned to the States for a ticker-tape parade.

Attorney for the Damned

Clarence Darrow (1857–1938) was a lifelong antagonist toward bigotry, prejudice, ignorance, and hate who won acquittals for the doomed, the hated, the hopeless, and the underdog. His passionate belief in justice for all became his life work. His famous cases included the Scopes evolution case, the Massie case in Honolulu, and the Sweet case in Detroit. Darrow knew that juries are more to be trusted than judges when it comes to the protection of the life and liberty of the citizen. He held that the freer we are to examine our values, the freer and more humane our society will be. He was, in many ways, a brother in spirit to H. L. Mencken (1880–1956), who wrote, "Moral certainty is always a sign of cultural inferiority. The more uncivilized the man, the surer he is that he knows precisely what is right and what is wrong," and "The truly civilized man is always skeptical and tolerant. . . . His culture is based on 'I'm not too sure.' "

America's First Billionaire

John D. Rockefeller (1839–1937) was born when Martin Van Buren was President, and he died in Franklin D. Roosevelt's second term. In those 98 years, he became rich as, well, Rockefeller—"America's first billionaire." He was the son of a peddler who had struck it rich by establishing centralized control in the oil industry through Standard Oil.

Unit 731

During the Sino-Japanese war (as of 1937) and during World War II, prisoners of war and civilian internees were sacrificed as human guinea pigs by Japanese army scientists. Victims were carved up, butchered without anesthetic, dissected until the last bloody scraps were washed off the operating tables. Men were staked out on proving grounds to test the effects of biological weapons. Formed by order of Emperor Hirohito, "Unit 731" was in remote northern Manchuria, commanded by General Shiro Ishii. Its innocuous designation was Kwantung Army Epidemic Prevention and Water Supply Unit.

The Burma Road

When the Sino-Japanese war erupted at the Marco Polo Bridge, in Beijing in 1937, Chinese engineers in just a year's time built a 700-mile-long road through rough mountain country from Yunan province in the south to the Burmese railhead of Lashio, to carry in war supplies that were landed at Rangoon, Burma, and shipped by rail to Lashio. "The Burma Road" became a vital lifeline for three years after the Japanese had taken effective military control of both the China coast and Indochina. It was captured by the Japanese in 1941.

The Rape of Nanking

Because almost all of the rules of morality could safely be broken on foreign soil, and because they looked on their foes as little more than animals, the Japanese army bore down on the Chinese city of Nanking in 1937 with repeated acts of indescribable cruelty, ruthlessness, and bloodshed during the Sino-Japanese war. Tens of thousands of Chinese were tortured and butchered by the Japanese in "the Rape of Nanking."

The Panay Incident

To keep the Yangtze (now called the Chang) clear for military operations, the Japanese military in 1937 ordered the sinking of all craft, regardless of nationality, near the mouth of China's longest river. The bombing, machine-gunning, and sinking of the US gunboat *Panay*, on patrol with American oil tankers, provoked momentary anger in the United States. But when Tokyo apologized profusely and agreed to pay an indemnity, the incident was put aside. Out of the episode, however, came the US decision to send a navy officer to London to discuss, informally, plans for cooperation with the Royal Navy in case of war with Japan.

The Marco Polo Bridge Incident

Five and a half years after occupying Manchuria and turning it into the puppet state of Manchukuo, Japanese soldiers, in 1937, clashed with Chinese forces at the Marco Polo Bridge in China's capital city of Beijing. The skirmish was the pretext for Hirohito's occupation of Beijing and Tientsin; the second Sino-Japanese war was on. It would continue for eight years until the atomic bombing of two Japanese cities and the end of World War II in August 1945.

The Trial of the Century. The Biggest Story Since the Resurrection

In 1936 the battered body of world-famous aviator Colonel Charles A. Lindbergh's kidnapped two-year-old son was found near the Lindbergh home in New Jersey. Two and a half years later, a German-born carpenter, Bruno Richard Hauptmann (born 1900), was nabbed in the Bronx, New York, with part of the $50,000 ransom that Lindbergh had paid. He was offered a life sentence in exchange for a confession, but he said he had nothing to confess. H. L. Mencken, the Baltimore editor and critic, was the first to call the kidnapping "the Trial of the Century" and "the Biggest Story Since the Resurrection." Many still believe that Hauptmann was railroaded into the electric chair in 1936 and that all evidence was bent to fit the preconception that Hauptmann was guilty.

The Sian Incident

Chinese Nationalist chief Chiang Kai-shek (1887–1975) was kidnapped in 1936 by warlord and former Manchurian Governor Chang Hsueh-liang (born 1898) and kept prisoner in Sian, in the Wei River valley, until he agreed to terminate the civil war against the Chinese Communists and establish a united front with them against the Japanese armies moving south from Manchuria. But within two years, Chiang resumed military harassment of the Reds, who were proving to be an effective fighting force against the Japanese.

Fifth Column

During the Spanish Civil War (1936–39), Nationalist General Emilio Mola (1887–1937) boasted in a radio broadcast that he had four columns of soldiers approaching the capital of Madrid and a "Fifth Column" of sympathizers within the city who would sabotage the Loyalist defenders from the rear.

The Ebony Express. The Ebony Antelope. The Track Star of the Century. The Fastest Man Alive

Jesse Owens (1913–1980) set five world records and tied a sixth within 45 minutes at the Big Ten Championships in Ann Arbor, Michigan, on May 25, 1935. In the 1936 Olympic Games in Germany, the black Ohio State University student ran and jumped to four gold medals and set three records.

The Rome–Berlin Axis

The Hitler–Mussolini partnership forged in October 1936 gave birth to "the Rome–Berlin Axis," which was solidified three years later by the Italian–German Alliance. This in turn was extended in September 1940 by a military alliance between Germany, Italy, and Japan—the so-called Berlin Pact, which Hungary, Romania, Slovakia, and Croatia later joined.

The Lincolns

About 2,800 Americans—acrobats, trade unionists, professors, artists, actors among them—went to Spain in 1936 as volunteers in the Loyalist army of the shaky young Republican government, just five years free of its ancient monarchy and now threatened by well-armed, rebellious, Fascist military leaders. Technically a battalion, the American unit was called the Abraham Lincoln Brigade—"the Lincolns." With rare exceptions, few of the Americans had military experience; more than half of them died in the 1936–39 civil war, won by Generalissimo Francisco Franco's troops.

The Most Dangerous Woman in America. The Lady of Hull-House. Saint Jane

The social reformer Jane Addams (1860–1935), once representative of the best of democracy, was called a traitor and "the most dangerous woman in America" because of her activities in the world-peace movement and her opposition to World War I. "Pacifist" had become synonymous with "Red," every criticism of the war was hysterically interpreted by isolation-ist superpatriots as un-American and disloyal, and so she was expelled from the Daughters of the American Revolution. More than a decade later, in 1931, "Saint Jane" was honored with the Nobel Peace Prize. (Hull-House was the name of her social settlement in Chicago.)

Butterfield 8

When New York City had telephone exchanges with names—TRafalgar, RIverside, MOnument, CHickering, CIrcle, WAdsworth—*BUtterfield 8*, the title of John O'Hara's popular 1935 novel about a promiscuous woman, became a code word for high-class call girls.

The Kingfish.
The Ungovernable Governor

In 1935, patronage-powerful Senator Huey Pierce Long (born 1893)—"the Kingfish"—was murdered in the state capital in Baton Rouge, Louisi-ana, by a young and brilliant surgeon, Carl Weiss, who was also accom-plished in music, painting, mathematics, and mechanics and was a new father. The reason for the assassination is unknown, for the gunman was shredded by 30 bodyguard bullets on the spot; but there has been specula-tion about a connection with the fact that Weiss was the son-in-law of a disappointed officeholder. Before his Senate career, Long had been a ruth-less dictator as governor of Louisiana, and he was still running the state from his seat in the US Senate—with sights on the presidency. Franklin D. Roosevelt called him one of the two most dangerous men in America. Southerners recognized "the Kingfish" as a colorful demagogue who played upon deep-seated economic grievances and racial hatreds of poor whites. Yet his actions were not those of a racist; as governor, he abolished the hideous poll tax; he was the only Southern governor of those times to treat blacks more or less as equals; and he told the head of the Ku Klux Klan to stay out of Louisiana. Long's undoing was his becoming corrupted by power. His two favorite slogans were "Share Our Wealth" and "Every Man a King."

His brother Earl Kemp Long (1895–1960), who also became a governor of Louisiana, in the 1940s and 1950s, was known as "the Ungovernable Governor."

The Pink Triangles

Homosexuals also suffered in Hitler's Germany; he felt that "that degener-acy" would poison the Aryan race and must be eliminated at all costs. Gay men were arrested and placed in concentration camps and forced to wear, as of 1935, a pink triangle, as a badge of shame (about 20,000, of an esti-mated German gay population of 1.5 million in 1933). "The Pink Triangles" were put to the hardest labor and fed the thinnest rations. They were ostracized, suffering the abuse and derision of guards and fellow internees alike. This unenlightened treatment was often continued by the American and British liberators of the camps; for example, one inmate, after spending three years in a Nazi camp, was required by the Allies to finish another five years of the Nazi-imposed sentence of eight years for sexual deviance. In the 1970s, the practice of marking people as homosexual was resumed in the jail of Polk County, Florida, in the form of pink bracelets that all male and female gay inmates have to wear. They, too, are suffering abuse and derision from guards and fellow prisoners. This policy was challenged, after 15 years, by the American Civil Liberties Union, in 1989.

The Nuremberg Laws

The Third Reich (1933–45) legitimized and legalized antisemitism with promulgation of the Nuremberg Laws, drawn up in 1935 at a congress of the National Socialist (Nazi) party in the Bavarian city of Nuremberg, in southwest Germany. German Jews, no matter how long their ancestry in the Fatherland, were deprived of their civil rights, their very citizenship. Jews could not marry non-Jews. Persons of partly Jewish descent were deprived of certain rights. (In World War I, 80,000 German Jews were at the front for the Kaiser, where 35,000 were decorated, 2,000 commissioned, and 12,000 killed in battle.)

The Dust Bowl

Born of a combination of climatic and human factors, "the Dust Bowl" in 1935 encompassed a 97-million-acre piece of high-level land in the southern portion of the Great Plains. It included parts of Colorado, New Mexico, Texas, Oklahoma, Nebraska, and Kansas. In the "dirty 30s," 20 states set records for dryness that still stand, and high winds caused "black blizzards."

Gloomy Gus

Richard M. Nixon (born 1913) was first called "Gloomy Gus" at Duke University Law School. He proposed marriage the night he met Thelma Catherine "Pat" Ryan (born 1912) in a local theater group playing *The Dark Tower*. "I thought he was nuts or something," Mrs. Nixon has since been quoted. "I guess I just looked at him. I couldn't imagine anyone ever saying anything like that so suddenly." President Harry S. Truman once said that "Richard Nixon is a no-good lying bastard." President Jimmy Carter, when he was governor of Georgia, declared, "he's the most dishonest President we've ever had." During the Watergate investigation, President Nixon maintained, "I am not a crook."

The Cherokee Kid.
The Cowboy Philosopher.
The American Prometheus

Will Rogers (1879–1935), who once said, "I would rather be the man who bought the Brooklyn Bridge than the man who sold it," may have been the most beloved man in America in his day. The cowboy-lariatist-columnist-humorist-philosopher-flying fanatic "Cherokee Kid" (he was part Oologah Indian) and "Cowboy Philosopher" was the nation's top motion-picture box-office attraction and the most popular after-dinner speaker ever, delivering such quotes as "Our municipal election ran true to political form. The sewer was defeated but the councilmen got in." "The Senate passed a bill appropriating $15 million for food, but the House has not approved it. They must think it would encourage hunger." Rogers boasted that he never met a man he didn't like.

The Long March

In 1935, Mao Tse-tung's army of about 90,000 men and women broke through the Nationalist army's siege and marched westward to Kweichow province, where Mao (1893–1976) gained supreme leadership of the Communist party. They moved on to the northern city of Yen-an, overcoming towering mountains, turbulent rivers, and constant harassment by Nationalists and local warlords. More than half of the original marchers survived the 6,000-mile trek.

The King of Swing

A year after forming his own band, Benny Goodman's search for a "big-band" jazz style finally bore fruit in 1936 when he introduced "swing," tightly woven ensemble work overlaid with brilliant improvisations of soloists, including Goodman himself on the clarinet. "The King of Swing" (1909–1986) introduced jazz to Carnegie Hall in 1938; the concert recording is a classic.

The Great Dissenter

Associate justice of the US Supreme Court Oliver Wendell Holmes, Jr. (1841–1935), was known for advocating "judicial restraint" but also for his frequent, eloquent (and sometimes outrageously misguided) disagreements with his colleagues. The son of the New England literary figure Oliver Wendell Holmes, MD, he believed that the life of the law was not logic but experience. His dissenting opinions inspired generations of lawyers and public servants. England honored him as the only person outside the British Empire ever to be made a member of the Honorable Society of Lincoln's Inn. Other "Great Dissenters" on the Supreme Court were John Marshall Harlan (1833–1911) and Louis D. Brandeis (1856–1941).

The First Lady of the American Stage. The Little Corporal

Helen Hayes (born 1900), the five-foot "First Lady of the American Stage," admits she's "bossy. I'm not imperious, I don't really want people to curtsy low before me and back out of rooms, but I do like to run things. My husband [the playwright Charles MacArthur] used to call me the Little Corporal, after Napoleon." The actress made her professional debut on Broadway as a shy eight-year-old in the role of Little Mimi in Victor Herbert's *Old Dutch*. Her favorite play was Laurence Housman's long-running *Victoria Regina* (1935), which solidified her reign.

The Keeper of the Nation's History

The National Archives—"the Keeper of the Nation's History" since 1934— catalogs and preserves documents like the Declaration of Independence and the Constitution, as well as the records of the presidency, the Congress, and the Supreme Court—the three branches of the federal government established by the Constitution (1787). Congress made the Archives, in Washington, DC, an independent agency after appointees of President Richard M. Nixon started to help him haul off White House tapes and records during the Watergate investigation in the early 1970s.

The Dord Edition

The first printings of *Webster's New International Dictionary, Second Edition,* 1934, became known as "the Dord Edition" because of the ghost entry "**dord**(dôrd), *n.* See *density.*" The error started with the note "D or d" on a 3x5 slip as two abbreviations of "density," which was correct; but another editor overlooked the spaces around "or," felt it must be a noun, and tentatively added "*n.*"; a third editor added the pronunciation "(dôrd)," still tentatively—but the word had begun breathing. "Dord" lived for five years. Today, a 1934–39 printing of Webster's Second is a collector's item because of the error and may bring upward of $1,000.

Baby Face

Pint-size George Nelson, born Lester N. Gillis (1908–1934), was known as "Baby Face Nelson" or just "Baby Face," seemingly in contrast to his activities as a bank robber and as one of the most notorious members of the John Dillinger gang. He was hunted in 10 states by 5,000 policemen, 300 infantrymen, the FBI, and several airplanes; and when he was finally mowed down in a gun battle in a Chicago suburb in 1934, he took two federal agents with him.

The Hays Office. The Hays Code

Following repeated scandals in Hollywood, the motion-picture industry, in 1934, decided to police itself, appointing the lawyer and former US Postmaster General Will H. Hays (1879–1954) movie czar. Long kisses, adultery, and nude babies were kept off the silver screen, and married couples (in the movies) had to sleep in twin beds. "The Hays Office" even lengthened the hemline of the cartoon character Betty Boop. The sultry Mae West complained, "We weren't even allowed to wiggle when we sang." Unexpectedly, the Hays office allowed Clark Gable to utter, "Frankly, my dear, I don't give a damn."

Little Napoleon

John J. McGraw (1873–1934) managed the New York Giants with an iron hand for 33 seasons—nearly 5,000 games—winning nine National League championships and three World Series. "Little Napoleon" was one of the first inductees into the National Baseball Hall of Fame. Perhaps his most unusual campaign was in 1916: The Giants put together winning streaks of 16 and 26 games and ended up in only fourth place, seven games behind the league champion Brooklyn Dodgers.

Fireside Chats.
The First Media President

President Franklin D. Roosevelt (1882–1945) was celebrated for his 15 or so "fireside chats" on the radio in his first two terms—he was "the First Media President." In one fireside chat, in 1934, he asked the American public: "Are you better off than you were last year? Are your debts less burdensome? Is your bank account more secure? Are your working conditions better? Is your faith in your own individual future more firmly grounded?"

The Lady in Red

Mrs. Anna Miller was wearing an orange dress, but it looked red under a light. To this day, it is believed that "the Lady in Red" fingered the gangster John Dillinger (1903–1934). FBI agents had waited for two hours outside a movie house on Chicago's North Side. When Dillinger, his current lover, Mrs. Rita Keele, and Mrs. Miller emerged from the gang-and-gun film *Manhattan Melodrama*—its moral was that crime doesn't pay—the agents mowed down "Public Enemy Number One."

The Fugu Plan

The highest councils of prewar Japan wanted to create an "Israel" in Asia. They planned in 1934 to convince European Jews to move to Manchukuo and provide creative energy, industrial skills, and cultural finesse to the emperor's puppet state. American and British Jews could even invest in the development. A Japanese military officer has been quoted as saying that "the plan is very much like fugu [the Japanese blowfish whose deadly poison must be removed before it can be eaten]. If we are indeed skillful in preparing this dish . . . if we succeed in our undertaking, we will create for our nation and our beloved emperor the tastiest and most nutrious dish imaginable." Nothing came of "the Fugu Plan." An expert on Japanese-Jewish relations is not sure it really existed.

The Gashouse Gang

The St. Louis Cardinals were called "the Gashouse Gang" because of their rowdy, feisty, aggressive baseballers, especially Dizzy Dean, Pepper Martin, Ducky Medwick, Leo Durocher, and Frankie Frisch, the second-baseman manager. The allusion seems to be to the Gashouse District, a rough Lower East Side neighborhood of Manhattan that was marked by several large gas tanks and whose vicious thugs were, in fact, called "the Gashouse Gang." The Cardinals won the National League title and the World Series in 1934 and finished second the following season.

The Week That Was

By coincidence, there were in the same week in December 1933 two shifts of moral standards in the United States: A federal judge ruled that James Joyce's novel *Ulysses* could be published and read in the United States, and the states repealed the Eighteenth Amendment to the Constitution, the only amendment to be repealed—Prohibition.

The Ulysses Case

Instead of finding "the leer of the sensualist," Federal Judge John M. Woolsey (1896–1977) found in James Joyce's classic novel an "honest," "sincere," "somewhat tragic but very powerful commentary on the inner lives of men and women," and he rendered a historic anticensorship decision (December 1933): "*Ulysses* may, therefore, be admitted into the United States."

The Coolidge Effect

After the death of Calvin Coolidge (1872–1933), his name, justifiably or not, became associated with the observation that when a man is too "spent" sexually to respond to the same female, he *is* turned on if a fresh

partner is available. The President and Mrs. Coolidge (who was much admired for her poise and charm) were said to have visited a chicken farm,
and when she was told that a rooster can "mount" many, many times, she
said, "Tell that to my husband"; but when *he* heard that the rooster did it
with a different hen every time, the "Do-Nothing President" said, "Tell
that to my wife."

The Lame-Duck Amendment

Until the Twentieth Amendment to the Constitution of the United States
was ratified, in 1933, defeated candidates for reelection to the federal government—senators, representatives, even Presidents—had to hang around
for four months: from early November to early March. They were "lame
ducks." The "Lame-Duck Amendment" cut that time in half: "The terms
of the President and Vice President shall end at noon on the twentieth day
of January, and the terms of Senators and Representatives at noon on the
third day of January, of the year in which such terms would have ended if
this article had not been ratified; and the terms of their successors shall
then begin."

Felix's Happy Hot Dogs

When Franklin D. Roosevelt became the 32nd President of the United
States, in 1933, hundreds of graduates of the nation's leading universities
moved to Washington, DC, to help run the administration's New Deal programs. Reporters nicknamed them "Felix's Happy Hot Dogs," after their
mentor, Professor Felix Frankfurter (1882–1965), of the Harvard Law
School, who became a Supreme Court justice in 1939.

The Townsend Plan

The most notorious phenomenon of the Depression years, Old-Age Re-
volving Pensions, Inc.—nicknamed "the Townsend Plan"—proposed to
retire every American over 60 years of age and pay each retiree a monthly
stipend of scrip worth $200, which had to be spent within the month. The
pensions would be financed by a national sales tax. Created in 1933 by the
physician–social reformer Francis Everett Townsend (1867–1960), the
Townsend Plan became a strong political force; it was incorporated into
bills put before Congress, which was overwhelmingly hostile, and the plan
never passed into law. But it was instrumental in the passage of the 1935
Social Security Act.

The Blue Eagle

The centerpiece of the first wave of President Franklin D. Roosevelt's New
Deal program in 1933 was the National Recovery Administration—NRA.
Its symbol was the blue eagle, and its goal was regulation of competition,

which would help the depressed economy to recover its strength. "The Blue Eagle" organized industries into groups, which would write codes, or sets of rules, governing prices and the quality of goods and wages. Within two years, the Supreme Court declared the NRA to be unconstitutional.

Hundred Days

President Franklin D. Roosevelt's famous "Hundred Days" began with his inaugural address (March 1933), when he declared that the Depression-besieged nation "asks for action, and action now. We must act and act quickly." And action the United States got: Government agencies were set up to revive the economy with a vast expenditure of public funds, the United States went off the gold standard, and finance and banking were regulated by a flood of anti-Depression measures. (*See also* 1815: Hundred Days.)

The Big Lie

A propaganda tool used by the Nazis, "the Big Lie," has been defined as "a falsehood of such magnitude and audacity that it is bound to have an effect on public opinion even if it is not given credence by a majority." It reflects Hitler's view that winners don't have to explain or to apologize for what they say or do.

A New Deal

Franklin D. Roosevelt (1882–1945), in Chicago, accepting the Democratic party's nomination to be its presidential standardbearer in 1932, per-orated, "I pledge you, I pledge myself, to a new deal for the American people." (The phrase was suggested by Brain Truster Raymond Moley, 1886–1975.) When FDR overwhelmed the incumbent, Herbert Hoover (1874–1964), in the Democrats' first lopsided national election victory in genera-tions, the "New Dealers" strove immediately to get direct aid to the victims of the Depression and to get the economy off the canvas.

The Little Tin Box

Bribe money is said to be kept by public officials in little tin boxes. One Manhattan sheriff bragged that he owed the impressive superiority of his lifestyle to the little tin box he had at home (à la Ollie North). In the Broad-way musical *Fiorello*, the little tin box, "a cushion for life's rude shocks," is celebrated in song.

The March King

John Philip Sousa (1854–1932) earned his dough-re-me with the compo-sition of a hundred marches, many of them popular to this day: "Semper

Fidelis," "The Washington Post March," "The Stars and Stripes Forever."
He also stole a march on other composers with the popular comic operet-
tas *El Capitán, The Bride Elect,* and *The Free Lance.* He was conductor of the
US Marine Band for a dozen years. He toured the world for two years with
his own band and was decorated with the Victorian Order by King Edward
VII.

The Bonus Army

In 1932, during the Depression, 17,000 World War I veterans—the Bonus
Expeditionary Force, "the Bonus Army"—marched on Washington, DC,
to demand cash compensation that they were legally entitled to under a
congressional act. President Herbert Hoover refused to hear their pleas. To
disperse the homeless veterans, and in challenge to the right of assembly,
Hoover called out Army Chief of Staff Douglas MacArthur and key aide
Dwight D. Eisenhower, and sent cavalry and tanks against men, women,
and children. Tear gas and flamethrowers demolished Hoovervilles. Two
police officers and two veterans were killed. The nation was stunned. The
veterans' claims were not settled for another four years.

The Scottsboro Trials

In 1931, nine black youths, one only eight or nine years old, were indicted
in Scottsboro, Alabama, on the charge of raping two white girls in a moving freight car. Northern liberals and radicals defended the boys through
several trials because they believed that the charge was unproved and that
the verdicts—death or up to 99 years in prison—were the backlash of an-
tiblack sentiment. The US Supreme Court twice reversed convictions on
procedural grounds: The youths' right to counsel had been infringed, and
no black had served on the grand jury or on the trial jury. Retrials resulted
in long prison terms, no death sentences, and acquittal for two.

The Wizard of Menlo Park

Thomas Alva Edison (1847–1931) transformed the everyday world as if by
magic. He invented the electric lamp and distribution system, the perfect
phonograph, an electric vote recorder, a stock printer, an alkaline storage
battery, a dictating machine, a mimeograph, the motion-picture camera,
and the fluoroscope used in the first X-ray operation in the United States.
He considered the electric lamp his greatest achievement—it turned night
into day. After completing an invention, in his laboratory in Menlo Park,
New Jersey, Edison would jump up and down in a kind of jungle dance. In
all, he held 1,093 patents.

The Miracle Worker

Annie M. Sullivan Macy (1866–1931), who was partially blind, helped the indomitable Helen Keller (1880–1968) overcome the triple handicaps of deafness, blindness, and speechlessness caused by a childhood illness, probably scarlet fever. "The Miracle Worker" was at Miss Keller's side when she was graduated from Radcliffe College with honors in German and English and when she traveled and "lectured" around the world.

The Man of a Thousand Faces

The silent-screen movie star (more than 150 flicks) Lon Chaney (1883–1930) was "the Man of a Thousand Faces," a master of the grotesque. Exchanging thoughts with his deaf and dumb parents by means of sign language led to Chaney's extraordinary skill as an actor with unusually expressive gestures, particularly body language. He first gained national "recognition" by playing a frog in *The Miracle Man* (1919), reshaping his face with plastic gum.

The Blond Venus

The German-American movie star Marlene Dietrich claimed she looked like a potato with hair, but she was indeed a "blond Venus," irresistible to men. Marlene—born (1901) Maria Magdalena von Losch—went everywhere with a monocle and a boa, sometimes with five red-fox furs. The ageless femme fatale entertained German prisoners in the United States during World War II.

Planet X

Astronomer Clyde W. Tombaugh (born 1906) was searching in 1930 for "Planet X"—the gravitational force that perturbs the giant planets Uranus and Nepture—when he spotted on his photographic plates a speck moving 3,577 billion miles from his telescope in the Lowell Observatory, in Arizona. But instead of "X," he had discovered the outermost planet so far seen in the solar system—Pluto. The search for "Planet X" continues. It may be a planet or something smaller, but *something* is out there causing unexplained gravitational perturbations.

Emperor Jones

Robert Tyre (Bobby) Jones, Jr. (1902–1971)—"Emperor Jones"—popularized golf all by himself. He won the US Open four times, the US Amateur five times, and the British Open three times. In 1930 he became the only player to cop the Grand Slam—winning the National Open, the National Amateur, the British Open, and the British Amateur. He quit tourney play at the age of 28 and became a practicing lawyer. He also founded the prestigious Masters tournament at the Augusta National Golf Club, which he had helped to lay out.

Hoovervilles

During the Depression, tar-paper housing for otherwise homeless Americans was called "Hoovervilles," for President Herbert Hoover (1874–1964), whose administration at first failed to grasp the enormity of the stock-market collapse. In March 1930, the President predicted that the worst effects of the crash on unemployment would pass by summer. Eleven summers later, when the United States entered World War II, the nation was still suffering pervasive Depression blues.

The Dishonest Decade

The self-delusion, the blunders, and the deceits on all sides as Hitler stormed to power in Germany have prompted historians to label the 1930s "the Dishonest Decade." Donald Cameron Watt (born 1928) believes that the democracies' willingness to consider last-minute negotiations probably stemmed from 1939's interpretation of 1914 as a series of diplomatic failures of communication that led to a war no one wanted. It seems that what the democracies could not quite believe in 1939 was that Hitler wanted war.

The 1920s

The American Earthquake

The Great Depression that began with the stock market crash in October 1929 rocked like an earthquake all assumptions that had been made, here and abroad, about the American economic way of life. Thomas Lamont (1870–1948), a J. P. Morgan banking-empire senior partner, had just written to President Herbert Hoover: "The future appears brilliant—we have the greatest and soundest prosperity and the best material prospects of any country in the world."

Black Tuesday. The Day the Bubble Burst. The Crash

The most catastrophic day in the history of the New York stock market was October 29, 1929, Black Tuesday. About 16 million shares were sold at declining prices. By mid-November, some $30 billion in the value of listed stocks was wiped out. On December 3, President Herbert Hoover, in his annual message to Congress, declared that confidence in the nation's business had been restored. Within four years, one third of the American labor force, 16 million people, were unemployed. The Depression lasted more than a decade.

The St. Valentine's Day Massacre

Seven associates of the Bugs Moran gang were rubbed out in a warehouse slaughter in Chicago on February 14, 1929—St. Valentine's Day. Chicago police believed that rival gang leader Al "Scarface" Capone had ordered the hit.

The Happy Warrior

Governor Alfred E. Smith (1873–1944), "the Happy Warrior," was the first Catholic to run seriously for the presidency of the United States, in 1928. For the first time, thousands of blacks in the North (very few of them Catholic) voted for the Democratic ticket, but the New York governor was still defeated by the Republican Herbert Hoover, by 357 electoral votes. Smith was celebrated for his brown derby and cigar and quick wit—"the Happy Warrior." He became the first chief executive of the Empire State Building corporation.

The It Girl. The Brooklyn Bombshell

Clara Bow (1905–1965), a tiny starlet with bee-stung lips, a flat chest, big eyes, and dimpled knees, personified the flapper in silent movies. "The hottest jazz baby in films" radiated "It," a vague euphemism for sex appeal, and for sexual intercourse, as in the 1928 Cole Porter hit tune *Let's Do It, Let's Fall in Love*. The "It Girl"'s sex appeal drove men mad with desire, until talkies revealed her thick Brooklyn accent: She no longer had it. (The movie *It*, starring Clara Bow, was based on the 1927 book *It* by the prolific English novelist and Hollywood scenario writer Elinor Sutherland Glyn, about 1864 to 1943, who not only coined but—to judge by a contemporary ditty—also *had* "it": "Would you like to sin / With Elinor Glyn / On a tiger skin? / Or would you prefer / To err / With her / On some other fur?")

Big Poison. Little Poison

Major-league baseball's best-hitting brothers, percentagewise, were the Waners. Paul Waner (1903–1965), "Big Poison," had a career batting average of .333; his brother Lloyd (1906–1982), "Little Poison," batted .316—for a combined average of .324.5. (The three DiMaggio brothers hit for a combined average of .290, the three Alou brothers hit for .292. The Aaron brothers, Hank and Tommie, combined for 768 home runs—Hank slugged 755 of them.)

The Good Shoemaker and the Poor Fish Peddler

After an emotionally charged trial and subsequent headline-making protests, two Italian anarchist draft dodgers, Nicola Sacco (born 1891), "the Shoemaker," and Bartolomeo Vanzetti (born 1888), "the Fisherman," were electrocuted in Massachusetts in 1927 for the murder of two men during a payroll holdup seven years earlier. Editorialists declared that the aliens were prosecuted chiefly because of their radical views, that it was obvious that the case pitted immigrants, workers, and the poor against the Protestant establishment and those who believed America should tolerate only certain people and certain ideas—and besides, "why all this fuss over a couple of 'wops'?" On the 50th anniversary of the execution, the governor of Massachusetts, Michael Dukakis, issued a public apology for the state's act; he was condemned in turn by many politicians and citizens. (The jury had seen evidence that a gang of professional bandits may have been the holdup men and killers.)

The Lone Eagle. Lucky Lindy

The first airman to fly solo across the Atlantic Ocean was "the Lone Eagle"—Charles A. Lindbergh (1902–1974). The year was 1927, only 24 years after the Wright brothers first flew for 59 seconds. "Lucky Lindy" took off in his single-engine monoplane from Long Island, New York, and touched down 33½ nonstop hours and 3,600 nonstop miles later at Le Bourget, near Paris. He later flew on to England, and he returned to America—aboard a naval cruiser—with a jubilant world's acclaim. He was *Time* magazine's first Man of the Year. A captain in the Air Corps reserve at the time of his flight, Lindbergh became one of only two men honored by the United States with the Medal of Honor for nonwartime service.

The Long-Count Fight. The Manassa Mauler

In 1927 Jack Dempsey (1895–1983)—"the Manassa Mauler"—pounded heavyweight champion Gene Tunney (1897–1978) to the canvas, but Dempsey didn't withdraw to a neutral corner right away. The 10-count couldn't start until he did. Tunney got to his feet after 14 seconds or so and went on to retain his crown. "Half the people thought he won," Dempsey said later, "the other half thought I won. They're still arguing about it." There are even fights about it. Dempsey (from Manassa, Colorado) scored 21 first-round knockouts in his heavyweight career.

The Murderers' Row

When the superlative New York Yankees baseball team of 1927 won 110 games, the batting order included Babe Ruth, Lou Gehrig, Earl Combs, Tony "Poosh 'em Up" Lazzeri, and Bob Meusel—"the Murderers' Row." The Yankees, the "Bronx Bombers," copped the World Series, as they did again the following year after winning 101 regular-season games. The appellation "murderers' row" has since been used to refer to any lineup of sluggers who "kill" the other team's pitchers. It may even refer to "heavy hitters" in other areas, especially in politics, as in 1952 when Republican presidential candidate Dwight D. Eisenhower was chided by the Democratic candidate Adlai Stevenson for his backing by a "murderers' row of reactionaries."

Little Miss Dead Shot. Peerless Lady Wing-Shot

Annie Oakley (1860–1926) was an incredible sharpshooter. She could split a playing card held edge-on and hit coins tossed into the air. As a teenager, she bested marksman Frank E. Butler (who also died in 1926), then married him; together, they shot the lights out on vaudeville and circus circuits. Anything he could do, she could do better. She shot a cigarette from the lips of the future Kaiser Wilhelm of Germany. Songsmith Irving Berlin hit the bull's-eye with his marvelous 1946 Broadway musical about "Little Miss Dead Shot," *Annie Get Your Gun.*

The Most Famous Little Boy in America

Eleven-year-old Johnny Sylvester may or may not have been dying from a forehead infection caused by a horse's kick, in 1926, when word reached his hero, the New York Yankees' Babe Ruth, that Johnny had "a last request": a baseball autographed by the great "Bambino." Back came two balls autographed by the Yankees and St. Louis Cardinals and a message from Ruth: "I'll knock a homer for you on Wednesday." Wednesday was game four of the World Series between the Yankees and the Cards, and the Babe clouted not one home run, but three. Ruth later made a well-publicized visit to the youngster in New Jersey. "The most famous little boy in America" managed to recover his health, and he lived into 1990, graduating from Princeton University, then serving in the US Navy during World War II and as president of a packing-machinery manufacturer.

The Latin Lover.
The Sheik

When Rudolph Valentino (1895–1926), the Italian-born former dishwasher, unexpectedly died a few days after contracting pneumonia and peritonitis, women around the world became hysterical. A few shot themselves. In Japan, two clasped hands and leapt into a fiery volcano. There were "grief riots" for the silent-screen star; "the Latin Lover"'s funeral in Hollywood was turned into a carnival. Were the last words of "the Sheik" really "Let the tent be struck!"? Or did he say, "I want the sunlight to greet me—don't pull the shades"? It would have been sacrilegious to doubt such lofty last words or to mention his effeminate gaze, his oleaginous sensuality, his cauliflower ear, his penchant for wearing corsets, his . . .

A Lost Generation

The description originated with a garage owner in the French Midi after World War I. Talking one day with the American expatriate Gertrude Stein, he referred to his young mechanics as *une génération perdue*. Ms. Stein (1874–1946) always knew a good thing when she heard it, or saw it, and passed along the phrase to her friend Ernest Hemingway, who then wrote "You are all a lost generation" as an epigraph for his first major novel, *The Sun Also Rises* (1926).

Mr. Green Thumb

Luther Burbank (1849–1926), the horticulturist often denounced for "interfering with nature," must have had a green thumb. He created 113 varieties of fruits and plants and 90 varieties of vegetables. His new potato and pitless plum made him world-famous. Burbank loved his work: "Can my thoughts be imagined when, after so many years of patient care and labor, . . . I look upon these new forms of beauty on which other eyes have never gazed?"

The Monkey Trial

Friendly, shy John Thomas Scopes (1901–1970), a high-school teacher of general science and coach of athletics in Dayton, Tennessee, became the focus of the historic freedom-of-speech "Monkey Trial" of 1925 when he answered an appeal by the American Civil Liberties Union for someone willing to challenge the new state law forbidding the teaching of Darwin's theory of ape-to-human evolution in contradistinction to the biblical interpretation of human creation. The jury's verdict of guilty was upset on a technicality, and Scopes was let go.

Ladies of Newport.
The Grand Young Man

Franklin D. Roosevelt's (1882–1945) political career nearly crashed in 1921 when, as assistant secretary of the Navy, he had to deal with "the perverted practices" (his description) of homosexual sailors stationed at the Naval Training Station in Newport, Rhode Island. Eighteen "Ladies of Newport," as the gay sailors called themselves, were entrapped by an eager vice squad of enlisted men, who had volunteered to have homosexual acts performed on them—the first and probably only time that US sailors have been officially commended for homosexual acts. A Senate subcommittee declared that FDR, who had tried to keep the matter secret, had committed perjury, and that the future President, by condoning the entrapment, was directly responsible for what the committee considered the most deplorable, disgraceful, and unnatural proceeding. The *New York Times* reportage was headlined: "Lay Naval Scandal to F.D. Roosevelt—Details Are Unprintable." His good name was besmirched, but "the Grand Young Man," as FDR was celebrated in those salad days, survived the near-fatal censure (and the crippling polio attack later in 1921) and kept his career on track.

Scarsdale Divorce

New York businessmen, especially show-biz types, cavorted on the Great White Way night after night while their wives vegetated in the suburbs, particularly in Westchester County towns such as Scarsdale. The "arrangement" came to be "a Scarsdale Divorce."

The Borscht Belt

The show-biz summer-hotel circuit in the Catskill Mountains, north of New York City, became known in 1925 as "the Borscht Belt" because many of the hotels (Grossinger's, the Concord) had a predominantly Jewish (Russian, German) clientele, and one of their favorite dishes was borscht, a Russian beet soup usually served with sour cream. The hills were alive with the jokes and the songs of well-known and beginner performers: Milton Berle, Moss Hart, Red Buttons, Danny Kaye, Pepper January (Joan Rivers), Jerry Lewis, Sid Caesar, Mel Brooks—and the boychik Eddie Fisher, who was married there in a big to-do.

A Collective Neurosis

Freud (and others after him) regarded religion—any kind of religion—as "a Collective Neurosis," convinced that humankind would have to outgrow it to attain maturity.

Genda's Circuses

General Minoru Genda (1904–1989), who helped plot the Japanese attack on Pearl Harbor, was an early advocate of naval air power over surface vessels. At the Japanese Naval Academy, he introduced aerobatics teams that were popularly known as "Genda's Circuses." He bombed and strafed cities in China in the 1930s before drafting Nippon's air tactics for the surprise assault on the American Pacific fleet in 1941.

The Norwegian Doll

Five-foot-two Sonja Henie (1912–1969) introduced the miniskirt to figure skating in 1924 when the charming whirling dervish was the unmatched queen of figure skating. "The Norwegian Doll" won 257 medals, cups, plates, and bowls, plus ten consecutive world titles and six European Olympic championships. On the side, she gathered one of the most important private collections of modern art, the Sonja Henie–Niels Onstad Foundation.

The Thrill Killers

The press dubbed as "the Thrill Killers" the wealthy and brilliant Chicago teenagers Richard Loeb and Nathan Leopold for having murdered—for the thrill of it (to assert their intellectual independence)—schoolboy Bobby Franks, in 1924. Both the *Chicago Tribune* and publisher kingpin William Randolph Hearst informed Freud that he could name his own price, including a chartered ocean liner, if he would travel to Chicago and psychoanalyze "the Thrill Killers." Herr Doctor declined the invitation. Leopold (1904–1971) was released from prison in 1958; Loeb (born 1907) was killed by another prison inmate in 1936.

The Divine Sarah

The French actress Sarah Bernhardt, born Rosine Bernard (1844–1923), made her debut at the age of 18 and soon became the most famous stage actress of her time, the queen of French romantic comedies and tragedies. It was Oscar Wilde who dubbed her "the Divine Sarah." In 1912 she became the first great stage actress to appear in the new medium of the motion picture. The amputation of a leg in 1915 did not stop her from giving stellar performances or from playing for French soldiers at the front in World War I. Among many eccentricities was her habit of sleeping in a coffin, even during numerous farewell tours.

The Beerhall Putsch

Hitler's Munich Putsch, November 9, 1923, became known as "the Beerhall Putsch" for the simple reason that this badly planned, premature, botched uprising was plotted in a beerhall. With the help of a World War I hero, General Erich von Ludendorff (1865–1937), Hitler tried to overthrow the Bavarian government, but the plot failed, 16 of Hitler's followers were killed, and he himself was captured. It was in Landsberg prison, high above the River Lech, that he dictated *Mein Kampf* (My Struggle) to Rudolf Hess and became Germany's all-time best-selling author. The British historian and then-ambassador to Germany, Edgar Vincent, first Viscount D'Abernon, referred to Hitler in a footnote in 1924 as "a political figure who, after leading an insurrection in Bavaria in 1923, faded into oblivion."

The House That Ruth Built

Yankee Stadium in the Bronx, New York, was built to accommodate the crowds that wanted to watch the New York Yankees and George Herman ("Babe") Ruth, baseball's all-time greatest player. Opening day was in 1923. (The Yankees had played their home games in the neighboring Polo Grounds, 1913–22.) With Ruth, the almighty "Sultan of Swat," at the plate, the Yankees won the American League title seven times. When the stadium was renovated in the mid-1970s, the Yankees played their home games in Shea Stadium, in Queens, New York—leading to the trivia question, "Who managed the Yankees for two full seasons and never won a game in Yankee Stadium?"

Charles Atlas

There really was a "Charles Atlas," a 97-pound weakling who was always getting sand kicked in his face at the beach in full-page body-building mail-order advertisements on the back covers of comic books and dime magazines. He became a bodybuilder and presently "the world's most perfectly developed man." Atlas (né Angelo Siciliano, 1894–1972) adopted his name when he began to resemble a statue of the Greek god who held up the heavens. Scrawny guys are still told to go out and get some physical culture and become "Charles Atlas."

The Cruelest Month

April has been "the cruelest month" since T. S. Eliot (1888–1965) so labeled it in 1922.

The Founding Fathers

Nearly a century and a half after John Hancock and Thomas Jefferson and John Adams and Benjamin Franklin and Alexander Hamilton and George Washington and James Madison et al. had promulgated the Declaration of Independence and created the United States of America and composed a four-page Constitution that is the supreme law of the land to this day,

President Warren G. Harding (in 1922) coined the description "the Founding Fathers."

Couéism

The 1922 method for curing one's ills by autosuggestion —"Couéism"—is named for the French psychotherapist Émile Coué (1857–1926), who is best remembered for the optimistic phrase he wants us to repeat endlessly: "Day by Day, in Every Way, I Am Getting Better and Better."

The Teapot Dome Scandal

The only cabinet member to go to jail (10 months) for misusing the President's trust was Warren G. Harding's secretary of the interior, Albert Bacon Fall (1861–1944). In 1921, he had received $408,000 and a herd of cattle in bribes for granting leases in naval oil reserves in California (Elk Hills) and Wyoming (Teapot Dome) without competitive bidding. The oil-and-political scandal broke, in 1922, when Harry Slattery, a conservationist who had opposed Mr. Fall's nomination, provided investigators with the tips that convicted the secretary. The Democratic opposition to President Harding had been about to give up efforts to prove fraud in the leasing of the naval oil reserves when Mr. Slattery stepped forward.

The Clown Prince of Baseball

After a three-year career as a pitcher with the Washington Senators (14 wins, 10 losses), the long-limbed Al Schacht (1892–1984) became a clown on the diamond. He was "the Chicken" of his day. During World War II, he went to various fronts and entertained the troops.

The Gipper

George Gipp (1895–1920), a rangy ball carrier weighing 175 pounds, led the Fighting Irish of the University of Notre Dame to undefeated football seasons in 1917, 1918, and 1920. He was a superlative punter, tackler, dropkicker, passer, and runner. He died of pneumonia. Coach Knute Rockne inspired a lowly Notre Dame eleven in 1928 to rally for a 12–6 decision over favored Army at Yankee Stadium, in New York, by exhorting them to "win it for the Gipper." (George Gipp was played by Ronald Reagan in the 1940 movie *Knute Rockne, All American*.)

The Secret City

After the Civil War, blacks and whites mingled in Washington, DC's restaurants, barbershops, theaters, and charitable and social organizations. But, gradually, Jim Crow became king in the nation's capital. By 1920, its black residents lived in "the Secret City," inferior preserves in sight of the Capitol.

The Pitch That Killed

A high, tight, hard pitch submarined, or sidearmed, by the New York Yankees Carl Mays (1891–1971)—one of the most detested players in baseball throughout his career—beaned the popular Cleveland Indians shortstop, Ray Chapman (born 1891), transfixed as he crowded the plate on a gray, drizzly day in 1920 in New York's Polo Grounds. The ball bounced back to Mays, who, thinking the pitch had hit the bat, threw Chapman out at first base. But Chapman had slumped to the ground, his skull fractured, blood pouring from his left ear. He died a few days later. Players didn't wear helmets in those days—it wasn't manly—helmets weren't mandated until the 1958 season. Mays suffered much abuse for the accident—the Cleveland team threatened not to play the Yankees when they next visited Cleveland—but he went on to win 26 games that year and 27 in 1921.

The Pacifist Candidate

When he was in prison, in Atlanta, for sedition (he had protested both the US military draft and involvement in World War I), the socialist labor leader Eugene V. Debs (1855–1926) netted 919,799 votes for President in 1920, about 3 percent of the popular vote. He was five times a candidate for the Oval Office; he won 6 percent of the vote in 1912. The great American "Attorney for the Damned," Clarence Darrow, once said of Debs: "There may have lived somewhere a kinder, gentler, more generous man than Eugene Debs, but I have not known him." Debs was pardoned by President Warren G. Harding, in 1921.

The 1910s

The "Say It Ain't So, Joe" Scandal

When the 1919 major-league World Series was supposedly "fixed" for gambling profits in the Chicago White Sox's "Black Sox Scandal," a boy is said to have approached the foremost Chicago player among the accused, the superstar "Shoeless" Joe Jackson, with the words "Say it ain't so, Joe," only to hear from his idol that, in fact, the games were fixed—although Jackson himself maintained his personal innocence to the end. The scandal is retold in the 1988 movie *Eight Men Out*.

The Little Group of Wilful Men.
The Reservationists

President Woodrow Wilson (1856–1924) battled "the little group of wilful men" in the US Senate who were opposed to the treaty of Versailles that Wilson had brought back in 1919 from the Versailles Peace Conference following the armistice of World War I. The Chief Executive declared that he would never make concessions to the "reservationists." The treaty was never signed by the United States.

The Noble Experiment

The Eighteenth Amendment to the Constitution of the United States, ratified in 1919, prohibited the manufacture, sale, or transportation of intoxicating liquors—"the Noble Experiment." It was the law of the land for only 13 years, or until it was repealed. The Eighteenth was the only amendment ever to be repealed.

Big Red

The racehorse Man o' War has been the greatest three-year-old thoroughbred of all time. Several times, "Big Red" went off at odds of 1 to 100. Only once was he beaten, and that was in a tremendous upset by—who else?— Upset, in the Sanford Memorial Stakes at Saratoga, New York, in 1919. He was retired to stud for $5,000, a record at the time, and sired 379 foals, which won a total of 1,300 races.

The Great Influenza.
Demographic Catastrophe

In just a year's time, the pandemic Spanish flu of 1918 killed twice as many people—over 21 million—as had died in World War I. (Some 5,100 perished in a two-week period in October in Philadelphia alone.) Victims would be feverish one day, dead the next. No country was exempt. The virus eventually died out.

Fourteen Points

Nine months after the United States entered World War I and five months before Yanks first saw combat "over there," President Woodrow Wilson proposed in an address before a joint session of Congress, January 8, 1918, a 14-point framework for peace discussions, confident that the Allies would be victorious. He called for free trade, disarmament, "open covenants openly arrived at," aid to Communist Russia, restoration to France of Alsace-Lorraine, and an end to secret diplomacy. The 14th point was a provision for "a general association of nations . . . under specific covenants," out of which came the League of Nations.

The Great War

What 21 years later was called World War I, or the First World War, 1914–18 (with about 10 million dead) was often referred to as "the Great War." The designation was made obsolete through the vastly greater cataclysms (50 or 60 million dead) of World War II, 1939–45.

The Lost Battalion

During World War I, Major Charles W. Whittlesey's luckless outfit from the US Army's 77th Division (1st Battalion of the 308th Infantry Regiment) became the chief castaway of a wretchedly coordinated battle line in the Argonne Forest, in France's Paris basin, in 1918. For five days, 600 Yanks were surrounded and besieged by German armies. When rescued, only 194 in "the Lost Battalion" had survived. Whittlesey, a New England lawyer, was awarded the Medal of Honor.

The Wolf Man

Freud's patient Sergej Pankejeff, a Russian aristocrat, who is referred to as "the Wolf Man," suffered from a phobia of wolves (and also from psychogenic constipation, from a religious obsession that alternated with blasphemous thoughts, and from anorexia). "The Good Doctor" showed that it was all a reaction to early experiences; the famous 1918 case helped Freud to confirm his theory of infantile sexuality.

Doughboy

The American serviceman in World War I was called a "doughboy." In World War II and the Korean conflict, he was a "dogface." In the Vietnam conflict, he was a "grunt."

The Red Baron

Manfred Baron von Richthofen (1892–1918), "the Red Baron," was Germany's most spectacular fighter pilot in World War I. He shot down 80 Allied aircraft before he himself was shot down in his red Fokker triplane over the Somme Canal, near Amiens, France. He was buried by the Allies with a wreath: "To our gallant and worthy foe." ("The Red Baron" was the brother-in-law of the novelist D. H. Lawrence.)

The Bathtub Hoax

Although it is pure fiction, H. L. Mencken's (1880–1956) account of the history of the first bathtub in America is often cited, to this day, as fact. He published it in 1917 as an amusing if somewhat vacuous whimsicality in the New York *Evening Mail*, with the title "A Neglected Anniversary," noting that it had flitted past absolutely without public notice—not a plumber had fired a salute or hung out a flag, no governor had proclaimed a day of prayer celebrating the first installation in Cincinnati 75 years earlier. Mencken wrote the piece of spoofing to relieve the strain of war days, but his satisfaction turned to consternation when even reference books took him seriously.

The Perfect Game*.
The Asterisk Game

The Boston Red Sox pitcher Ernest Shore's (1891–1980) perfect no-hit, no-run, no-man-on-base, 4–0 victory over the Washington Senators in 1917 has an asterisk next to it in baseball's record books because he didn't pitch the whole game. Babe Ruth had pitched to the first Senator, Ray Morgan, walking him; Ruth argued the base on balls so vociferously that he was thumbed out of the game. Shore came in to pitch. Morgan was thrown out stealing second, and Shore retired the next 26 Senators in a row.

The Green-Corn Rebellion

Subsisting on raw green corn, several hundred poor, pacifist—but armed—Oklahoma tenant farmers and sharecroppers marched on Washington, DC, in 1917, to protest the Great War raging in Europe. They clashed with patriotic posses along the way. About 450 of the marchers were arrested, and their leaders were sentenced to 3- to 10-year jail terms.

Big Berthas

The German long-range howitzers of immense caliber and 100-foot-long barrels that shelled back areas of the western front in 1917, and Paris in 1918, were popularly called "Big Bertha" by the Germans, referring to the ample waistline of Frau Bertha Krupp von Bohlen, a scion of the munitions maker. The Big Berthas were not built by Krupp, however; they were manufactured by Skoda, in Austria-Hungary, a German ally in the Great War.

The Kerensky Government

The Russian Socialist Aleksandr Feodorovich Kerensky (1881–1970) was for a few months Russian premier in the wake of the February revolution of 1917, which overthrew the czarist government. His own government fell before the Bolsheviks when he insisted on Russia's staying in World War I and failed to deal with urgent economic problems, particularly land distribution.

The King of Ragtime

Scott Joplin (1868–1917) was "the King of Ragtime." He played in Missouri honky-tonks (a euphemism in those days for whorehouses), where he was the resident "professor," or pianist, setting the rhythm for stripping in many a bordello. His piano rags are hailed as "the precise American equivalent, in terms of a native style of dance music, of minuets by Mozart, mazurkas by Chopin, or waltzes by Brahms." His "Maple Leaf Rag," composed in 1899, scored an instant hit.

The Zimmermann Telegram. The Zimmermann Note

German Foreign Secretary Arthur Zimmermann sent a telegram on January 16, 1917, to his ambassador in Washington, DC, saying that in the event that the United States was drawn into the war, Mexico should be promised the "lost" territories of Texas, New Mexico, and Arizona if Mexico became Germany's ally (and assuming, as Zimmermann no doubt did, that Germany would be victorious). British intelligence intercepted and deciphered the telegram, and President Woodrow Wilson released it to the press the next day. It helped to prepare American public opinion for US entry into the war against Germany in April.

Ten Days That Shook the World

Lenin urged the Bolshevik-dominated soviet to seize power from the Kerensky government, and it did, in "Ten Days That Shook the World." The 1917 armed coup d'état by cossacks and White Guards was masterminded by Leon Trotsky. Lenin (1870–1924) became chairman of the Council of People's Commissars; Trotsky (1879–1940), foreign commissar; Stalin (1879–1953), commissar of nationalities.

The Black Tom Case

Before the United States entered World War I, it sent shiploads of munitions to friendly European nations, prompting nearly 200 acts of sabotage by German agents. The most devastating exploded at 2:08 AM on Sunday,

July 30, 1916. A thunderous blast, like the discharge of a great cannon, shattered the silence of New York harbor and terrified millions. The Black Tom supply depot on the New Jersey side of the harbor had been blown up. Thousands of cases of ammunition and projectiles exploded, raking the harbor with shrapnel for hours. Miraculously, only five people were killed, and not a single person on the streets of New York or New Jersey was injured by flying weaponry.

The Bloodbath

On reclaimed marshland in Picardy, on the English Channel, in northern France, and along the Somme River, more than one million men died in 1916 as Allied armies gained a few thousand yards against the Central Powers in the middle months of World War I. The war was to last two more years, ending without a truly decisive battle having been fought and with the Kaiser's troops still occupying territory from the Crimea to France. No enemy soldier set foot in Germany.

Winston's Folly.
The Weapon of the Future

At the insistence of the First Lord of the Admiralty, Winston Churchill (1874–1964), Britain built the first tanks during World War I. He wanted an armored car that could smash over German trenches on the western front. What he got at first was "Winston's Folly"—rumbling, weird contraptions on caterpillar treads. They made their debut in the battle of Flers-Courcellette, on the Somme River in northern France, in 1916, and appeared to be a failure. Fourteen months later, at Cambrai, 300 British tanks changed modern warfare, liquidating German defenses in a dawn attack and becoming "the Weapon of the Future."

The Lafayette Escadrille

A small group of American volunteer aviators established the "Lafayette Américaine" in the French air service during World War I. At the end of 1916, it was renamed "Lafayette Escadrille." It saw front-line action and suffered heavy casualities. In January 1918, with the United States now in the Great War, the Escadrille was reorganized in the US Army as the 103 Pursuit Squadron.

Easter 1916

A band of nationalists seized the post office in Dublin and proclaimed an Irish Republic—the "Easter 1916" action. The insurrectionists were captured by the British, and the leaders were put to death. William Butler Yeats (1865–1939), a nationalist himself, who was angered that friends had needlessly sacrificed their lives, wrote their eulogy: a world "changed, changed utterly: A terrible beauty is born." The deaths of his friends had become ennobled in Yeats' mind.

Ford's Peace Pilgrims

In the second year of World War I, self-appointed war-enders in the United States sailed to Europe on industrialist Henry Ford's "Peace Ship." The peace pilgrims' mission of 1915 failed dismally, and Ford himself left Europe's inhospitable shores with a head cold five days after he had landed. When the United States entered the war, in 1917, Ford's company became a leading producer of armaments.

Asiatic Annies

During World War I, an Allied expedition assaulted Gallipoli in west Turkey for the purpose of gaining control of the Dardanelles and Bosporus straits. Turkish shells fired at British soldiers were called "Asiatic Annies."

Dora

The term "Dora" became a popular English acronym of the Defense of the Realm Act of 1914, which legislated many temporary restrictions in Great Britain at the beginning of World War I. "D.O.R.A.," which soon became "Dora," was portrayed as an elderly woman personifying the spirit of restriction.

The Big Cut. The Path Between the Seas. The Great Enterprise

Apart from war efforts and space programs, construction of the Panama Canal, "the Path Between the Seas," was the largest, most costly single project since antiquity—the Moon shot of its era. Excavating 262 million cubic yards for "the Big Cut" cost 25,000 lives—500 for every mile—and $639 milion when that was real money. When the first vessel, the steamer *Ancon*, passed through the canal, in August 1914, it marked the first voyage ever through the American land mass, and the United States became a two-ocean global power.

The Hundred-Thousand-Dollar Infield

Eddie Collins, Jack Barry, Home Run Baker, and Stuffy McInnis played for manager-owner Connie Mack's Philadelphia Athletics. Mack (1862–1956) eventually broke up his famous "Hundred-Thousand-Dollar Infield" because of the salaries, sending Collins (1887–1951) to the Chicago White Sox, Barry (1887–1961) and McInnis (1890–1960) to the Boston Red Sox, and Baker (1886–1963) to the Yankees. Today the average annual salary of a single major-league infielder is $500,000. (The Hundred-Thousand-Dollar Infield played in the Baker Bowl between two death-causing collapses of dilapidated stands. Twelve people died when the balcony gave way in 1903, and one died and scores were injured when a section in right field fell in 1927.)

The Black Hand

Gavrilo Princip (1895–1918) was a teenage Serbian political agitator and member of the nationalist secret society Union of Death—"the Black Hand"—when, on June 28, 1914, he drew a revolver instead of the bomb that he had in his belt and fired two shots. Princip's assassination of Archduke Francis Ferdinand of Austria and the duchess, in Sarajevo, in central Yugoslavia, precipitated World War I.

The Moses of Her People

Harriet Tubman (c.1820–1913) was the most famous "conductor " on "the Underground Railroad," a route so called because runaway slaves secretly traveled from "station" to "station" furnished mainly by sympathetic whites. A price of almost $40,000 on her head didn't keep "the Moses of Her People" from going into the South time and time again to lead hundreds of other blacks to freedom.

The Pollyanna Mechanism

The attitude that all is well and life is good despite the reality that it is not was given the name "the Pollyanna Mechanism" in psychology from the complacent heroine of the 1913 novel *Pollyanna* by Eleanor H. Porter (1868–1920). The girl Pollyanna merely played the innocent "glad game," meaning that she always looked at the bright side in her numerous trials. But to cynics, a Pollyanna is a person who is foolish enough to think that the world we live in is in pretty satisfactory condition. (The term has been applied to Presidents Reagan and Bush, among others.)

A Chamber of Horrors

Americans accustomed to traditional and provincial paintings saw modern art for the first time at the 1913 Armory Art Show in New York City—and were shocked out of their socks, to say the least. Duchamp, Picasso, Cézanne, Matisse, Kandinsky, Brancusi, Braque—"a Chamber of Horrors" to many visitors. Former President Theodore Roosevelt, on a private visit, peremptorily charged: "This is not art!" Duchamp's *Nude Descending a Staircase*—"an explosion in a shingle factory," declared one critic, ". . . a brick factory," vituperated another—was the show's most talked-about painting.

Snodgrass Muff

A dropped fly ball is called a "Snodgrass Muff" in baseball, for the New York Giants outfielder Fred Snodgrass (1887–1974). He dropped a fly ball in the bottom of the tenth inning that opened the door for a Boston Red Sox come-from-behind 3–2 victory in the seventh, and deciding, game of the 1912 World Series. The boner had put the tying run on base.

A Night to Remember.
The Wilhelm Gustloff Paradox

On her maiden voyage, the "unsinkable" White Star liner *Titanic* struck an iceberg near foggy Newfoundland on the night of April 14, 1912, and slipped to the bottom of the Atlantic Ocean, with the loss of about 1,500 lives—it was "a Night to Remember." (The *Titanic's* sister ship, the *Olympic*, had entered service the year before, and in her long career experienced three notable collisions, including one with the Royal Navy cruiser HMS *Hawke* in broad daylight on a calm sea within sight of land.)

The *Titanic* disaster is dwarfed by the sinking of the German ship *Wilhelm Gustloff*, which was torpedoed by the Russian submarine *S-13* off Danzig in the Baltic Sea on January 30, 1945, with the loss of about 7,700 men, women, and children—more than five times the death toll of the *Titanic*. But the disaster has never gotten the same attention in the United States. Among the reasons for the disproportionate publicity seem to be that (1) the victims, though mainly civilians, were a "mere" 7,700 out of the 50 million to 60 million dead of World War II, (2) the victims were "only" Germans, enemies at the time, (3) the victims, quite unlike the *Titanic's*, did not include the rich and famous.

Pangaea. Laurasia. Gondwanaland

The German geophysicist and explorer Alfred Wegener (1880–1930) first proposed, in 1912, the now generally accepted theory of "continental drift": About 225 million years ago, in the Paleozoic era, all of the continents were united in a vast supercontinent, which Wegener called "Pangaea"; it broke into subcontinental masses: "Laurasia" to the north, "Gondwanaland" to the south. The resulting "continental shelves" are in motion at this very moment.

Three Principles of the People

The San Min Chu I—"Three Principles of the People"—was Sun Yat-sen's guiding light as he founded the Republic of China in 1912 and became its first president. The principles are usually translated as nationalism, democracy, and livelihood. Sun (1866–1925) is celebrated as the spiritual father of Chinese democracy.

The Livermore Party

In 1911, a black man charged with murder was tied to a stake on the stage of the opera house in Livermore, Kentucky, and tickets were sold to witness his execution, even to participate in it. The amount that gunmen paid for their seats also determined the number of shots they could fire at the victim.

The Great White Hope

Until Jack Johnson (1878–1946) became the heavyweight champion, in 1908, battering James J. Jeffries (1875–1953) in 14 rounds, in Reno, Nevada, no black man had won boxing's most prestigious title. On the heels of Johnson's crowning achievement, riots erupted around the country, resulting in eight deaths and injury to many more, and generating the search for "the Great White Hope" to put Johnson in his place: his back on the canvas, stars swimming in his head.

The Five-Foot Library.
Dr. Eliot's Five-Foot Shelf

After Charles William Eliot (1834–1926) resigned from the presidency of Harvard College, he startled the scholarly world, in 1910, by stating that a five-foot shelf is large enough to hold all of the books required for a liberal education (the "Harvard Classics"). His rather personal choices: *The Autobiography of Benjamin Franklin*, *Journal of John Woolman*, *Fruits of Solitude* by William Penn, *Essays* and *New Atlantis* by Francis Bacon, *Areopagitica* and *Tractate on Education* by Milton, *Religio Medici* by Thomas Browne, *Apology*, *Phaedo*, and *Crito* by Plato, *Golden Sayings* by Epictetus, *Meditations* by Marcus Aurelius, *Essays* and *English Traits* by Emerson, *Complete Poems* by Milton, *Volpone* by Ben Jonson, *The Maid's Tragedy* by Beaumont and Fletcher, *The Dutchess of Malfi* by John Webster, *The Changeling* by Thomas Middleton, *All for Love* by Dryden, *The Cenci* by Shelley, *A Blot in the 'Scutcheon* by Browning, *Becket* by Tennyson, *Faust* by Goethe, *Doctor Faustus* by Marlowe, *The Wealth of Nations* by Adam Smith, *Letters* by Cicero, *Letters* by Pliny, *Pilgrim's Progress* by Bunyan, *Tam O'Shanter* by Burns, *The Compleat Angler*, *The Life of John Donne*, and *The Life of George Herbert* by Izaak Walton, *The Autobiography of St. Augustine*, *Lives* by Plutarch, *Aeneid* by Dryden, *The Canterbury Tales* by Chaucer, *Imitation of Christ* by Thomas à Kempis, *The Divine Comedy* by Dante, *The Origin of Species* by Darwin, and *Arabian Nights*. (Several of these 42 titles were bound into one volume.)

The Oregon System

In 1910 the state of Oregon adopted reforms that included the initiative, referendum, recall, direct primary, and woman suffrage—"the Oregon System."

Baghdad-on-the-Subway

O. Henry (pseudonym of the short-story writer William Sydney Porter, 1862–1910) used to refer to Manhattan as "Baghdad-on-the-Subway." The New York borough was the setting of several of his short stories, whose hallmarks were the ironic coincidence and the surprise ending. He called everyday New Yorkers "the four million." (Baghdad, the capital of Iraq, was once the home of eminent scholars and artists, as was Manhattan in O. Henry's day.) Today, Manhattan is sometimes referred to as "Shanghai-on-the-Hudson" and "the Calcutta of the West."

The Sage of Hannibal

Mark Twain (1835-1910), who came in with Halley's comet and, as he himself predicted, went out with it, was the "Sage of Hannibal," Missouri, with an insight about everyone and everything. He believed that the Democratic party was a "good and motherly old benevolent National Asylum for the Helpless" and that President Theodore Roosevelt was "clearly insane in several ways, and insanest upon war and its supreme glories." He was born as Samuel Langhorne Clemens. ("Mark Twain" had been the pseudonym of Isaiah Sellers, c. 1802–1864, who was a journalist with the *New Orleans Daily Picayune* and one of the leading pilots of the early steamboat days on the Mississippi.) Twain, the first novelist to use a typewriter, was the best-known author in the United States in the late 19th century, but he wasn't the most read—*Tom Sawyer* and *Huckleberry Finn* were constantly being banned. His lectures were very popular, for such pearls of wisdom as: "Familiarity breeds contempt—and children." "The calm confidence of a Christian with four aces." "Good breeding consists in concealing how much we think of ourselves and how little we think of the other person." "Truth is the most valuable thing we have." "The difference between the right word and the almost right word is the difference between lightning and the lightning bug." "Let us endeavor so to live that when we come to die even the undertaker will be sorry." "I am different from Washington. I have a higher and grander standard of principle. Washington could not lie. I *can* lie but I won't." "My books are water; those of the great geniuses are wine. Everybody drinks water."

The 1900s

The Wagner Card.
The Flying Dutchman

Specimens of the Wagner baseball card in mint condition go for at least $100,000. It was issued in 1909 by the makers of Sweet Caporal cigarettes, but Honus Wagner (1874–1955)—the bowlegged Pittsburgh Pirates short-stop, "the Flying Dutchman"—whom it depicts, insisted that the card be withdrawn: The future Hall of Famer was opposed to smoking. There are only 50 known "Wagner Cards" around today. Wagner is considered by many to have been baseball's best all-around player. He enjoyed 17 con-secutive .300 seasons, and he won the National League batting title eight times. He broke into the majors in 1897 with a .344 batting average.

The Peary Myth

Did the American explorer Robert E. Peary (1856–1920) reach the North Pole—the first human to do so, in 1909—as he claimed he did? Is his claim wrong? Did he deliberately lie, first to his crew, then to the public? The lat-est "authority" to assert that he was at, or very near, the pole was a De-cember 1989 report commissioned by the National Geographic Society. Equally "conclusive" arguments are advanced on the "hoax" side, based on the facts: on Peary's own data and on his suspicious behavior on his re-turn to the United States, and taking into account other, proven lies of Peary's. Whatever the truth, "Peary at the North Pole" has gained, in the American mind, mythical proportions that put it in a league with Wash-ington chopping down the cherry tree and Doubleday inventing baseball. (Known for a fact are Peary's earlier work as a surveyor of a proposed At-lantic–Pacific canal route through Nicaragua and repeated explorations of Greenland and "the great ice of the Arctic.")

Wheat Heaven

In the decades before the 1930s Dust Bowl turned their dreams into night-marish dust, farmers saw the Great Plains of the United States as "Wheat Heaven." The prairie was lush; rain fell in abundance. In the Texas Pan-handle, for example, about 82,000 acres were planted in wheat in 1909. Two decades later, the acreage was two million. The wheatfields were "goldmines." But then it stopped raining, and greed turned out to have been touched by Midas.

Little Hans

Reported by Freud in *Analysis of a Phobia in a Five-Year-Old Boy*, in 1909, a boy's phobia of horses was traced by the father, with Freud's help, to castration anxiety stemming from masturbation, to repressed death wishes toward the father because of rivalry with the mother, and to fear of retaliation, which in the boy's mind was displaced onto horses. "Little Hans" (Herbert Graf, son of the musicologist Max Graf) is a landmark case in the history of psychoanalysis.

The Dirty Letters

Correspondence between James Joyce (1882–1941), vacationing in Dublin, and his common-law wife, Nora Barnacle (1884–1951), at their home in Trieste, is known to Joyce scholars and fans as "the Dirty Letters" for their exhortations on relieving sexual frustration. They also reveal that the author of *Ulysses* and *Finnegans Wake* got notions from Nora. In his correspondence, Joyce limned a florid anal fantasy: a girl with her white drawers pulled apart and "a fat brown thing" protruding from her bottom. Nora told Joyce to masturbate twice on reading her letter, and she reminded him she liked "being fucked arseways." Joyce invited his "darling brown-arsed fuckbird" to "write more and dirtier, darling."

The Tin Lizzie

Henry Ford's sturdy Model T car, "the Tin Lizzie," was "so low in price," he said, that "no man making a good salary will be unable to own one." One of the first American automobiles (1908), it was offered to the public "in any color, so long as it's black." More than 15 million Tin Lizzies were produced, their second-order consequences virtually revolutionizing American life in the process. (Henry Ford [1863–1947] is the only Westerner mentioned admiringly in Hitler's *Mein Kampf*, published 1925–26. In the 1930s, Ford pumped millions of dollars into the burgeoning treasury of the Nazis, as an outright contribution, seeing Nazi Germany as a bulwark against communism's advance toward western Europe, that is, against the loss of the European market.)

The Rat Man

Freud traced a lawyer's obsessional fear of rats to repressed death wishes toward his father. Among "the Rat Man"'s (Ernst Lanzer's) obsessions was his belief that a rat that seemed to have come out of his father's grave had eaten the corpse. The analysis of this 1907 landmark case laid the groundwork for Freud's interpretation of obsessional neurosis.

A Merkle Boner

The New York Giants and the Chicago Cubs were tied, 1–1, with two out in the last of the ninth inning in New York's Polo Grounds. There was a Giant runner on third base, and 19-year-old rookie Fred Merkle was on first. The batter hit a single to center, and the runner on third scored what should have been the game-winning run. But Merkle seemingly failed to go all the way to second base; he trotted off to the clubhouse. In the chaos that followed, he was ruled to be the inning's third out by a generally accepted technical violation not penalized until that instance: He had to touch second base for the run to count. The game was declared a 1–1 tie, to be replayed if both clubs ended the season with identical first-place records. (They did.) "Bonehead" Merkle was vilified on the spot and hounded for the rest of his 16-year baseball career. (The Cubs won the playoff and the 1908 National League title.)

The Ellis Island of the West. The Galveston Movement

By the tens of thousands, European-Jewish refugees entered the United States at the turn of the century through Ellis Island, in New York Harbor. Another ten thousand found their way to "the promised land" via "the Ellis Island of the West," the port of Galveston, Texas. Their recruitment and then their settlement throughout the American West was supervised by organized teams of agents in "the Galveston Movement."

The Girl in the Red Velvet Swing

The exquisite 22-year-old artist's model and showgirl Evelyn Nesbit (1884–1967)—"the Girl in the Red Velvet Swing"—declared, "Stanny White was killed, but my fate was worse. I lived." Her lover—a voluptuary, and the nation's most prominent architect, Stanford White (born 1853)—was shot in 1906 by Evelyn's insanely jealous husband, Harry Thaw (1871–1947). At the sensational trial, she was described as a "tigress between two men, egging them on." When she died, at age 82, she knew only too well that her lovely young self had died that night 60 years earlier at the roof garden of Madison Square Garden in New York.

The Hitless Wonders

The Chicago White Sox won 93 games in the 1906 baseball season, but they smacked only seven home runs and batted a mere .228—"the Hitless Wonders." Fortunately, the pitchers fired 32 shutouts. After winning the American League championship, the Windy City nine set back its cross-city rivals, the Chicago Cubs, in the World Series, four games to two. (The first game of the Series was contested in bitterly cold weather and snow flurries.)

Tinker to Evers to Chance

The most famous double-play combination in major-league baseball—Joe Tinker (1880–1948) to Johnny Evers (1881–1947) to Frank Chance (1877–1924)—has given its name to any event that several hands touch successfully. Interestingly, the Chicago Cubs infielders averaged only 14 double plays each season from 1906 to 1909. (But when the Philadelphia A's Frank Baker was celebrated as "Home Run Baker," the most four-base clouts he ever hit in a season was 12, in 1913. So much for legends.)

The Great Earthquake

In the lore and legend of great American disasters, "the Great Earthquake" stands out. It struck San Francisco at 5:12 AM on April 18, 1906, and the fires it caused killed between 800 and 1,000 people and did more than $420 million worth of damage, leaving a quarter of a million people homeless. The tremor lasted about 40 seconds and probably would have registered between 7.9 and 8.3 on the Richter scale of ground motion. (The Richter scale was devised years after the quake.)

The Niagara Movement

Four decades after the end of the Civil War, 29 militant black intellectuals from 14 states were not allowed to meet in a New York manor—none would accept them as guests—so they gathered on the Canadian side of Niagara Falls. "The Niagara Movement" of 1905 declared that America's 10 million blacks—"struggling up through difficulties and oppression—need help but are given hindrance, need protection but are given mob violence, need justice but are given charity, need leadership but are given cowardice and apology, need bread but are given a stone."

Quai d'Orsay

As 1600 Pennsylvania Avenue, its address in Washington, DC, connotes the White House, and 10 Downing Street, the London residence of the prime minister, connotes the British government, "Quai d'Orsay" in Paris is often the reference for its principal occupant, the French ministry of foreign affairs. The quay, on the left bank of the Seine River, extends from the Eiffel Tower to the National Assembly, the Palais Bourbon.

Louisa

The nickname "Louisa" was given Major General Lewis (Lew) Wallace (1827–1905) by his men in the Civil War. He sat on the military court that convicted the members of the conspiracy that assassinated President Abraham Lincoln a few days after Appomattox, in 1865. Besides his military career, Wallace was also a governor, a legislator, a diplomat (Turkey), and the author of several popular books, including *Ben Hur; A Tale of the Christ* (1880) and *The Boyhood of Christ* (1888).

The Dora Case

One of Freud's most celebrated cases (reported in his *Fragment of an Analysis of a Case of Hysteria*, in 1905), "Dora" was a woman with multiple symptoms (including headaches, suicidal impulses, and amnesic episodes) that contributed both to his theory of repression and to his use of dream interpretation as an analytic tool. ("Dora" was Ida Bauer, the sister of the Austrian socialist leader Otto Bauer.)

The Wobblies

The radical industrial labor union, the Industrial Workers of the World (IWW)—"the Wobblies"—was founded in 1905 principally by one-eyed William ("Big Bill") Haywood (1869–1928) after he had led the Western Federation of Miners (WFM) through a violent five-year period of warfare between labor and mine owners. The Wobblies made an indelible mark on the history of American labor with their pamphlets, songs, and poems and with their free-speech fights and strikes. (Haywood fled the United States after being convicted in a 138-day trial for sedition—he had denounced World War I as a capitalist attack on the worldwide working class—and was then for the most part ignored by the new Soviet leaders when he sought sanctuary in Moscow. But the Salt Lake City native is one of two Americans buried in the Kremlin wall.)

The Bloody Sunday

On Sunday, January 22, 1905, Russian troops fired on unarmed workers, led by a priest, marching to the Winter Palace in St. Petersburg to petition Czar Nicholas II. The bloodbath signaled the beginning of the first Russian revolution. After months of strikes, riots, assassinations, naval mutinies, and peasant uprisings, the government promised to establish a consultative Duma, or assembly, elected by limited franchise.

The Black Hundreds

Russian reactionary forces, in the wake of the aborted revolution earlier in 1905, instituted the most brutal series of pogroms in the country's history. "The Black Hundreds" were virulently antisemitic and antiliberal; their cry was "Down with the constitution and with the Jews." Soldiers and police often looked on without interfering as the Black Hundreds killed, wounded, and left homeless thousands of Jews all over Russia (about 50,000 killed—many by hanging—from 1905 to 1909 alone). The pogroms ceased with the success of the Bolshevik Revolution 12 years later, but they were revived in Germany and Poland when Hitler reached power.

The Floating Inferno

On the sunny Wednesday morning of June 15, 1904, the excursion steamboat *General Slocum* churned up New York City's East River with a Sunday-school outing. The vessel caught fire and became a "floating inferno." The death toll was 1,021. It was the worst fire in New York history. Seven years later, a fire that swept through the Triangle Shirtwaist Company in Manhattan's Greenwich Village killed 146 workers (and touched off a national movement for safer working conditions). On the 79th anniversary of the Triangle disaster, a deliberately set fire in an illegal nightclub in the Bronx killed 87 patrons.

The Forbidden City

Until 1904, foreigners rarely set foot in the remote Tibetan capital of Lhasa, the second-highest (11,800 feet) city in the world. "The Forbidden City" was well off the beaten path, and the Lamaist clergy there was hostile to outsiders. (Lhasa was the center of Tibetan Buddhism, and about half of the city's population were Lamaist monks.) China's capital also had a "Forbidden City." It was the Inner, or Tartar, section of Beijing where China's emperors and retinues were housed and foreign nations had their legations. Today it is a vast museum, its palaces replete with art treasures.

The Town a Candy Bar Made. Chocolatetown U.S.A.

Hershey, Pennsylvania, the world's largest chocolate-making plant and town, was built in 1903 near the birthplace in Derry Township, in southeastern Pennsylvania, of Milton Snavely Hershey.

Calamity Jane

The famous frontier character Martha Jane Burke (c. 1852–1903) dressed in men's clothes and boasted of her marksmanship. It was always a calamity for the person who offended her. She is buried beside Wild Bill Hickock, in Deadwood, South Dakota. ("Calamity Jane" is the main character in a series of dime novels that was named for her.)

The Great White Way

Broadway, from Times Square to 48th Street, the theater district in New York City—"the Great White Way"—is a "bouquet of luminous advertising," said a French visitor in 1903. "An immense blaze of legends and pictures, most of them in motion . . . the finest free show on Earth," said another observer seven years later. In 1917, "fabulous glow-worms crawl up and down . . . zig-zag lightnings strike an acre of signboard . . . household words race with invisible pen across a whole city block"—luminous epilepsy, incandescent hypnotism. Electricity was the turn-on.

The White Elephants

Early in the 1902 baseball season, John J. "Little Napoleon" McGraw, manager of the National League New York Giants, declared that the owners of the American League–charter member Philadelphia Athletics had a "white elephant" on their hands. Some white elephant! Manager Connie Mack's pachyderms won the pennant with 83 triumphs, and McGraw's description, which was intended as an insult, became a logo for the A's. (McGraw's Giants were like pygmies that year—they finished in last place—but they did beat the A's three years later, in the 1905 World Series.) "The White Elephants" won nine league titles before packing their trunks and moving to Kansas City in 1955.

The Bully Pulpit

Theodore Roosevelt (1858–1919) recognized that he could use the presidency as a "Bully Pulpit" to inspire or moralize. "A President has a great chance," TR said after leaving office; "his position is almost that of a king and a prime minister rolled into one; once he has left office, he cannot do very much; and he is a fool if he fails to realize it all and to be profoundly thankful for having had the great chance. No President ever enjoyed himself in the presidency as much as I did." He enjoyed it so much that four years out of office he ran for another term, but finished third.

The Bruins

The Chicago baseball team that in 1901 was given the name Chicago Cubs (for its many young players) was earlier called the White Stockings, then the Colts, then the Cowboys, then the Broncos, then the Rainmakers. "Cubs" soon gave rise to the nickname "the Bruins," which means the bears, from the medieval character Sir Bruin, the bear in the German epic *Reynard the Fox*. (Chicago's National Football League entry is called, not coincidentally, the Bears.)

Red Emma

The American anarchist Emma Goldman (1869-1940) was arrested when the assassin of President William McKinley, in 1901, told authorities that he had been influenced by her speeches and writings. When she was released, having had absolutely nothing to do with Leon Czolgosz's fiendish act, she expressed sympathy with the gunman's motives but offered to nurse the dying President. "Red Emma" was deported to Russia 18 years later, expecting to be called back to "Soviet America."

The Oil Century

The worker became the consumer in "the Oil Century," the 20th century. Unlike the 19th, or "Coal Century," in which they were left out of "progress," workers have been paid well enough to consume what they made, and they gradually became genuine participants in the economy, both economically and politically. The writer David Halberstam (born 1934) has also observed that the oil age was well suited to America because it was designed for a society that considered itself free of class restraints. (*See also* 1801: The Coal Century.)

The Esthetic Singer

The Irish poet, dramatist, and novelist Oscar (Fingal O'Flahertie Wills) Wilde (1856–1900) was given the sobriquet "the Esthetic Singer" because of his espousal of the principle of "art for art's sake" and his founding of the esthetic movement that reflected it. When Wilde called on Walt Whitman, "the Good Gray Poet," in Camden, New Jersey, in 1882, he was urged by the American to go ahead in his mission to shatter the ancient idols. Laying a hand on Whitman's knee, Wilde said, "I can't listen to anyone unless he attracts me by a charming style or by beauty of theme." Whitman (1819–1892) found Wilde to be "like a great big splendid boy." It may have been after this visit that Wilde wrote, "Of course, America had often been discovered before Columbus, but it had always been hushed up." He summarized his principle of estheticism with the dictum: "In matters of grave importance, style, not sincerity, is the vital thing."

The Nietzsche Irony

"The Nietzsche Irony" is that the Nazi movement adopted Nietzsche as one of its idols, whereas it could not have been more wrong. The German philosopher Friedrich Wilhelm Nietzsche (1844–1900) would have scorned everything the Nazis stood for. He was consistent over the years: "How refreshing it is to see a Jew among the Germans! All this dullness, all these flaxen heads, these blue eyes; the absence of esprit in their faces, words, demeanor." "When I try to picture the type of being that runs counter to all my instincts, it is always a German." "Mixed races are the source of great civilizations." "It is a matter of honor to me to be absolutely clear and unequivocal regarding antisemitism, namely, *opposed*, as I am in my writings."

In the United States, a different kind of misunderstanding surrounds Nietzsche in that his name seems to evoke the "Superman," a secondary Nietzsche concept that should be perceived in context (it has nothing to do with any notion of racial superiority). Nietzsche was one of history's most subtle observers of human nature; he recognized, before Freud, the extent to which sexual and unconscious factors are likely to affect even seemingly unrelated actions and our most lofty thoughts. He generally anticipated the modern human being. The French Nobel Prize–winning author André Gide (1869–1951) went so far as to write, about Nietzsche, that "nothing remains to be said and it is enough to quote him."

Clever Hans

The famous "thinking horse," "Clever Hans," in Germany in 1900, was reputed to be able to solve mathematical problems, spell words, and the like by tapping a hoof. The psychologist Oskar Pfungst (1874–1932) proved that "Clever Hans" was merely responding to "minimum cues" in the form of involuntary movements on the part of its owner.

The Goncourt

The French novelist Edmond Louis Antoine Huot de Goncourt (1822–1896) willed the bulk of his fortune for the creation of the Académie des Goncourt. Annually, it awards the most coveted literary prize of France, the Prix Goncourt—"the Goncourt." (In Goncourt's day, top-quality authors often became rich, had influence, and were honored with titles of nobility.)

The 1890s

A Message to García

An essay published in 1899 by Elbert Hubbard (1856–1915) in his avant-garde periodical *The Philistine*, "A Message to García," was the most famous piece Hubbard ever wrote; it is still in print today, with a cumulative circulation of more than 40 million copies. It was based on an incident in the Spanish-American War and begins with the words, "In all this Cuban business there is one man who stands out on the horizon of my memory like Mars at perihelion"—a Lieutenant Andrew Rowan, whom President William McKinley had sent with a vital message to General Calixto García Iníquez, in charge of the Cuban forces fighting Spain. The essay stresses the importance of perseverance and was designed to improve morale among workers. "No man who has endeavored to carry out an enterprise where many hands were needed . . . has been well-nigh appalled at times by the imbecility of the average man—the inability or unwillingness to concentrate on a thing and do it." "Self-interest prompts every employer to keep the best—those who can carry a message to García."

Palmetto Slices

In 1899, thousands of people traveled on excursion trains to Palmetto, Georgia, to witness the lynching of a black man. The victim was sliced apart, and the pieces—"Palmetto Slices"—were sold for souvenirs.

The Royal Road to the Unconscious

The Austrian psychiatrist and cofounder of psychoanalysis, Sigmund Freud, described dreams as "the Royal Road to the Unconscious." They express repressed impulses and ideas that exert influence on behavior. "The Good Doctor" considered his turn-of-the-century volume, *The Interpretation of Dreams*, to be his most important achievement: "Insight such as this falls to one's lot but once in a lifetime." Nevertheless, it took eight years to sell the first printing (1899) of 600 copies. (Freud was paid $209.) Since those days, however, the work has seen reprint after reprint, in many countries, and there are currently at least three editions, two in hardcover and one in paperback, in the United States alone. (*See also* 1274: The Angelic Doctor.)

The Hague Tribunal

The Permanent Court of Arbitration, founded by the First Hague Conference, in The Hague, the Netherlands, in 1899, was popularly called "the Hague Tribunal." A case was initiated when two or more nations signed a *compromis*, an agreement to submit a dispute to arbitration. The Hague Tribunal was superseded by the World Court after World War I, and the World Court in turn was superseded after World War II by the International Court of Justice, which meets in The Hague.

Tin Pan Alley

At first around 28th Street in downtown Manhattan, now on Broadway, north of Times Square, "Tin Pan Alley" is where music publishers, songwriters, song pluggers, and piano pounders gather and pass around notes. Why Tin Pan Alley? A lyricist had put paper on the strings of his piano to create a twanging sound. A journalist, in 1899, saw the arrangement and thought they were tin pans—and he coined the name.

Opium Wars.
The Great White Plague

A few thousand British marines, then joint British and French forces and corrupt, greedy Chinese officials and warlords humiliated the Chinese people, and British merchants legally flooded China with opium. It was like feeding poisoned milk to children. At the end of the 19th century, about 90 million Chinese were addicted to opium. Total eradication of opium, by decreasing the demand, cutting off the supply and meting out capital punishment to offenders, occurred only in 1949, when the civil war ended and Mao's Communist party assumed power.

The Waltz King

The Austrian conductor and composer Johann Strauss (1825–1899), son of the famous conductor and composer Johann Strauss (1804–1849), created more than 400 waltzes, some of which are popular to this day, such as "The Beautiful Blue Danube" of 1866 (used brilliantly in the 1968 movie *2001: A Space Odyssey*) and "Tales from the Vienna Woods" of 1868. Among opera fans he scored with his hit *Die Fledermaus* (The Bat), 1873. He pursued his career against the wishes of his father.

The Illustrious Infidel.
The Great Agnostic

Robert G. Ingersoll (1833–1899) was a lawyer, a lecturer, a politician, a statesman, and "the most brilliant speaker of the English tongue of all men," but above all he was the outstanding American freethinker of his time. He felt that "An honest God is the noblest work of man," rather than assuming that man is the creation of a God. You do not need religion, he wrote, "to love justice, to long for the right, to love mercy, to pity the suffering, to assist the weak, to forget wrongs and remember benefits—to love the truth, . . . to cultivate hope, to see the calm beyond the storm, the dawn before the night, to do the best that can be done and then be resigned—this is the religion of reason, the creed of science." (George Washington wrote, in 1797: "The government of the United States is not, in any sense, founded on the Christian Religion.")

The White Man's Burden

A euphemism for the type of imperialism predominant in America, continental Europe, and especially Great Britain at the end of the 19th century and the early years of the 20th century was "the White Man's Burden." Imperialists in "superior civilized nations" saw a moral duty devolving upon them in their colonies.

The Man of Blood and Iron.
The Iron Chancellor

Otto Eduard Leopold von Bismarck (1815–1898) was called "the Man of Blood and Iron" for his remark that the conflict between Prussia and Austria could be settled only by "blood and iron" (and it was, in their war of 1866). The appellation "the Iron Chancellor" alludes to the inflexible purpose and indomitable will that the Prussian leader showed all of his life. He is eminently quotable. Well circulated is "The less people know about how sausages and laws are made, the better they'll sleep at night."

The Society of Harmonious Fists

The so-called Boxer Movement in China, 1898–1900, was an antiforeign rebellion that began with a peasant secret society and was diverted by xenophobic officials against the policies of their imperial government, against Western missionaries, and against Chinese converts. The movement has been referred to as "the Society of Harmonious Fists," which is the more or less literal translation of the Chinese name for the Boxer Movement (*I Ho Ch'uan*). In June 1900, some 140,000 "Boxers" occupied Beijing. China emerged from the uprising with a greatly increased debt and subject-nation status.

Yellow Kids

Journalistic freebooters, or hired pens, "Yellow Kids," moved into the path of fire in Cuba, in the Spanish-American War (1898), and on other war fronts so that they could help their jingoist newspaper publishers beat the opposition with "I was there" news. Their dispatches indeed helped to sell papers.

A Splendid Little War

As the brief two-ocean Spanish-American War of 1898 approached its end, the US ambassador to England, John Hay (1838–1905), wrote to Colonel Theodore Roosevelt of the Rough Riders, celebrated for their operations in Spanish-run, revolution-shattered, Cuba: "It has been a splendid little war; begun with the highest motives, carried on with magnificent intelligence and spirit, favored by that fortune which loves the brave." Only the incredible ineptitude of the Spaniards and the phenomenal luck of the Americans kept the war from stretching into a struggle as long and as full of disasters as the Boer War became for the British. As it was, it was grim, dirty, and very bloody. (President William McKinley told news reporters, "God told me to take the Philippines." But he admitted he had no idea in which part of the world they were.)

The New York Journal's War

The Spanish-American War of 1898 was not instigated solely by the sensationalism of the jingo press and yellow journalism, but newspaper major-domo William Randolph Hearst (1863–1951) always took credit for "the *New York Journal*'s War." Its daily headlines reflected America's restlessness and its desire to see the country function as a great nation, complete with a powerful navy and well-armed overseas bases. The *Journal* never let its readers forget the *Maine*, the US battleship that had blown up in Havana harbor, with 260 sailors killed. To this day, the cause of the disaster is unknown, but it was the spark that prodded President William McKinley to send troops into Cuba.

The Yellow Press

All the trash that's fit to print became a hallmark in 1898 of "the Yellow Press," American newspapers that would do just about anything for a story. The characterization "yellow" for sensational publications in general had been in use for half a century, from the yellow covers of cheap books and magazines.

Klondike Fever. The Klondike Stampede

The last great gold rush was triggered in 1897 by the discovery of rich placer gold deposits in Bonanza (Rabbit) Creek (a tributary of the Klondike River), a small stream that enters the Yukon River from the east at Dawson, in the Klondike region of Yukon Territory, in northwest Canada. The stampede of about 25,000 "overnight" prospectors with "Klondike Fever" brought on a serious food shortage. The gold still in "them thar hills" is being mined at less than a feverish pitch.

The Flying Teapot

In 1897 the identical twins Francis Edgar and Freeland O. Stanley (born 1849) produced the first working steam motorcar. Two years later, they drove "the Flying Teapot" to the top of 6,288-foot-high Mount Washington, the highest peak in New England, in two hours and ten minutes; five years later, they did it in 28 minutes, and with minimal pollution. The Stanley Steamer could surpass the speed of 100 miles per hour.

The Veto President

Many Presidents have not vetoed a single bill. The first to veto more than 100 was "the Veto President," Grover Cleveland, who served two nonconsecutive terms (1885–89, 1893–97). He vetoed 584 bills. The only four-time Chief Executive, Franklin D. Roosevelt, is the champion, with 631 vetoes; only nine of the bills were then enacted into law by Congress. (Congress did not override a presidential veto until 1845, when the issue was payment for naval vessels, ordered by President John Tyler, the first Vice President to succeed to the presidency on the death of the President.)

The Beehive State

The history of the state of Utah has been the history of Mormonism. The beehive is a symbol of the Mormons, known for their great industry, and Utah is called "the Beehive State." It entered the Union in 1896 as the 45th state, after the Mormon church had withdrawn sanction of polygamy.

Gibson Girls

The ideal woman came to life in the illustrations of Charles Dana Gibson (1867–1944)—"the Gibson Girl." His incisive drawings of fashionable life and his delineation of aristocratic social ideals, mainly in *Life* magazine and *Collier's Weekly*, made Gibson a foremost illustrator of his time.

The Royal Disease

Hemophilia is called "the Royal Disease" because the families of Queen Victoria of England, King Alfonso XIII of Spain, and Czar Nicholas of Russia were plagued with it. It is indeed hereditary.

Anna O. The Talking Cure

"Anna O." is the famous pseudonym of the physician Josef Breuer's landmark hysteria case. (Her condition had been brought on by her father's lingering death.) Breuer's "Talking Cure" became a precursor to psychoanalysis. The case was cited by Breuer and Freud (though Freud never saw her as a patient) in their joint *Studies in Hysteria* (1895). Fifty-eight years later, "Anna O." was revealed to have been Bertha Pappenheim (1859–1936), a pioneer social worker, writer, and feminist. She lectured throughout central Europe and in Moscow and New York and personally conducted municipal officials to brothels in Constantinople and Alexandria for a firsthand look at man's inhumanity to woman.

Darwin's Bulldog

Thomas H. Huxley (1825–1895) was known to the newspaper-reading public as "Darwin's Bulldog," the Englishman who marshaled the scientific evidence underlying the theories of the great biologist and evolutionist Charles Darwin (1809–1882).

The Street of Forgotten Men

New York's Bowery, on the lower East Side, became "the Street of Forgotten Men." The neighborhood had the cheapest beer in the city. One could put down five-cents-a-glass whiskeys until the cows came home. Half of the city's cheap lodging houses were there. A 15-cent "bum's roost" was a bunk in a dormitory.

Coxey's Army

Numbering at one time 20,000 unemployed men, "Coxey's Army" walked with Mayor Jacob Coxey of Massillon, Ohio, from that town to Washington, DC, to demand jobs, in 1894. Before Coxey (1854–1951) could make his speech demanding public building programs, he was arrested by police for walking on the grass. He ran for President on the Farmer-Labor ticket twice, in 1932 and 1936.

Bad Old Man

The nickname "Bad Old Man" was given half affectionately by Confederate soldiers to their Civil War General Jubal Anderson Early (1816–1894). He defeated Union General Lew Wallace (the future author of *Ben-Hur*) in the battle of Monocacy, and took his troops within sight of the Capitol in Washington, DC. He ordered Chambersburg burned when the Pennsylvania town refused to pay a ransom. After the war, the West Point graduate fled the country, returning in 1869 to practice law. He became a president of the Southern Historical Society.

The Autocrat of the Breakfast-Table

Oliver Wendell Holmes, Sr. (1809–1894), was a professor at Harvard Medical School, a poet (who wrote "Old Ironsides"), an essayist, the author of pioneering psychological novels, and the father of Oliver Wendell Holmes, Jr., of the US Supreme Court. The sobriquet "Autocrat of the Breakfast-Table" was actually the title of a series of witty discourses on social, scientific, and theological matters. He said: "Man has his will—but woman has her way," "Insanity is often the logic of an accurate mind overtaxed," and "Sin has many tools, but a lie is the handle that fits them all."

The Quaker Poet

The poet John Greenleaf Whittier (1809–1892) was a lifelong devout Quaker, and for the last half century of his life he was devoted to the cause of abolitionism. He helped to found the *Atlantic Monthly* (1857), and his most famous work, *Snow-Bound*, was published in 1866. His ballad "Barbara Frietchie" (1864) is still memorized by many schoolchildren: "Up from the meadows rich with corn, clear in the cool September morn . . ." (Whittier fabricated Frietchie's facing down of Confederate troops: She was actually 95 years old at the time and bedridden.)

The Man on Horseback.
A Robespierre on Horseback

The French soldier and political adventurer Georges Ernest Jean Marie Boulanger (1837–1891) is best remembered for his almost succeeding in becoming dictator of France. He was seldom seen in public except when riding a black charger and therefore was popular as "the Man on Horseback." The phrase came also to mean any person who curbs the violence of mob rule and reestablishes law and order. If he is ruthless, trampling the people underfoot, such a man may be referred to as "a Robespierre on Horseback."

The Bucs

The Pittsburgh Pirates baseball team used to be the Alleghenies (1886), then the Innocents, becoming the Pirates in 1891 for their skill in "pirating" players from other teams. The formal name Pirates was accompanied by the synonymous word Buccaneers—or "the Bucs," as they're still called by tabloid-headline writers: "Bucs Walk Plank, 7–0," "Bucs Stopped Here."

Cump. Old Tecumseh

General William Tecumseh Sherman (1820–1891) ("Tecumseh," for the Shawnee Indian prince, c.1768–1813) was affectionately called "Cump" by his friends; to his troops, he was "Old Tecumseh." The garrulous Civil War leader, celebrated (or notorious) for his march through Georgia to the sea, may be America's most quoted military man. In 1880 he declared that "war is hell," and he informed the Republican national convention, wanting him to be its presidential candidate, "I will not accept if nominated and will not serve if elected."

The Prince of Showmen.
The Prince of Humbugs

P.T. (Phineas Taylor) Barnum (1810–1891) was perhaps the greatest showman of all time, but he was also a member of the Connecticut legislature, a mayor of Bridgeport, and a lecturer on temperance and other popular topics. The impresario exhibited "George Washington's 161-year-old black nurse," the Fejee Mermaid, the two- to three-foot dwarf General Tom Thumb (Charles Sherwood Stratton, 1838–1883), and the 6 1/2-ton elephant Jumbo (hence the use of "jumbo" for very large), and he promoted the concert tour of "the Swedish Nightingale," Jenny Lind-Goldschmidt (1820–1887). He could have said, "There's a sucker born every minute."

Bergstrasse 19

The cofounder of psychoanalysis, Sigmund Freud, saw his patients, beginning in 1891, in a treatment suite in his home at Bergstrasse 19, in Vienna, rather than at an office elsewhere in the city. The reason that he chose Bergstrasse 19—now perhaps the most famous address in psychiatry—for a combination home and office was that it had been the home of Viktor Adler, the future Social Democrat, with whom Freud had argued as a student and whom he had visited there. Before moving to Bergstrasse, Herr Doktor had hired a carriage to see patients.

Old Sparky. America's Hot Seat

The electric chair has been dubbed many things—it all depends on where you're coming from—but "Old Sparky" and "America's Hot Seat" have been the most "popular" sobriquets. The first American to be executed by electrocution was William Kemmler, on August 6, 1890, in New York. The state put three brothers to death in the chair on the same day in 1903. Six hundred ninety-five New Yorkers have been killed by "Old Sparky."

The Pathfinder of the West

John C. Fremont (1813–1890) mapped the western United States. The illegitimate son of a refugee from the French Revolution, he was truly "the Pathfinder of the West." He surveyed the region between the Mississippi and Missouri rivers and explored the Des Moines River, the Oregon Trail, the Sierra Nevadas, and the Sacramento Valley. He struck gold, was one of California's first US senators, and was the Republican party's first presidential standard-bearer (1856).

The 1880s

The Head, and Heart, and Soul of the Mightiest Rebellion of Modern Time

Jefferson Davis (1808–1889), the compromise president of the Confederate States of America in revolt against the Union, was so described first by Mark Twain. A Democratic senator from Mississippi, Davis had led out of Congress the parade of senators from the 11 seceding southern slave states a few months before the war erupted. He was captured a month after the South had surrendered and was held in irons in a military prison. He was never brought to trial because of legal complications. He was given a hero's funeral, in New Orleans.

The Johnstown Tragedy.
The Torrent of History

A group of wealthy Pittsburghers, among them Andrew Mellon and Henry Clay Frick, and New York steel tycoon Andrew Carnegie neglected the maintenance of an earthen dam they had built 15 miles above Johnstown, Pennsylvania, to make a private 70-foot-deep lake for their summer pleasure. In 1889 the dam broke in the heaviest rainstorm recorded in western Pennsylvania, loosening a torrent that swept away 2,209 lives; a third remained unidentified. The worst such disaster in US history was recorded by the editor of the *Johnstown Tribune* as "not the hand of Providence. Our misery is the work of man." Americans were angry that once again barons of industry could literally get away with murder.

Wimbledon

"Wimbledon" was synonymous with the annual meeting of the English National Rifle Association from 1860 to 1889, which was held at a place of that name, an open heath seven miles southwest of London.

The Mountains of the Moon

Discovered in 1889 by the British explorer and journalist Henry Morton Stanley (né John Rowlands, 1841–1904), the semifabulous, snowcapped "Mountains of the Moon"—Mount Ruwenzori—are in the east-central African mountain range in the western arm of the Great Rift Valley, between Lake Albert and Lake Edward. They are constantly shrouded in an eerie mist nurtured by extensive glaciers and glacial lakes. In ancient times, they were erroneously thought to be the source of the Nile. The range was first climbed, in 1906, by the Italian explorer, naval officer, and mountaineer Prince Luigi Amedeo of Savoy-Aosta (1873–1933), Duke of Abruzzi (who also was the first to climb Mount St. Elias in Alaska and several elevations in the Himalayas; he was leader of the 1899–1900 polar expedition on the *Stella Polare* and commander of the Italian Adriatic fleet in World War I).

The Father of Gerontology

The French chemist Michel Eugène Chevreul (1786–1889) improved the quality of candles, recognized diabetes as a disease of sugar metabolism, worked to expose spiritualism, and was a pioneer in gerontology, a study for which he was uniquely qualified. In his 90s, he studied the psychological effects of old age. He lived into his 103rd year.

The Apostle of Culture

The English critic, poet, and essayist Matthew Arnold (1822–1888) sought a culture that would pursue perfection through a knowledge and an understanding of the best ever thought and said. He is known for his abundant use of the phrase "sweetness and light" (which he admittedly borrowed from Jonathan Swift): "The pursuit of perfection, then, is the pursuit of sweetness and light. He who works for sweetness and light, works to make reason and the will of God prevail. He who works for machinery, he who works for hatred, only works for confusion."

Jack the Ripper

The London butcher of women known as "Jack the Ripper" struck five times, twice in one night, between August 31 and November 9, 1888, and was never heard from again. The case is still open in Scotland Yard.

Mighty Casey

It's what a person is called for "striking out," for failing to come through in a clutch situation, from the 1888 baseball poem by Ernest Lawrence Thayer (1863–1940), "Casey at the Bat": "Oh! somewhere in this favored land / The sun is shining bright; / The band is playing somewhere, / And somewhere hearts are light; / And somewhere men are laughing / And somewhere children shout, / But there is no joy in Mudville— / Mighty Casey has struck out." (The final score was 4 to 2.)

The Great American Traveler

Daniel Pratt (1809–1887) was known for his harmless eccentricities, lecturing throughout the eastern United States. Originally a carpenter, he was under the illusion that he had been elected US President. He was particularly popular on college campuses.

La La Land. Tinseltown.
Cocaine Gulch. The Dream Factory

Hollywood (1886–   )!

The Mother of Exiles

The Statue of Liberty in Upper New York Bay (dedicated in 1886) is usually the first "American" that millions of immigrants have seen. The world's tired and poor, its "huddled masses yearning to breathe free,/ the wretched refuse of your teeming shore,/ . . . the homeless, tempesttossed," have embraced the colossal figure as "the Mother of Exiles."

The Haymarket Square Convulsion

During a street demonstration demanding a reduction of the 10-hour workday and six-day workweek to eight hours a day six days a week, a bomb exploded and rioting ensued in Chicago's Haymarket Square in 1886. Seven policemen were killed and 100 persons injured. Though no evidence was produced that they had made or thrown the bomb, eight anarchists were tried and convicted of inciting the violence; four were hanged, and one committed suicide; the remaining three were pardoned (after being imprisoned for seven years) on grounds that the trial had been unjust.

Black Jack

John Alexander Logan (1826–1886), a radical congressman from Illinois and an unsuccessful Republican vice-presidential candidate (1884), served with distinction as a Union general in the Civil War. Because of his long black hair and his swarthy complexion, he was given the affectionate nickname "Black Jack" by his troops. He was the House of Representatives' manager in the impeachment trial of President Andrew Johnson (1868), the founder of Memorial Day (1868), and the founder and three-times president of the Grand Army of the Republic. (*See also* 1948: Black Jack.)

The City That Was Built on Gold

The city that was built on gold is South Africa's largest city, Johannesburg. The world's most desired metal was discovered in the Transvaal, in northeastern South Africa, in 1886; by the turn of the century, about 100,000 people called Johannesburg their burg.

The Birthplace of American Architecture

Chicago became "the Birthplace of American Architecture" as the site of the world's first skyscraper, the 16-story headquarters building designed and put up in 1884–85 by William Le Baron Jenney (1832–1907) for the Home Insurance Company. Skeletal construction freed design; massive walls no longer had to hold up buildings. The Windy City's architects became world-famous: Jenney, Louis Sullivan, Frank Lloyd Wright, Henry Hobson Richardson, and Daniel Burnham.

Old Three Stars

Ulysses S. Grant (1822–1885), victorious commander of the Union army in the Civil War and 18th President of the United States, was called "Old

Three Stars" by his troops in allusion to the number of stars that indicated his rank of lieutenant general. In 1866 he became the first American soldier since George Washington to hold the rank of full general. He was the first Chief Executive to visit China, and his memoirs, published by Mark Twain, rank among the great military narratives.

The White Cross

In England, in 1882–83, a Miss Ellice Hopkins and several Anglican prelates organized a "moral purity" society that became known as "the White Cross." Besides a set of personal-purity principles that may strike us as rather quaint, one of the tenets was quite modern for its time, namely, that the same law should be equally binding for everyone—"one law for men and women."

The Ring of Fire

Seventy-five percent of the 850 active volcanoes in the world are within "the Ring of Fire," a zone running along the west coast of the Americas from Chile to Alaska and along the east coast of Asia from Siberia to New Zealand. Twenty percent of these volcanoes are in Indonesia, where Krakatoa literally blew its top in 1883: The 2,640-foot-high peak of the volcano collapsed to 1,000 feet below sea level.

The American Montaigne.
The Sage of Concord

Both "the American Montaigne" and "the Sage of Concord" were popularly used for the essayist, poet, and lecturer Ralph Waldo Emerson (1803–1882). The references are to the wisdom of the 16th-century French essayist and philosopher Michel Eyquem de Montaigne and to Emerson's place of residence, Concord, Massachussetts. He once noted: "To laugh often and love much; to win the respect of persons and the affection of children . . . to know that even one life has breathed easier because you have lived—this is to have succeeded." He also believed that "the reward of a thing well done, is to have done it." But he also said: "I hate quotations. Tell me what you know." (His observation that "the human body is the magazine of inventions . . . all the tools and engines on earth are only extensions of its limbs and senses" became Marshall McLuhan's classic "the medium is the message.")

The Man Who Made Such a Noise in the World

He was Charles Darwin (1809–1882). England may have made a monkey of itself by not knighting the originator of the revolutionary theory of organic evolution, but it did honor him with burial in Westminster Abbey.

The Elephant Man

The German pathologist Friedrich Daniel von Recklinghausen (1833–1910) described, in 1882, what became known as "von Recklinghausen's disease," or, formally, neurofibromatosis—characterized by surface tumors that may be accompanied by hearing and vision impairment and by mental retardation. The most popular name of the disorder became "Elephant Man's disease," from one of its supposed victims, the twisted, grotesque John (Joseph) Merrick (1862–1889), in Victorian England who was known as "the Elephant Man." "The most disgusting specimen of humanity anyone had seen" claimed he was "happy every hour of the day." He radiated affection and gratitude, reflecting much love received from his mother in his early years.

The Law West of the Pecos

Judge Roy Bean (c.1825–1903)—"the Law West of the Pecos"—had been a cattle rustler in Mexico. During the Civil War (1861–65), he joined a band of lawless irregulars fighting for the Confederacy. In Langtry, Texas, he set up a combination saloon and courtroom and handed down justice with a law book in one hand and a six-shooter in the other—his verdicts were unorthodox and arbitrary.

The Liberator of Italy

Giuseppe Garibaldi (1807–1882), the Italian patriot and soldier and the leading figure in the Risorgimento, fought in civil wars in South America, then returned to Europe to join uprisings that were breaking out there. He lived in the United States for a time, selling candles in Staten Island, New York. In 1860 Garibaldi led the conquest of the Two Sicilies. "The Liberator of Italy" twice turned down President Abraham Lincoln's bid to lead a Union army in the American Civil War.

Dizzy

"Dizzy" was the nickname of Benjamin Disraeli (1804–1881), first Earl of Beaconsfield, founder of England's modern Conservative party, and twice prime minister. He was Jewish but baptized a Christian, and he was a great favorite of Queen Victoria. He was very quotable: "Every woman should marry—and no man." "Ignorance never settles a question." "All power is a trust; that we are accountable for its exercise; that, from the people, and for the people, all springs, and all must exist."

Emperor of the United States

Joshua Norton (c.1819–1880), an Englishman raised in South Africa who came to the United States to seek his fortune during the California gold rush of 1849, went from riches to rags to fame as one of the nation's most colorful eccentrics. When he lost his wealth, he lost his reason and proclaimed himself Norton I, "Emperor of the United States," an illusion he maintained for 20 years. "Loyal subjects" made him a popular tourist attraction. In the streets of San Francisco he enjoyed mock-imperial privileges. When he died, in a gutter, the *Chronicle* wrote "Le Roi est mort" (the king is dead), and flags flew at half-mast. Mark Twain and Robert Louis Stevenson put him in novels.

The 1870s

The Liberator

The Liberator was the name of the journal published for 35 years by William Lloyd Garrison (1805–1879), the best-known antislavery leader of the 19th century, and the term "Liberator" has been used in referring to the man himself. The journal's motto was "My country is the world; my countrymen are all mankind." And on the pedestal of his statue in Boston are inscribed his words: "I am in earnest / I will not equivocate / I will not excuse / I will not retreat a single inch / and I will be heard." He once publicly burned a facsimile of the Constitution because it condoned slavery.

The Learned Blacksmith

The American reformer Elihu Burrit (1810–1879) presents a heroic example of self-education in the face of adversity. He "acquired a mastery of eighteen languages and twenty-two dialects, not by rare genius, which he disclaimed, but by improving the bits and fragments of time which he could steal from his occupation as a blacksmith" (William Mathews, *Getting On in the World*, 1873). Burrit published proficiently, lectured widely, and became the chief exponent of international peace of his era, organizing many peace groups and congresses in the United States and Europe.

Re Galantuomo

Literally meaning "honest king," the title "Re Galantuomo" was conferred upon Victor Emmanuel II (1820–1878), king of Sardinia (1849–61) and afterward of united Italy (1861–78). The allusion is to the generous manner in which he fulfilled his promise to maintain a constitutional government, a free press, and a fair degree of religious liberty. He indeed personified the Risorgimento.

His Fraudulency. The Deal

Threat of a new civil war hung over the House of Representatives in 1877 when its specially created electoral commission, voting along strict party lines, gave the Republican Rutherford B. Hayes (1822–1893) the controversial 19th presidency by one vote; it is thought by many to this day that the Democratic candidate, Samuel Jones Tilden (1814–1886), the reform governor of New York, had really won the election. An investigation into "His Fraudulency's" election was aborted, and, in turn, Reconstruction government came to an end in the South: It was "the Deal."

Lemonade Lucy

Mrs. Rutherford B. (Lucy) Hayes (1831–1889), the first First Lady to be called the First Lady, refused to serve alcohol at state functions in the White House, earning her the name "Lemonade Lucy." Tobacco was also banned. There was one exception to the liquor prohibition: the reception for Grand Duke Alexis Alexandrovitch, of Russia, in 1877, when wine was served. Mrs. Hayes was the first President's wife to be graduated from college (Wesleyan Women's, in Cincinnati). She inaugurated the custom of the annual Easter egg roll on the lawn of the White House.

The Jewel in the Crown

Established over three centuries, the British Empire, on which the sun never set, considered India its prize possession, its "Jewel in the Crown." Control there was symbolized and reinforced when Queen Victoria (1819–1901) was crowned empress of India in 1877.

The Triple Crown of Baseball

Only 13 times has a player led one of the major baseball leagues in home runs, runs batted in, and batting percentage—"the Triple Crown"—in the same year, and only Ted Williams (in 1942 and 1947) and Rogers Hornsby (1922, 1925) have each won the title twice.

The Territory of Jefferson.
The Centennial State

Colorado was called "the Territory of Jefferson" before it joined the Union in 1876, the 100th anniversary of the Declaration of Independence, and became "the Centennial State." It is the highest state: 53 snow-capped Rocky Mountains there soar to more than 14,000 feet.

The Solid South

With but one exception—1928, when a Catholic (Governor Alfred E. Smith, of New York) was the party's standard-bearer—Southern states have tended to vote solidly for the Democratic presidential nominee from the 1876 Reconstruction election through Harry S. Truman's unexpected triumph in the 1948 campaign. The Republicans Dwight D. Eisenhower (1952, 1956) and Richard M. Nixon (1960) splintered "the Solid South." These days, the South tends to vote Republican in national elections, Democratic in local elections.

The Plumed Knight

The prominent Maine legislator and unsuccessful presidential aspirant James Gillespie Blaine (1830–1893) became known as "the Plumed Knight" after Colonel Robert G. Ingersoll used this sobriquet when nominating him at the 1876 Republican convention: "Like an armed warrior, like a plumed knight, [he] marched down the halls of the American Congress and threw his shining lance full and fair against the brazen forehead of every traitor to his country and every maligner of his fair reputation." Blaine won his party's nomination in 1884 but lost the presidency by a whisker to Grover Cleveland.

Custer's Last Stand

Any foolish and hopeless situation may be referred to as "Custer's Last Stand"—"inspired" by the massacre of foolhardy General George Armstrong Custer (1839–1876) and 225 of his men by Sitting Bull and 40,000 Sioux and Cheyenne in the battle of Little Bighorn, in Montana, in 1876.

The Hanging Judge

Congressman Isaac Charles Parker (1838–1896) was appointed in 1875 a judge of the western district of Kansas, an unruly area that included in its jurisdiction the Indian Territory. Because of the many death sentences he meted out, he became known as "the Hanging Judge." His rigorous justice did help to bring law and order to the area.

The Four Hundred

Mrs. Caroline Schermerhorn Astor's mansion at 34th Street and Fifth Avenue had one of the few private ballrooms in New York. It held only 400 people, but they were always the crème de la crème, the bluebloods, *the* 400 in the fashionable social order. It was said that "if you go outside that number, you strike people who either are not at ease in a ballroom or else make other people not at ease."

The Triple Crown of Horse Racing

The Kentucky Derby, in Louisville (as of 1875), the Preakness Stakes in Baltimore (as of 1873), and the Belmont Stakes in New York (as of 1867) represent "the Triple Crown of Horse Racing." Only 10 horses have won the three races, which are held in May and June each year.

The Siamese Twins

The name "Siamese Twins" was popularly given to Chang and Eng, of Chinese heritage, born in Siam in 1811. Their bodies failed to separate completely; they shared a single navel and a cartilaginous band between their breast bones. An American, Robert Hunter, bought them from their mother, and they began a long career of public exhibits. They led a relatively normal life, married two sisters, and had 22 children between them. Chang and Eng died in 1874, within 2½ hours of each other. Many of their descendants, all entirely normal, live in North Carolina to this day.

The Young Roscius. Master Betty

William Henry West Betty (1791–1874) became famous as an actor in London when very young. At the age of 12, "Master Betty" made £34,000 in 56 nights—unheard of for an actor in his time. He played the then-popular roles of Oswyn, Douglas, Rolla, Romeo, Tancred, and Hamlet with "unknown perfection." William Pitt (the Younger) had the House of Commons pass a motion that the House adjourn so that its members could attend Betty's performance as Hamlet. His career lasted only from 1803 to 1807, when he retired, a rich man, 16 years old. (His retirement, for the last 67 years of his life, was interrupted by a part-time, half-hearted return to the stage between 1812 and 1824.)

Betty was not the only English actor who was referred to as "Roscius" as a mark of distinction. The allusion is to Quintus Roscius, who died about 62 BC, the greatest of Roman comic actors. His friend and disciple Marcus Tullius Cicero (106–43 BC) defended him in a noted lawsuit.

Soapy Sam

The English bishop Samuel Wilberforce (1805–1873) was known all of his life for his cleverness and persuasiveness. When a little girl once asked him why he was called "Soapy Sam" (a nickname he did not like), he replied: "Because, dear, when I get into hot water I always come out clean." Yet he did not escape being killed by a fall from his horse. (His father, William Wilberforce, 1759–1833, campaigned successfully for the abolishment of slavery in the British Empire.)

The Black Governor

The first black governor of the United States was P. B. S. Pinchback (1837–1921), son of a white father and a free black mother. During Reconstruction, when there was a national effort to elect blacks to important political positions, Pinchback, a lawyer, became lieutenant governor of Louisiana and in 1872 succeeded to the acting governorship when the elected chief executive was impeached. Louisiana's population was about 50 percent black at the time. In 1873 Pinchback was elected senator from Louisiana, but he was not seated. (Virginia's L. Douglas Wilder [born 1931], grandson of slaves, a Korean War hero, and a millionaire trial lawyer, became in 1989 the first *elected* black governor.)

Whistler's Mother

The American painter, wit, and eccentric James Abbott McNeill Whistler (1834–1903) created a picture in 1871 to which he gave the title *Arrangement in Gray and Black No. 1* to deemphasize the subjective content of the work. It became one of his most famous paintings, but hardly anyone calls it by its true name. It is best known as "Whistler's Mother."

The Railway King

George Hudson (1800–1871), of York, England, amassed an enormous fortune in the most daring railway speculations of his era. But after the panic of 1847–48, he lost all of his wealth and spent the last 10 years of his life on the European continent in straitened circumstances.

The Canal Opera

To help celebrate the opening of Ferdinand de Lesseps's Suez Canal, the Italian composer Giuseppe Verdi (1813–1901) was commissioned to write an appropriately grand opera. The dramatically popular *Aida* had its first performance in 1871, two years after the artificial waterway had opened— "the Canal Opera."

The Week of Blood

After the victorious German troops withdrew from France in 1871 at the end of the Franco-Prussian War, a Socialist government (the Commune) was set up in Paris. It was besieged by regular French government troops (the Versaillists), and its overthrow resulted in "the Week of Blood." Reprisals included the execution of about 17,000 people, including women and children.

The Newspaper of Record.
The World's Greatest Newspaper

The *New York Times* made its reputation as "the Newspaper of Record" in 1871 by printing stories that exposed the Tweed ring, which was defrauding New York City. As "the World's Greatest Newspaper," it has published historic documents, usually in full. Among them are Soviet premier Nikita Khrushchev's "secret speech" (1956) revealing the crimes of his dictatorial predecessor, Joseph Stalin; the Pentagon Papers (1971); and the Warren Report on the assassination of President John F. Kennedy (1964).

Mrs. O'Leary's Cow

According to legend, one of the most celebrated disasters in US history, the destruction by fire of the city of Chicago, in 1871, was initiated when a cow owned by a Mrs. O'Leary kicked over a lantern and the flame swept over a pile of hay. The conflagration killed about 200 people, rendered 90,000 homeless, and destroyed about $200 million worth of property, including 17,000 buildings. The once wooden city was rebuilt as a city of steel and stone, "the Birthplace of American Architecture," the city of big shoulders. (Two hundred miles to the north of the great Chicago fire, Peshtigo, Wisconsin, was also in flames. Twice as many people burned to death, but somehow the disaster didn't get the same attention.)

The Reconstruction Amendments

In the first five years after the Civil War, the states ratified three amendments to the Constitution of the United States that reflected goals of the North during the war and came to be known as "the Reconstruction Amendments": the Thirteenth, in 1865, abolished slavery; the Fourteenth, in 1868, protected the citizenship of slaves freed after the war; and the Fifteenth, in 1870, concerning the right of suffrage, was necessary because the Supreme Court alone cannot always protect rights guaranteed by the Constitution.

The Pigeon Post

During the two-year Prussian siege of Paris (1870–71), communications links (rail and underground telegraph) with the French still free to the west of the capital were severed, so hot-air balloons carried messages and homing pigeons out of Paris. The plan was to have the pigeons carry messages back to their rooks in Paris. The success rate of return flights was not high. By one estimate, only 59 of the 302 enlistees in "the Pigeon Post" made it.

The Prisoner of the Vatican

The appellation "the Prisoner of the Vatican" was given to Pope Pius IX (Pope from 1846 to 1878) by his adherents when, in 1870, he was deprived of his temporal possessions and was assigned the Vatican, in Rome, as a place of residence in which, he claimed, he remained a prisoner. It turned out that the loss of the Papal States in 1870 was a blessing for the papacy, although it took 60 more years to solve "the Roman Question," namely, how to assure "the Vicar of Christ" nonnational status in a nationally organized world. (The First Vatican Council, in 1870, enunciated the doctrine of papal infallibility.)

Old Faithful

You could set your watch by "Old Faithful": Every 64.5 minutes, the ancient geyser in Yellowstone National Park, in the American West, would shoot about 11,000 gallons of water some 150 feet into the air. These days, it pops up irregularly.

The 1860s

Black Friday

Friday, September 24, 1869, thousands of American financial speculators were ruined when their efforts to corner the gold market were deflected by the federal government's release of gold for sale. That Friday became known as "Black Friday."

The Golden Spike

Northwest of Ogden, Utah, in 1869, the driving of "the Golden Spike" connected trackage of the Union Pacific and the Central Pacific, completing the first transcontinental railroad. A cry of "Done!" echoed through the mountains.

Homosexual

The word *homosexual*, referring to a person who is sexually attracted to someone of his or her own sex, was coined in 1869 by the Hungarian physician Karoly Maria Benkert (from Greek *homo*, "same," and Latin *sexus*, "sex"). The coinage took the place of a number of vague or makeshift terms. In ancient Greece, where it was common for men to be at least bisexual, no term, oddly, existed for homosexuality, only a variety of expressions referring to specific homosexual roles and attitudes.

The Big Three of the North

The Hudson's Bay Company, the Royal Canadian Mounted Police, and religious missions—these white Canadian groups, "the Big Three of the North," dominated the eastern Arctic before the Canadian government took control of the region in 1869.

The Big Ditch

Twenty-five thousand Egyptians dug out 97 million cubic yards of earth to build the 105-mile-long Suez Canal connecting the Mediterranean Sea, the Gulf of Suez, and the Red Sea, cutting the nautical miles between London and Bombay by 41.2 percent and between London and Hong Kong by 25.8 percent. "The Big Ditch" opened in 1869.

Old Buck. The Last President of the United States

"Old Buck" was James Buchanan (1791–1868), the 15th US President, who called himself "the last President of the United States" as war between the states loomed. He was a "doughface," a Northern Democrat allied with proslavery Southern Democrats. The only bachelor President, Buchanan was wealthy and was a serious drinker. He had defeated the first Republican presidential candidate (John C. Fremont), in 1856. Buchanan believed that secession by Southern states would violate the Constitution but that the government lacked the constitutional power to prevent any from leaving the Union. His proposed constitutional amendments, which protected slavery in the South as a solution to the crisis, would have been no solution at all. When he was succeeded by the Republican Abraham Lincoln, in 1861, the nation was a month from Civil War.

Seward's Ice Box. Seward's Folly

President Andrew Johnson's secretary of state, William H. Seward (1801–1872), arranged in 1867 for the purchase of Alaska from Russia—586,400 square miles for $7.2 million, or two cents an acre. Because few people thought it was worth the investment, the Alaska Purchase came to be called "Seward's Ice Box" and "Seward's Folly." Alaska turned out to be a bonanza. (Seward also wanted to annex Hawaii and Santo Domingo.)

The Great Lone Land

The second largest country in the world (six time zones) is Canada, "the Great Lone Land" (a self-governing dominion as of 1867). Nearly 90 percent of the country's nearly four million square miles is economically useless for any purpose other than growing trees or providing minerals. A million square miles is tundra. Two of the 10 provinces—Yukon and the Northwest Territories—constitute more than a third of the land area, but they have less than 1 percent of the (1990) population of about 25 million.

The Good Gray Poet

The sobriquet of the great American poet Walter ("Walt") Whitman (1819–1892)—"the Good Gray Poet"—came into use after a pamphlet in his defense, titled *The Good Gray Poet*, was published by William Douglas O'Connor in 1866. Whitman once wrote: "I will not have in my writing any elegance or effect of originality to hang in the way between me and the rest like curtains. I will have nothing hang in the way, not the richest curtains." "I am as bad as the worst, but thank God I am as good as the best."

Prince John

John Van Buren (1810–1866), a lawyer, was called "Prince John" not because his father, Martin, "the Little Magician," was the eighth President of the United States—as some reference sources have been asserting—but because of what many saw as his "princely" figure and manners.

The Fabulous Invalid

Season after season, probably beginning with the very first production, the musical *The Black Crook* (1866), the Broadway theater claims that it is on its last legs, that the box-office is dying, despite the tens of millions of dollars that now pour through the wickets. Yet somehow "the Fabulous Invalid" revives each September, the start of another season, and limps along to another record-breaking year. There is no business like show business! (About eight million tickets are sold annually, for a gross of about $250 million. Thirty to 35 new shows open each year.)

The Reconstruction Riot

In 1866, whites assaulted the convention hall in New Orleans, Louisiana, where black radicals and carpetbaggers were challenging the suffrage clause of the new state constitution. In gun battles, 38 persons were killed, 146 wounded. In the 1870s, about 3,500 Louisianians, mostly blacks, were slain or wounded. Victims included Republican officeholders.

White Man's Country

Andrew Johnson (1808–1875), the only US President to be impeached, had as one of his aims when he succeeded the assassinated Abraham Lincoln, in 1865, the preservation of the South as a "white man's country." He had been the only southern senator to denounce the Confederacy and to uphold the Union, but he failed to keep his state, Tennessee, from joining the Confederacy. He was military governor of Tennessee before becoming Lincoln's second Vice President. He is the only erstwhile President to be elected to the Senate after leaving the White House and one of two former Chief Executives to sit in Congress.

Scalawags

Southern whites who cooperated with the Union's occupying forces after the Civil War and were presumed to be in favor of treating the former slaves as equals were called "Scalawags." Their voice in Congress was the dominant radical Republican factor. Most white southerners considered "Scalawags" (which had meant rascals or rogues in general) even more reprehensible than "Carpetbaggers."

The Black-Pay Proviso

During the American Civil War (1861–65), black soldiers in the Union forces were paid $10 a month, less $3 that was withheld for clothing; white troops received $13 a month *plus* a $3 clothing allotment—thus, actually, $16 versus blacks' $7. (Approximately 10 percent of the Union soldiers were black—about 180,000 men in all—and about one third of the Union navy's 3,222 casualties were black. The best-known black fighting unit was the 54th Massachusetts Regiment, commanded by white Colonel Robert Gould Shaw (1837–1863); its most spectacular success was leading the bloody assault on Fort Wagner, at the mouth of Charleston Bay, on the afternoon and evening of July 18, 1863; the 1990 movie *Glory* celebrates its fate.)

Old Abe. Honest Abe. Father Abraham. The Rail Splitter. The Great Emancipator

Many names have been conferred on Abraham Lincoln (1809–1865), the 16th President of the United States. "Old Abe" referred to his presence in the White House (but he did not like his name shortened to "Abe"); "Father Abraham" became popular in the Civil War; "the Rail Splitter" stems from the account that he had once supported himself by splitting rails for his father (splitting as many as 3,000 rails with the help of one laborer). Lincoln's career was an extraordinary personal history of failure, yet he became the foremost symbol of American democracy.

The Fire Eater

Virginia-born Edmund Ruffin (1794–1865), a fire-eating partisan of slavery and secession, was given the honor (as he called it) of firing the first shot of the Civil War, aiming the Confederate cannonball at Union forces in Fort Sumter, in the harbor of Charleston, SC, in 1861. The old man enlisted with rebel forces as a symbolic gesture. When he heard the news of the surrender of the Confederacy, Ruffin wrote, "I hereby declare my unmitigated hatred to Yankee rule . . . and to the perfidious, malignant, & vile Yankee race." He placed the barrel of a silver-mounted rifle in his mouth and pulled the trigger.

The Surrender Table

The small, oval, varnished-pine "surrender table" used by Generals Ulysses S. Grant and Robert E. Lee at Appomattox Courthouse, Virginia, to end the Civil War, in 1865, was given as a gift to Major General George Armstrong Custer (1839–1876), who had demonstrated daring and brilliance in Union cavalry victories. (Custer was to make negative headlines in April 1876.)

The Wagon Boy

Thomas Corwin (1794–1865) remained "the Wagon Boy" even when he was a US senator, secretary of the treasury, and minister to Mexico. As a youngster, he had driven wagonloads of provisions to the front lines for General William Henry Harrison in battles with Native Americans on the northern frontier. Young Corwin was "a good whip and an excellent reinsman."

Bluebacks. Greenbacks

The paper money of the Confederate States during the American Civil War was referred to as "Bluebacks" to distinguish it from the Union paper money, which was known as "Greenbacks." When the "Bluebacks" became worthless in 1865, the money of the South was called "shucks." ("Greenbacks" are said to have been named thus by S. P. Chase, secretary of the treasury, when they were first issued in 1862. Their green tint, originally produced in Canada, is difficult to counterfeit or to photograph.)

Bluebellies. Graybacks

Because of the light blue overcoats and cloaks worn by Union soldiers during the American Civil War, the Confederates often referred to the Northerners as the "Bluebellies." On the Union side, the Southerners were sometimes called the "Graybacks," for their gray uniforms.

The Knights of the Golden Circle. Copperheads

The secret order of Southern sympathizers in the North during the Civil War was called "the Knights of the Golden Circle," and its 300,000 members were "Copperheads." Sometimes they called themselves "Sons of Liberty," after the American revolutionists (Samuel Adams, Paul Revere, et al.) of nearly a century earlier. The Golden Circle dissolved in 1864 as Union victories mounted and agitation for a negotiated peace lost its appeal.

The Angel of the Battlefield. The Mother of the Red Cross

The American philanthropist and former schoolteacher and patent-office clerk Clara (Clarissa Harlowe) Barton (1821–1912) was in charge of Union front-line hospitals in the Civil War in 1864, then went on to organize military hospitals in the Franco-Prussian War, the Spanish-American War, and the Boer War, and to supervise relief actions in major disasters. She was one of the organizers of the American Red Cross (1881), and she became president of the International Red Cross Society.

The Ice King

Frederic Tudor (1783–1864) figured out how to "harvest" and keep ice from melting and to ship it successfully to the warmest ports, from Martinique to India. Hailed as a miracle worker, the flamboyant, defiant, energetic, reckless, imperious, vain, contemptuous "Ice King" believed this creed: "He who gives back at the first repulse and without striking the sec-

ond blow despairs of success, has never been, is not, and never will be a
hero in war, love, or business."

The Five-Day Riot

For five days in July 1863—the middle of the Civil War, as it turned out—
mobs ran amok in New York in protest against the first federal conscription
passed by Congress. Antiwar sentiment was already high, and voluntary
enlistments were low when the rampagers began setting fire to draft offices. But it was more than a draft riot. It was also a challenge to labor and
capital relations and a fight for political dominance—and it was a race riot.
The mobs, principally immigrants, looted upper-class homes, torched fac-
tories, and destroyed any property they could lay hand on, bringing the
city to a halt. And they also hunted down and tortured and lynched black
workmen. The most violent civil disorder in 19th-century America was
quelled by five Union Army regiments, armed with howitzers, which had
been ordered back from Gettysburg. The death toll was at least 105.

Old Stars

Ormsby MacKnight Mitchel (1809–1862), a prominent professor of astronomy, and an author of popular books on astronomy, was a major general during the Civil War. To his Union troops, not surprisingly, he was
"Old Stars."

The Little Magician. Whiskey Van. Old Kinderhook

Martin Van Buren (1782–1862), the eighth President of the United States,
was given the name "the Little Magician" for his mastery of the politician's
art; "Whiskey Van" originated among his political opponents (who may
not have drunk any less); he was born in Kinderhook, New York. Van
Buren was President Andrew Jackson's most trusted adviser, and he was
the last sitting Vice President before George Bush, in 1988, to run successfully for the presidency.

The Mother of the Beautiful Child

Despite her accomplishments as a poet, Elizabeth Barrett (Mrs. Robert)
Browning (1806–1861) was said to have been more proud of being "the
Mother of the Beautiful Child." The child was her son, a model of beauty
and grace. In a letter to a friend, she wrote that her son's beauty and her
sobriquet were worth her novel in verse, *Aurora Leigh*, times 20. (The
work was published in 1857, seven years after her best-known collection,
Sonnets from the Portuguese—"How do I love thee? Let me count the
ways.")

The Little Giant

Stephen A. Douglas (1813–1861)—"the Little Giant"—won the Lincoln–Douglas debates of 1858 and reelection to the US Senate, but two years later he lost the presidential election to Abraham Lincoln. Before the inauguration, in 1861, he told "the Great Emancipator," "In our devotion and attachment to the Constitution we have never differed—in this we are one—this must and shall not be destroyed," and he held Lincoln's hat during the inauguration address. Douglas had a broad national vision. When he was fatally stricken with typhoid, he was representing Lincoln in rallying the Northwest.

48 Hours

The nickname of Abner Doubleday (1819–1893), the Civil War commander—"48 Hours"—was coined because it seemed as though he needed a "double day" to make a decision. Doubleday fired back the first Union shot from Fort Sumter in the very first clash of the Civil War, in April 1861, and he was a hero in the turning-point Union victory at Gettysburg, which turned back Confederate General Robert E. Lee's invasion of the North.

That Peculiar Institution.
Execrable Commerce

Before the Civil War, President Abraham Lincoln struck upon a compromise over "That Peculiar Institution," namely, slavery: free the slaves right away and pay off their owners with a large loan floated for the purpose. His stroke of genius was thought to be merely a political gimmick and was dismissed. ("Execrable Commerce" was Thomas Jefferson's term for the slave trade; he signed into law the legislation prohibiting the legal importation of slaves after January 1, 1808.)

The Colonizer of Nicaragua.
The Gray-Eyed Man of Destiny

William Walker (1824–1860) was the most famous American before the Civil War, a symbol of the nation's spirit of self-confidence. His swashbuckling exploits in Central America got him as far as becoming "the Colonizer of Nicaragua" and its president (1855). He proceeded to set up a military empire (with the use of slave labor) and to declare himself dictator, a title and position that US President Franklin Pierce officially recognized. After five years of ups and downs in new adventures, Walker was captured by the British, who turned him over to Honduras, where "the Gray-Eyed Man of Destiny" was executed by a firing squad, at age 36. He fell into near-total oblivion as fast as he had risen to fame.

The Wide-Awakes

"The Wide-Awakes" were campaign clubs of the Republican party formed during the presidential election of 1860. Inspired by a speech that the ardent abolitionist and Lincoln supporter Cassius Marcellus Clay (1810–1903), of Kentucky, had delivered in Hartford, Connecticut, in the preceding year, they paraded at night, wearing black oilskin hats and capes and carrying torches. There were about 500,000 "Wide-Awakes" nationwide. Their candidate won the election.

Metternich's Maxim

The Austrian statesman Prince Klemens Wenzel Nepomuk Lothar von Metternich (1773–1859) was an "enlightened" friend of absolutism and a foe of democracy, believing that the king and his council should make the laws, which, however, should be in the interest of the people: "All *for*, but not *through*, the people." The English historian John Sherren Brewer (1809–1879) remarked that "in schools and private families, Metternich's maxim is acted on; but nations are clubs, not schools or families; and in clubs the members, not the elected chairman, make the laws."

The 1850s

The English Opium Eater

Thomas De Quincey (1785–1859) is famous for *Confessions of an English Opium-Eater* (1822), a fascinating memoir distinguished by great imaginative power and prose that is splendid and elaborate without stiffness. He began his opium habit while at Oxford and had bizarre and spectacular dreams while under its influence. In 1827, he wrote: "If once a man indulges himself in murder, very soon he comes to think little of robbing; and from robbing he comes next to drinking and Sabbath-breaking, and from that to incivility and procrastination."

The Mile High City

Denver, settled 1858, is exactly 5,280 feet above sea level.

Old Bullion

Thomas Hart Benton (1782–1858) was given the name "Old Bullion" because the five-time senator from Missouri strongly advocated gold and silver as the only remedy for the country's financial ills. "Old Bullion," who delighted in his sobriquet, was defeated for a sixth term because of his opposition to the proslavery features of the Compromise of 1850.

The Mother of Three Seas. The Land of 11,000 Lakes. The North Star State. The Gopher State

Minnesota (the 32nd state, admitted in 1858) has the greatest water area of any of the 50 states, if Hawaii doesn't count its Pacific Ocean realm. About 4,800 square miles of the state's total of 84,068 square miles is wet. It is indeed "the Land of 11,000 Lakes." The watersheds are in a sense "the Mother of Three Seas." Channels run to Hudson Bay and the Arctic, to the Atlantic, and to the Gulf of Mexico.

The Great Bonanza

The Comstock Lode, "the Great Bonanza," discovered in 1857 in western Nevada, on Mt. Davison, was the richest silver deposit ever found in the United States. It was laid claim to in 1859 by Henry Tomkins Paige Comstock, "Old Pancake" himself. Near the end of the century, the mine was virtually abandoned as a result of wasteful mining methods and the decline of the value of silver.

Religion of Humanity

The French Positivist philosopher Auguste Comte (1798–1857) proposed the worship of Humanity as an object of love and reverence, in place of a deity whose existence it is impossible either to affirm or to deny. Comte's conception of Humanity is that of a collective entity, comprising all human beings, past, present, and to come, whose lives have been, are, or will be devoted to the well-being of humankind. Love is the leading principle of the Religion of Humanity, and progress is its object.

The Apostle of Temperance. The Sinner's Friend

The Irish Franciscan priest Theobald Mathew (1790–1856) waged a temperance campaign that involved as much as one half of the population of Ireland. He also campaigned in England and North America. He himself had taken the pledge in 1838.

Beecher's Bibles

Sharps rifles were frequently called "Beecher's Bibles" during the era of "Bleeding Kansas" before the Civil War, when the territory was contested by proslavery and free-state forces. The name had its origin in an 1856 speech by the clergyman, reformer, and author Henry Ward Beecher (1813–1887); he said that a Sharps rifle had more moral force than a Bible as a weapon against slavery. Beecher, a brother of Harriet Beecher Stowe, whose novel *Uncle Tom's Cabin* helped ignite the Civil War, once said, "Where is human nature so weak as in the bookstore." His last words: "Now comes the mystery."

The Big D

Dallas, Texas, incorporated in 1856, now with nearly a million residents, was probably named for the American statesman who was President James K. Polk's Vice President—George Mifflin Dallas (1792–1864).

Black Republicans

The term of reproach "Black Republicans" was applied by the proslavery side to members of the Republican party when it was founded in 1856 because the party was organized to prevent the extension of slavery into any new state or territory. It denounced the Supreme Court's decision in the Dred Scott case, and it favored admission of Kansas as a free state. Its first presidential candidate was defeated; its second was Abraham Lincoln.

A New Jerusalem

The German poet Heinrich Heine (1797–1856) predicted that Jews and Germans would create "a New Jerusalem" in Germany, "a modern Palestine that would be the home of philosophy, the mother soil of prophecy, and the citadel of pure spirituality." Heine—more or less a lifelong agnostic—said, a moment before his death, "God will pardon me—it is his profession." (*See also* 1534: The New Jerusalem.)

Big Ben

The 13½-ton Great Bell, installed in the clock tower of the British Houses of Parliament in 1856, became popularly known as "Big Ben" with reference to Sir Benjamin Hall, who was chief commissioner of works when it was cast and who had a deep booming voice. In calm weather, "Big Ben" may be heard over most of London.

The Lady with a Lamp

Care of the sick and of the war-wounded—that was the lifetime career of Florence Nightingale (1820–1910), the Italian-born "Lady with a Lamp," who in 1854 headed a unit of 38 British women nurses in the Crimean War with Russia. "Nursing is a noble profession for women," she asserted. Nightingale founded modern nursing and was a pioneer in preventive medicine. She lived to be 90 years of age, and she was the first woman to receive Britain's Order of Merit.

The Land of the Rising Sun.
The Floating Island

Nippon, the native name of Japan, is derived from the phrase for Great Japan, *Dai Nippon*—"from the place where the Sun comes from": "the Land of the Rising Sun." One of its ancient names is "the Floating Island."

The Know-Nothings

Militantly patriotic, anti-Catholic, and anti-immigrant members of the American party replied "I don't know" when asked about their organization. Especially popular in the midwestern United States, "the Know-Nothings" elected more than 40 congressmen in 1854; two years later, their presidential candidate, former Whig President Millard Fillmore (1800–1874), received 21 percent of the national popular vote and all of the electoral votes of Maryland. Know-Nothings successfully interrupted construction of the Washington Monument for two decades when they objected to a gift of granite from the Pope.

The Pacific Overture

Eager to secure for President Millard Fillmore an open-door treaty with Japan, which was encased in a policy of isolation from the West, Commodore Matthew Perry (1794–1858) determinedly sailed his squadron of black ships into Tokyo (then Edo) Bay "to demand as a right, and not to solicit as a favor, those acts of courtesy which are due from one civilized country to another." The 1854 agreement capping Perry's "Pacific Overture" provided for hospital treatment of shipwrecked American sailors and for fueling and supply privileges at two Japanese ports.

The Great Pacificator. The Great
Compromiser. The Apostle of
Liberty. A Second Washington.
The Old Chief. The Mill Boy
of the Slashes

The American statesman Henry Clay (1777–1852) was known for his skill in reconciling sectional differences, especially in the Missouri Compromise of 1820. On his very first day as a representative, in 1811, he was named Speaker of the House. The affectionate appellation "the Mill Boy of the

Slashes" refers to his humble beginnings: The Slashes were a low swampy region in Hanover County, Virginia, which he continued to visit.

The Achilles of England. Europe's Liberator. The Great Duke. The Iron Duke

Many names were conferred upon the soldier-statesman Arthur Welles-ley, Duke of Wellington (1769–1852), one of Britain's greatest heroes. His most famous victory was as commander of the allied forces that defeated Napoleon at Waterloo. He became British prime minister in 1828, and in 1842 was made commander in chief for life.

The American System

Congressman Henry Clay (1777–1852), "the Great Compromiser," had a dream: a vast network of roads, bridges, and other internal improvements that would be paid for by the federal government and would knit the Union together—"the American System." Tariff protection of American industries would also help to foster their growth in competition with European mills.

The Little Woman Who Made the Great War

On meeting Harriet Beecher Stowe (1811–1896), President Abraham Lincoln greeted her as "the little woman who wrote the book that made this great war." Her novel *Uncle Tom's Cabin* (1852) had stimulated abolitionists to do all they could to get rid of slavery in the South. She itemized the moral evils of bondage, for example, the separation of black families. She repeated the theme in her next book, *Dred, A Tale of the Great Dismal Swamp* (1856). The setting was the Utopian life on a Canadian farm. An abolitionist guides his slaves toward gradual freedom. Mrs. Stowe argues that free markets were so much better for the businessman than was slavery.

Sister of Shakespeare

The title "Sister of Shakespeare" was conferred upon Joanna Baillie (1762–1851), the Scottish poet and dramatist, because of her extraordinary insight into human nature, as demonstrated in her cycle of *Plays on the Passions*, which include *De Monfort* (1800) and *Family Legend* (1810). Sir Walter Scott's praise of her in his *Marmion* ends with the lines: "Awakening at the inspired strain / Dreamed their Shakespeare lived again."

The Poet of Bran Bread and Pumpkins

Ralph Waldo Emerson's sobriquet for the father of the graham cracker, the social reformer Sylvester Graham (1794–1851), was "the Poet of Bran Bread and Pumpkins." Graham was also a minister (Presbyterian) and a temperance lecturer, as well as a bug on health and personal hygiene. He advocated coarsely ground whole wheat for bread, hard mattresses, open bedroom windows, cold showers, looser and lighter clothing, daily exercise, vegetables, fresh fruits, rough cereals, pure drinking water, and cheerfulness at meals.

Black Thursday

On Thursday, February 6, 1851, an enormous bush fire, destroying much animal life, raged in the British colony of Victoria, in southeast Australia. The one-day fire covered immense areas, and the heat was felt far out at sea, where many birds fell dead onto the decks of vessels. It was the year that Victoria was made a separate colony and the discovery of gold generated a rapid population increase in the country.

Disney Professor

The appellation "Disney Professor" has nothing to do with specializing in the knowledge of Walt Disney creations (or, as one wit tried to put it, with the proliferation of "Mickey Mouse" courses at American schools and colleges): The term designates a chair of archeology, at the University of Cambridge, founded in 1851 by John Disney, Esq., of The Hyde, Ingatestone, in England.

The Citizen King. The King of the French. The King of the Barricades. The Napoleon of Peace

Louis Philippe (1773–1850), the future king of France (1830–48), lived for three years in one room over a bar in Philadelphia. He had deserted the army of the French Revolution and lived in exile for a score of years before returning to France when the Bourbons were restored to the throne. He became "the King of the Barricades" because his rule was preceded by a three-day revolution, during which the people of Paris erected 10,000 barricades. He was called "the Citizen King" and "the King of the French" (not "of France") to show that he reigned not by divine right but by the will of the people. His 18-year reign was marked by peace and prosperity—"the Napoleon of Peace."

El Pueblo de Nuestra Señora la Reina de Los Ángeles de Porciúncula

This was the original name of Los Angeles (incorporated in 1850)—in translation: The Village of Our Lady the Queen of the Angels of "Little Portion."

Old Rough and Ready. Old Buena Vista. Old Zach

At least three names have been labels for Zachary Taylor (1784–1850), the 12th President of the United States. "Old Rough and Ready" was what he was first called by his soldiers in the Mexican War. "Old Buena Vista" alludes to his victory at Buena Vista, in Mexico, where, with only 5,000 men, he held 20,000 of Mexican President Santa Anna's men in check for two days, then defeated them. The name "Old Zach" originated during his four-decade military career. He died from a gastrointestinal upset five days after laying the cornerstone for the Washington Monument on a blistering Fourth of July. (He was the first President in whose election voting took place nationwide on the same day, in 1848.)

The Paris of the Orient. Sin City

Shanghai became "the Paris of the Orient" and China's largest city in only 150 years. Via the sleepy fishing village near the East China Sea in the 1850s, foreign troops and unscrupulous Chinese officials opened the nation to an inundation of opium. The white "barbarians" carved out choice areas of real estate for themselves, and the welcome mat in Shanghai was out for all, no questions asked. The "Sin City" became wicked, mysterious, debauched; the grossest of appetites could be gratified with impunity there.

The Bard of Rydal Mount

The English poet laureate William Wordsworth (1770–1850) was given the name "the Bard of Rydal Mount" for the spot where he lived much of his life and where he died. Hartley Coleridge (1796–1849) wrote, "He lived amidst th' untrodden ways / to Rydal Lake that lead / A bard whom there were none to praise, / And very few to read." A century later, Bertrand Russell (1872–1970) concluded that "in his youth, Wordsworth sympathized with the French Revolution, went to France, wrote good poetry, and had a natural daughter. At this period, he was a 'bad' man. Then he became 'good,' abandoned his daughter, adopted correct principles, and wrote bad poetry."

The 1840s

The Dismal Science

"The Dismal Science" is the designation that the British social critic Thomas Carlyle (1795–1881) gave to economics, or, as it was called, social science. In 1849 he wrote, in *On the Nigger Question:* "The social science—not a 'gay science,' but a rueful—which finds the secret of this Universe in 'supply and demand' . . . what we might call, by way of eminence, the dismal science." His view of the stars in the universe was that they are "a sad spectacle. If they be inhabited, what a scope for misery and folly. If they be not inhabited, what a waste of space."

Old Man Eloquent

The sixth President of the United States, John Quincy Adams (1767–1848)—a son of the second President, John Adams—was called "Old Man Eloquent" mainly for his vivid, forceful attacks on any measure that would extend slavery. He was the most successful American diplomat of his time and the only former President to be elected to the House of Representatives. Adams advocated "charity to all mankind, bearing no malice or ill will to any human being, and even compassionating those who hold in bondage their fellow men, not knowing what they do." "My toast would be, may our country be always successful, but whether successful or otherwise, always right." (Carl Schurz [1829–1906] would say, "Our country, right or wrong. When right, to be kept right; when wrong, to be put right.")

The Liberator

The Irish political leader Daniel O'Connell (1775–1847) was instrumental in bringing about the Catholic Emancipation Act of 1828, then sat in the British Parliament, where he fought for Irish independence and reforms of the government of Ireland. In 1841 he became the first Catholic lord mayor of Dublin since the time of James II.

The National Game

"The game of base ball" became "the National Game" at the end of the Civil War, as the most popular and most widely played team sport in America. It had been played in army camps on both sides. It evolved from the English game of "rounders." The first rules were established by a surveyor and amateur athlete, Alexander J. Cartwright (1820–1892), who umped the first game, in Hoboken, New Jersey, on June 19, 1846. (It is

Cartwright, not Abner Doubleday, who finally has been credited with this supreme American invention.) There are 26 major-league baseball teams. More than 13,000 men have played in the big time.

The Santa Claus Story of Baseball

The yarn has long been believed and is still widely believed that Abner Doubleday (1819–1893) invented baseball. The West Pointer *did* organize ball games in Cooperstown, New York, in the late 1830s, but the national pastime as it is known today was conceived by Alexander Cartwright.

America's Attic

The Smithsonian Institution—"America's Attic"—was founded, in 1846, "for the increase and diffusion of knowledge among men"; it had taken Congress a decade to accept English chemist James Smithson's start-up gift of half a million dollars. Everything from soup to nuts, and including the kitchen sink, has been on display in the huge complex of museums and galleries in Washington, DC. Among the historic Americana, treasures, and trivia: Francis Scott Key's star-spangled banner and a silk purse made from a sow's ear.

The No Month

"No warmth, no cheerfulness, no healthful ease, / No comfortable feel in any member— / No shade, no shine, no butterflies, no bees, / No fruits, no flowers, no leaves, no birds, / November!"—Thomas Hood (1799–1845), the British poet.

Johnny Appleseed

Anyone who fructifies the earth is a "Johnny Appleseed," after the frontiersman whose real name was John Chapman (1774–1845). He collected seeds from apple orchards and cider presses in Pennsylvania and headed west, sowing them in Ohio, Indiana, and Illinois. Nineteenth-century migrants, the legend goes, followed his trail of seedling orchards.

Manifest Destiny

Nineteenth-century expansionists believed that it was God's will to spread democracy from the Atlantic Ocean to the Pacific, and then across the Pacific with the annexation of Hawaii. "Our manifest destiny," the diplomat and journalist John Louis O'Sullivan (c.1813–1895) wrote, justifying the annexation of Texas, "is to overspread the continent allotted by Providence for the free development of our yearly multiplying millions." With its racist, imperialist, and mercenary overtones, "Manifest Destiny" resounded during the Mexican War, the quest for Oregon, the slavers' interest in Cuba, and "Seward's Ice Box."

The Great Hunger

A scientific commission appointed by Prime Minister Robert Peel failed to discover that Ireland's potato blight (1845–49) was actually a fungus growth and not a disease of the potato itself. In addition to having its principal crop ravaged, Ireland was also experiencing the harshest and longest winter in memory. About three-quarters of a million people died in "the Great Hunger" of 1848, and hundreds of thousands emigrated.

Old Hickory

The seventh President of the United States, six-foot-tall Andrew Jackson (1767–1845), started his political career when quite young, fighting in the American Revolution at the age of 13. He was called "Tough," then "Tough as Hickory," and finally, "Old Hickory." He was the hero of the Battle of New Orleans (1815), which was fought after the War of 1812 was over because word of peace had not reached the combatants in Louisiana. Jackson was the first to plunge the presidency into the thick of party politics, and he was the first Chief Executive to be the target, in 1835, of an assassination attempt.

Old Glory

"Old Glory" was the popular name for Sir Francis Burdett (1770–1844), the English politician and member of Parliament, who was arrested—after barricading his house for four days—for publishing a speech that would deny the House of Commons the right to imprison delinquents. He was the father of the philanthropist Angela Georgina Burdett-Coutts, Charles Dickens's friend.

The Dark-Horse President.
The Napoleon of the Stump

James K. Polk (1795–1849), the 11th President of the United States, was known as "the Napoleon of the Stump," a Tennessee congressman for seven consecutive terms. He was the unexpected presidential nominee of the Democratic party in 1844—the first "dark-horse" selection—and he won, turning back Henry Clay, "the Great Compromiser." The first Chief Executive to be photographed (1849, by Mathew Brady), Polk kept at least five of his campaign promises: the acquisition of California from Mexico (he actually acquired much of the southwestern and western land); the settlement of the Oregon dispute; the lowering of the tariff; establishment of the sub-Treasury; resignation after one term in the White House. He died three months after leaving office.

The Lion of the Lord

Under the leadership of Vermont-born Brigham Young (1801–1877), "the Lion of the Lord," the Mormons headed west after their founder, Joseph Smith (1805–1844), had been murdered by a mob in Carthage, Illinois. They set out from Nauvoo (Commerce, Illinois), and moved across Iowa, along the north side of the Platte River, over part of the Oregon Trail, through South Pass in the Rockies to Fort Bridger in Wyoming, and on to the "Great Basin"—Salt Lake Valley. Young was the supreme authority in the cooperative Mormon theocracy, and he directed phenomenal growth and prosperity. He became governor of the Territory of Utah (1850), formerly the Mormons' provisional state of Deseret. He took 27 wives and was survived by 17—and by 47 children. (The Mormons' doctrine of plural marriage had to be abandoned before Utah was admitted into the Union, as the 45th state, in 1886.)

The Schoolmaster of the Republic

The American lexicographer Noah Webster (1758–1843) has had far-reaching educational influence through his dictionaries and schoolbooks. In 1828 he published, in two volumes, his 20-year labor of love, *An American Dictionary of the English Language*, the first truly American dictionary (12,000 of the entries had never been listed in a dictionary before). His *Blue-Backed Speller* of 1783 is still in print; in fact, it is the best-selling book of all time (besides, obviously, the Bible). He said that "America must be . . . as famous for its arts as for arms." The words "Webster" and "dictionary" have become synonymous.

The Alphabet Maker

Realizing that feelings and passions are conveyed by sounds, the Cherokee silver craftsman and warrior Sequoyah (c. 1770–1843) distinguished the sounds, then conveyed them through pictorial signs: images of birds and beasts. He made the cultural leap from hieroglyphics to an alphabet or syllabary, reducing the number of pictorial signs to 81 characters. The Cherokee proved to be quick learners, and almost their entire nation in the southeastern United States was soon literate. "The Alphabet Maker" is the only person in recorded history to conceive and perfect an alphabet from the resources of his own mind.

The Grace Darling of America

Ida Lewis Williams (born 1841), the keeper of the Lime Rock lighthouse at Newport, Rhode Island, became well known for saving lives in shipwrecks. Her nickname derives from her famous English prototype, Grace Horsley Darling (1815–1842), who, as the daughter of the keeper of the Longstone lighthouse in Northumberland, helped to rescue many lives. (Benjamin Franklin once wrote, "Lighthouses are more helpful than churches.")

The Dorrites

A half century after the US Constitution was framed, Rhode Island (which was not represented at the federal convention in 1787) still restricted suffrage to substantial landowners and their oldest sons. About half of the adult male population did not have the right to vote. Thomas W. Dorr (1805–1854), a well-to-do lawyer, headed the People's party, which in 1841 drafted a constitution that was popularly approved, and the party elected Dorr governor. The legal chief executive proclaimed martial law and dispatched militia units against "the Dorrites." Dorr was convicted of treason but was soon released from life imprisonment.

The One-Month President.
Old Tippecanoe. Old Tip.
The Washington of the West

The ninth President of the United States, "the One-Month President," William Henry Harrison (1773–1841), earned the nicknames "Old Tippecanoe," "Old Tip," and "the Washington of the West" during his military career. As General Harrison, he won the famous battle against Tecumseh at Tippecanoe, in Indiana (1811), which put an end to organized Indian resistance to white settlement in the region, and he whipped the British repeatedly in the War of 1812. At 68, he was the oldest man before Ronald Reagan (in 1981) to be sworn President. He delivered his 100-minute inaugural speech in raw March weather, then got caught in a downpour, came down with a cold, developed "bilious pleurisy," and died a month to the day after taking office. A year earlier, he had noted, "All the measures of the Government are directed to the purpose of making the rich richer and the poor poorer."

The 1830s

The Pork-and-Beans War

The Anglo-American Aroostook "war" of 1838–39 was declared by the governor of Maine, the only time that someone other than the President has issued a declaration of war against another nation. The issue was border claims by both Maine and the Canadian province of New Brunswick in the Aroostook Valley, an unpopulated, lumber-rich wilderness. Bloodshed was averted when President Martin Van Buren dispatched General Winfield Scott to arrange a truce, and the British government agreed to refer the dispute to a boundary commission. The Webster-Ashburton Treaty (1842) fixed the present border, with the Aroostook region under American control. (The overburdened inhabitants of the region could spare little food for the militia troops, who had to make do with hardtack, salt pork, and simple food like beans.)

The Trail of Tears

Federal troops under General Winfield Scott evicted 20,000 Cherokee from their homes in the southeastern United States in 1838 and marched, or escorted, them at gunpoint 1,000 miles to Indian land in Oklahoma. Four thousand died along the way. A minority of the Cherokee nation, over the protest of the majority, had surrendered land in Georgia by the Treaty of New Echota, in 1835. A century and a half after the march, President Ronald Reagan designated ''the Trail of Tears'' as a National Historic Trail.

The Pickwickian Syndrome

Falling asleep at unexpected times, even during meals, and having the need for a nap at any time of the day, even in the morning shortly after rising, was the curse of a boy in Charles Dickens's *Posthumous Papers of the Pickwick Club* (1837), from which ''the Pickwickian syndrome'' was coined by 20th-century psychiatrists.

Bible Communists

The American religious leader John Humphrey Noyes (1811–1886) in 1836 founded the Community of Putney, Vermont, which became known as the ''Bible Communists'' for its avowed communism combined with the propagation of religious views. Noyes, a Yale theology student and a believer in Perfectionism (Matthew 5:48) and the Second Coming of Christ, had declared himself sinless in 1834. A second Utopian community was established at Oneida, New York; its members practiced an elaborate form of polygamy.

The Coonskin Congressman.
The Munchausen of the West

David (Davy) Crockett (1786–1836) was both frontiersman and politician. The nickname ''Munchausen of the West'' was given him in allusion to the many improbable tales he used to relate. He was a three-term Tennessee congressman and a popular figure in Washington. He was captured at the Alamo and later slain. (*See also* 1951: The Munchausen syndrome.)

The Moon Hoax

Every day for a week, during a heat wave and a newspaper circulation war in 1835, the *New York Sun* reported that the astronomer Sir John Herschel (1792–1871), son of the discoverer of the planet Uranus (in 1781), had sighted life on the Moon through the world's largest telescope, in South Africa: "Furry batlike creatures gesticulated, appeared impassioned and emphatic . . . capable of producing works of arts and contrivance."

The House Painter's Misfirings

From a distance of only six feet, the monomaniacal house painter Richard Lawrence (c.1803–1835) aimed two pistols at President Andrew "Old Hickory" Jackson attending a funeral service in the Capitol rotunda, in Washington, DC. Both pistols misfired, and the Chief Executive was unhurt. The assassin manqué was committed to a jail, then to a mental hospital.

Malthusianism

The English political economist Thomas Robert Malthus (1766–1834) tried to demonstrate that the human population would increase faster than the planet's natural resources to support our species, a theory that became known as "Malthusianism." Little did he know that in our contemporary usage "Malthusianism" would also come to mean masturbation—as one certain way of keeping the population increase down. Still, it is expected that humankind will leap from 5.2 billion to 6.2 billion by the end of the century.

The Hero of the Worlds

Dozens of towns and counties throughout the United States bear the name Lafayette, for the French general, political leader, and early foe of slavery, Marie Joseph Paul Yves Roch Gilbert du Motier, Marquis de Lafayette (1757–1834), who for decades was the popular symbol of the bond between France and the nascent United States. He was only 20 years old when, having bought a ship and landed in America with a troop of soldier-adventurers, he impressed George Washington so much that he was made a major general, by far the youngest major general in US history. Lafayette was wounded at Brandywine, fought at Gloucester, Barren Hill, Monmouth, and Rhode Island, and was at Washington's side during the crucial winter of 1777–78 at Valley Forge. He was instrumental in getting French support for the American enterprise.

In 1779, after France had declared war on England, Lafayette returned home as a hero, but soon came back to his command in America. As a token of gratitude, he was given a vast land grant in Louisiana, in 1803. When he again returned from France, as a visitor, in 1824–26, he was given a jubilant reception on a tour through the United States; Congress voted him a gift of the then huge sum of $200,000 and a township in Florida; and Lafayette became the first of only four foreigners not head of their countries who have ever addressed a joint session of Congress. Throughout most of his life, he was an effective, and celebrated, politician and general in France as well. It was Lafayette who designed the modern French tricolor flag.

The Great Magician. The Great Minstrel. The Northern Homer. The Minstrel of the Border. The Border Minstrel. The Black Hussar of Literature. The Wizard of the North. The Great Unknown

Many names were popularly conferred upon the eminent, and prolific, Scottish poet and novelist Sir Walter Scott (1771–1832). "The Great Unknown" indeed!

The Black Hawk War

The war between the United States and the Sac and Fox nations in 1832 became known as "the Black Hawk War" because the Native Americans fought under the leadership of Black Hawk (1767–1838), their chief. The war was waged by the Indians—in vain—for the recovery of lands that had been ceded to the whites under doubtful circumstances. After Black Hawk was defeated and captured, he was taken on a grand tour of the principal American cities and to meet President Andrew Jackson, to be impressed with the greatness of the nation. The *Autobiography of Black Hawk* (1833) is considered to be a classic statement of Native American resentment against white interlopers.

The Addison of the North

The Scottish novelist Henry Mackenzie (1745–1831) was given the label "the Addison of the North" as the author of *The Man of Feeling* and *The Man of the World*. The allusion is to the 17th–18th-century essayist-statesman Joseph Addison of *Tatler* and *Spectator* fame.

The Liberator. The Washington of South America

Simón Bolívar (1783–1830) has been hailed as "the Liberator" of South America from the dominion of Spain. He was the first president of Greater Colombia, which he formed through the union of the provinces of New Granada and Venezuela. The ardent, headstrong patriot also organized the government of Peru and gave his name to the inland country in west-central South America—Bolivia. He also initiated Pan-Americanism. His spiritual mentor was Jean Jacques Rousseau.

Old Ironsides

The wooden US frigate *Constitution*, "Old Ironsides," saw action in the Tripolitan War and the War of 1812 and was rebuilt twice, in 1833 and in 1877. Millions of schoolchildren, inspired by Oliver Wendell Holmes's poem "Old Ironsides," published in the *Boston Daily Advertiser* in 1830, contributed pennies for restoring the unfit vessel. "Old Ironsides," which got its nickname because of the strength of its oak construction, is the oldest commissioned warship afloat in the world—now a museum in the Charleston (Massachusetts) Navy Yard.

The Kitchen Cabinet

When President Andrew Jackson's cabinet, except for Secretary of State Martin Van Buren, a widower, snubbed the wife of his friend, Secretary of War John H. Eaton, "Old Hickory" abandoned regular cabinet meetings and instead began discussing and formulating policy with an informal group of advisers, "the Kitchen Cabinet" (1830). They included a journalist, an editor, and a nephew, as well as Van Buren and Eaton.

The Five Civilized Nations

Under the Removal Act of 1830, five tribes, or nations, of Native Americans were forced from their lands in the eastern United States and settled in the Indian Territory, in eastern Oklahoma. Two of the nations—the Cherokee and the Creek—had developed advanced agricultural methods in the southeast. Together with the Choctaw, Seminole, and Chickasaw, they were "the Five Civilized Nations." The Indian Territory was held communally, and the tribes were recognized as domestic dependent nations. Today their governments serve mainly in an advisory capacity.

The 1820s

The Cicero of the British Senate

The English orator and statesman George Canning (1770–1827) was given the name "the Cicero of the British Senate" for his eloquence—Cicero was Rome's greatest orator (106–43 BC). Canning once declared, "Give me the avowed, erect, and manly foe, / Firm I can meet, perhaps return the blow; / But of all plagues, good heavens, thy wrath can send, / Save, save, oh save me from the candid friend." Ciceronean indeed.

The Sage of Monticello. The Apostle of Liberty. Long Tom

"The Apostle of Liberty" is among the names bestowed on the third President of the United States, Thomas Jefferson (1743–1826). He wrote his own epitaph: "Here was buried Thomas Jefferson, author of the Declaration of Independence, of the Statute of Virginia for Religious Freedom, and father of the University of Virginia"—omitting the fact that he was a two-term President. (The Federalist press had said that if Jefferson were elected President, "Murder, robbery, rape, adultery, and incest will be openly taught and practiced.")

The Colossus of Independence. The Atlas of Independence. His Rotundity

John Adams (1735–1826), the second President of the United States, was known both for his leading role in the fight for American independence and for his lifelong stance of independence as an individual. For example, although he was allied with the powerful Alexander Hamilton and the conservative Federalists, he remained independent of them when they struggled with the Jeffersonians. The physician-educator Benjamin Rush once observed of Adams, "You stand nearly alone in the history of our public men in never having had your integrity called in question or even suspected. Friends and enemies agree in believing you to be an honest man." (He was "His Rotundity" because he was chubby and five feet six inches "tall," sandwiched in his presidency between the six-foot-two Washington and the six-foot-two-and-a-half Jefferson. His oldest son, John Quincy Adams [1767–1848], became the sixth President.)

The Fourth Estate

Thomas Macaulay (1800–1859) coined the phrase in 1826: "The gallery in which the reporters sit has become a fourth estate of the realm." Thirteen years later, Thomas Carlyle (1795–1881) wrote, "Burke said there were Three Estates in Parliament; but, in the Reporters' Gallery yonder, there sat a Fourth Estate more important far than they all. It is not a figure of speech, or witty saying, it is a literal fact—very momentous to us in these times."

The Decembrists

Russian military officers who were influenced by Western liberal ideas during the Napoleonic wars when they served in Europe formed secret revolutionary societies advocating the establishment of representative democracy. In December 1825, a poorly organized rebellion was crushed by the czar's artillery fire in St. Petersburg, and five of "the Decembrist" leaders were captured and executed. The government increased police terrorism when revolutionary activity spread among the educated classes.

Gentleman Cow

The euphemism "gentleman cow" is used to refer to extreme cases of censorship (bowdlerisms) such as the "cleaning up" done by the English editor Thomas Bowdler (1754–1825). In Tennyson's *The Wreck of the Hesperus*, he substituted "gentleman cow" for the offensive term "bull." This ultimate Victorian also produced a 10-volume *Family Shakespeare*, excising hundreds of sexual references from Shakespeare's language. He similarly expurgated the Old Testament.

Clinton's Ditch. Clinton's Folly

In 1811, De Witt Clinton (1769–1828) served as the mayor of New York, the lieutenant governor of New York, and a state senator—all at the same time—before going on to become US senator (he introduced the Twelfth Amendment) and governor of New York. He spent more than a decade enlisting public and legislative support for construction of the 363-mile-long Erie Canal connecting the Hudson River and the Great Lakes. When "Clinton's Ditch" or "Clinton's Folly" opened in 1825, it was clear sailing for New York City to become "the emporium of commerce, the seat of manufacturers, [and] the focus of great moneyed operations."

Ararat

Mordecai Manuel Noah (1785–1851), who was a Philadelphia lawyer, a journalist, and a playwright, tried to establish, in 1825, a homeland for Jews—"Ararat"—on an island in the Niagara River, in northern New

York. It would be a 48-square-mile, white-oak-forested city of refuge. A dedication ceremony was held, but Noah soon left the area, and his dream evaporated. Noah had been President James Monroe's consul at Tunis but had to be recalled because he was Jewish; his religion was belatedly seen by Washington to be an obstacle to the exercise of his consular functions.

The Era of Good Feeling

"The Era of Good Feeling" was eight years long, from 1817 to 1825— James Monroe's two-term presidency. The frustrating three-year War of 1812 was dead and buried, and America's future was looking bright. Monroe (1758–1831) was so popular that only one negative vote was cast by electors in his 1820 reelection, and that was cast because the elector believed that George Washington should be the only unanimously elected President. (In 1823, the Monroe Doctrine proclaimed that the United States would view as an unfriendly act any attempt of a European nation to intervene in American affairs or to increase its holdings in the New World.)

The Werther of Politics

Robert Stewart, 2nd Marquis of Londonderry (born 1769), British statesman with high achievements as foreign secretary, committed suicide in 1822, earning himself the appellation "the Werther of Politics." Werther, the *Weltschmerz* protagonist of Goethe's 1774 novel *The Sorrows of Young Werther*, also took his own life. (*Weltschmerz* is a sentimental melancholy and pessimism over the state of the world, accompanied by a romantic acceptance of this sadness as a natural aspect of human life—a quintessentially German word, meaning, literally, "world pain.")

The Charleston 35

In 1822, 35 black men, including the freeman Denmark Vesey, were hanged on charges of conspiring to take over the city of Charleston, South Carolina. Vesey (born about 1767) had acquired much wealth and influence after purchasing his freedom in 1800. His well-planned slave insurrection might actually have succeeded had he not been betrayed by informers.

The Father of Texas

Stephen Austin (1793–1836) founded the first Anglo-American community in Texas, in 1822. Because he believed that Texas did not have the resources either to win or to maintain its independence, Austin argued that Texas should remain a Mexican state. His mottoes were the redemption of Texas from the wilderness, fidelity and gratitude to his adopted country, and inflexible truth to the interests and just rights of the settlers.

Man of Destiny. The Colossus of the Nineteenth Century. The Gallic Caesar. The Armed Soldier of Democracy. The Little Corporal. Le Petit Caporal. Corporal Violet. Father Violet. The First Consul. Jupiter Scapin. The Corsican Ogre. The Corsican Sesostris. The Nightmare of Europe. The Antichrist. Boney. Nappy. The Tiddy-Doll. The Code Giver.

Many more than 18 names were bestowed on the Corsican-born French soldier and emperor Napoleon I (Napoleon Bonaparte, 1769–1821), one of the greatest conquerors—thus inflicters of suffering—of all time and yet a great promoter of liberalism through his lasting reforms in law and administration. (He declared he was the chosen instrument of destiny. To his admiring soldiers he remained "the Little Corporal" because of his small stature and youthful appearance. Violet was the floral device of the emperor, worn by his adherents during his exile on Elba. "Jupiter Scapin"—used also by Ralph Waldo Emerson in speaking of Napoleon—refers to the mixture of greatness and pettiness in Napoleon's character, from the knavish and thievish valet in Molière's comedy *Les Fourberies de Scapin*. Sesostris, the Egyptian king in Greek mythology, was proverbial for the rapidity and extent of his conquests. "Boney," a derogatory diminutive of Bonaparte, was popular among English writers and speakers, as was the diminutive "Nappy," from Napoleon. "The Tiddy-Doll" is what the English cartoonist James Gilbray called him in one of his most famous cartoons. The "Code Napoléon" [civil code] and four related codes [civil-procedure, commercial, criminal-procedure, and penal codes] are perhaps his most remarkable legacy, replacing the Roman civil law, which had still prevailed in most of Europe, and affecting the laws of many countries to this day.)

The French poet-philosopher Paul Valéry (1871–1945) thought that "It is a pity to see a fine mind like Napoleon devoted to meaningless things such as empires, world events, the noise of cannons and voices, and the belief in history, in glory, in posterity, in Caesar."

The Royal Brute. Farmer George

"O! ye that love mankind! Ye that dare oppose not only tyranny but the tyrant, stand forth!" Thus, Thomas Paine (1737–1809), the erstwhile

Englishman, urged the colonists to declare their independence from the tyrannous King George III (1738–1820), whom he described as "the Royal Brute." After Americans were rid of the monarch, Paine wrote, in 1783, "The times that tried men's souls are over and the greatest and completest revolution the world ever knew gloriously and happily accomplished." As for "Farmer George" (known to have rather rustic tastes and habits), the English author Edmund Clerihew Bentley (1875–1956) quipped: "George the Third / Ought never to have occurred. / One can only wonder / At so grotesque a blunder."

Doughface

Coined in a speech castigating abolitionists in 1820, "Doughface" came to be defined four decades later as "a contemptuous nickname applied to the Northern favorers and abettors of Negro slavery." A Doughface during the Civil War was a Northern politician who sympathized with Southern views on slavery; many Doughfaces became known as "Copperheads," Northerners who sympathized with the South during the War Between the States.

Prince of Princes. Beau of Princes. The First Gentleman of Europe

George IV (George Augustus Frederick, 1762–1830), king of Great Britain and Ireland from 1820 to his death 10 years later, was first called "Prince of Princes" by the poet Lord Byron. "Beau of Princes" was a nickname that originated while he was still Prince of Wales. But he is perhaps best known as "the First Gentleman of Europe" in allusion to his courtly manners and exquisite taste in dress. He was hated, though, for his extravagance and dissolute habits.

The 1810s

Light-Horse Harry

The implacable Henry "Light-Horse Harry" Lee (1756–1818) fought with distinction in many campaigns and participated in the siege of the tobacco port of Yorktown, Virginia, in 1781, which essentially ended the American Revolution. He wrote the most famous eulogy in American history, hailing George Washington as "first in war, first in peace, and first in the hearts of his countrymen." He was the father of Robert E. Lee (1807–1870), who led the army of the Confederacy.

The Cradle of Liberty

Faneuil Hall became known as "the Cradle of Liberty" because Bostonians in the years before the Revolution protested unpopular British measures in the public meeting place. It was Beantown's only polling place from 1743—the year after a wealthy merchant of Huguenot extraction, Peter Faneuil, made a gift of it to the community—to 1817.

The Cat Hoax

A prankster in Chester, England, in 1815, distributed handbills saying that the British Isles were overrun with rats and that, to fight them, 16 shillings would be paid for every full-grown tomcat, 10 shillings for every female, and 2½ shillings for every kitten, if turned in at a certain date. When the day came, the city was filled with people carrying cats, and a riot ensued. Five hundred cats were killed, but most escaped and plagued the city and the neighboring houses and barns for many weeks afterward.

The White Terror

After the second restoration of the French Bourbon kings, in 1815, in the reactionary period that followed, many atrocious acts were committed officially and unofficially, especially by the Jesuits. Although the Jesuits were known for their black garments, the period came to be referred to as "the White Terror."

The Waterloo Hero

The English General Rowland Hill, first Viscount Hill (1772–1842), was five times wounded in the battle of Waterloo, on June 18, 1815, yet led his troops in the triumphant charge at the close of the day—the last action of the Napoleonic wars. In 1828 "the Waterloo hero" became commander in chief of the British army, holding the post until his death 14 years later.

Hundred Days

"Hundred Days" as a historical time frame was from March 20, 1815, when Napoleon arrived in Paris, to June 28, when Louis XVIII—in the wake of Napoleon's "Waterloo"—was restored as king. (*See also* 1933: Hundred Days.)

The Pearl of the Orient

Sri Lanka is Sinhala for "resplendent land," which it is. Its beauty has earned the pear-shaped Indian Ocean island off southern India the title "the Pearl of the Orient." Sri Lanka used to be Ceylon; before that, Serendip.

The Polish Franklin

The Polish historian and philosopher Thaddeusz Czacki (1765–1813) has been called "the Polish Franklin," a title that was meant to compare him to the protean Benjamin Franklin. Czacki, who wrote a then-definitive work on the laws of Poland and Lithuania, was above all a promoter of education.

The Great Triumvirate

Three regional political giants were celebrated in Congress as "the Great Triumvirate" (from the Latin words *tres*, three, and *vir*, man): Henry Clay (1777–1852), "the Great Pacificator," the Kentucky "war hawk" and proponent of slavery; Daniel Webster (1782–1852), "the Yankee Demosthenes"; and John C. Calhoun (1782–1850), the flamboyant South Carolinian who resigned the vice presidency (1832) so that he could represent South Carolina in the Senate.

The Battle of the Nations

"The Battle of the Nations," more formally called the Battle of Leipzig, was one of the most sanguinary battles of modern times. It was fought from October 16 to 19, 1813, between the French and their allies (180,000 strong), commanded by Napoleon, and the combined forces of Austria, Russia, and Prussia (almost 300,000 in number), under Field Marshal Gebhard Leberecht von Blücher (1742–1819—"Marshal Forward"), and Crown Prince Jean Baptiste Bernadotte (c.1766–1844), founder of the present Swedish dynasty. Napoleon was defeated, at a combined loss of 80,000 men. (Another "Battle of Leipzig" was fought in 1631, during the Thirty Years' War.)

Uncle Sam

During the War of 1812 with Great Britain, Samuel ("Uncle Sam") Wilson (1766–1854) was an inspector at Elbert Anderson's storehouse in Troy, New York, which supplied crates of meat to American troops fighting British forces quartered in Canada. The crates were stamped prominently "EA—US" for "Elbert Anderson—United States," which prompted workers and longshoremen to joke that "US" stood for "Uncle Sam" (Wilson). The joke caught on, and "Uncle Sam" and "United States" became one.

Mr. Madison's War. The Second War of Independence

The three-year War of 1812 was touched off when Britain seized US ships trading with France (Britain's foe) and impressed 4,000 naturalized US sailors and also armed Indians raiding the western US borders. Congress declared war by only a small majority: The western states favored war; New England opposed it. President James Madison (1751–1836), in his second term as the nation's fourth President, fled Washington, DC, just before British troops set fire to the Capitol and to the building that after the war came to be called "the White House." The war didn't settle much, but it quickened the growth of American nationalism and spurred westward expansion.

The Louisiana Horrors

Black slaves burned several plantations and marched on New Orleans, Louisiana, in 1811. Sixteen were killed or executed, their heads cut off and displayed on poles along the Mississippi River. Slave rebellions had also been aborted two decades earlier in Louisiana. In the 1791 uprising, inspired by the successful slave revolt in Haiti, 23 slaves were hanged. Four year later, in Point Coupée Parish, 25 slaves were killed and 25 "judicially" executed by militia units.

The Wife-Hater Bible

An 1810 printing became known—and sought-after as a collectors' piece—as "the Wife-Hater Bible" because of an error in Luke 14:26: "If any man come to me, and hate not his father and mother . . . yea, and his own wife also" (for "his own life also").

Aldiborontesphoscophornio

The Scottish publisher John Ballantyne (1774–1821) was first called by a 25-letter name by the prolific novelist Sir Walter Scott (1771–1832) in allusion to his pomposity and dignity of manner. (Scott was edited and published by Ballantyne.) Aldiborontesphoscophornio was a then well-known character in Henry Carey's burlesque tragedy *Chrononhotontho-logos*—the name of another pompous individual in that theatrical bombast.

The 1800s

The Maid of Saragossa

When pretty, 22-year-old Augustina saw her fiancé die in Napoleon's 1808–09 siege of Saragossa (Zaragoza), Spain, she calmly mounted the battery and used a gun with such great effectiveness against the besiegers that she became known as "the Maid of Saragossa." Robert Southey wrote about her in his *History of the Peninsular War*, and Lord Byron devoted several pages to her in *Childe Harold*, including the line, "Her lover sinks—she sheds no ill-timed tear."

The Burr Conspiracy

Former Vice President Aaron Burr (1756–1836), who had dueled with and killed Founding Father Alexander Hamilton (1755–1804) four years earlier, was charged with treason because, so it was asserted, he had tried to separate the western lands from the rest of the country, establish his own rule there, and join up with Mexico. In a trial in 1808, presided over by Chief Justice John Marshall, Burr was acquitted when federal prosecutors could not prove the complaint.

The Raft Conference

On July 9, 1807, Czar Alexander I (1775–1825) met Emperor Napoleon Bonaparte (1769–1821) on a raft in the Neman River, off Tilsit, now Sovetsky, in Russia, to negotiate peace between their two countries.

Gotham

Washington Irving (1783–1859) introduced the name "Gotham" for New York City in a letter, of February 13, 1807, in the *Salmagundi Papers*: "Oh! Gotham, Gotham! most enlightened of cities!" (He was a native "Gotham-ite.") Gotham was the name of a village in southern England at the time of King John (1167–1216); the citizens were said to have feigned stupidity so that the king would not want to come and live in that area.

The Financier of the American Revolution

George Washington's long-time friend Robert Morris (1734–1806) was "the Financier of the American Revolution." His great organizational ability and his own personal credit prevented the new government's bank-

complishments, which earned her the more flattering epithet "the Semiramis of the North." The allusion is to the ninth-century-BC Assyrian Queen
Semiramis, or Sammu-ramat, the legendary wife of Ninus, the founder of
Nineveh; as the daughter of the Syrian goddess Derketo, she was endowed
with extraordinary beauty and intelligence; she was said to have built
many cities during her 42-year reign, and she is the only Assyrian queen
who is included by name on the monuments. (*See also* 48 AD: The Messalina Complex.)

The Ayrshire Poet.
The Bard of Ayrshire

The Scottish poet Robert Burns (1759–1796), born in Ayrshire County,
began writing very early but first published only at age 27 (10 years before
his death) in the hope of raising money to emigrate to Jamaica. He became
famous immediately and stayed in Scotland—"The best laid schemes o'
mice and men / Gang aft a-gley." His still popular songs include "Comin'
thro' the Rye," "My Heart's in the Highlands," and "Auld Lang Syne." He
was "truly sorry man's dominion / Has broken Nature's social union."

The Unspoken Farewell Address

George Washington never delivered his Farewell Address. It was written
with the help of his longtime colleague Alexander Hamilton and published
in newspapers in September 1796, six months before the end of Washington's second term. "The Father of His Country" used the address to dis-
courage further pleas for him to serve a third term. He warned against
permanent alliances with foreign powers, a big public debt, a large military
establishment, and devices of a "small, artful, enterprising minority" to
control or change government.

Count Cagliostro

The famous Sicilian charlatan and impostor Giuseppe Balsamo (1743–
1795), known as "Count Cagliostro," practiced every form of deception,
from medicine to divination to political intrigues throughout European
countries. Occasionally, he was imprisoned and once was sentenced to
death. In 1783 he made a dupe of the French Prince Cardinal de Rohan in
"the Affair of the Diamond Necklace," for which he was imprisoned in the
Bastille; he escaped. He was "the quack of quacks, the most perfect scoun-
drel that, in these latter ages, has marked the world's history" (Thomas
Carlyle).

Batavia

"Batavia" was the ancient Roman name for Holland, and it is still occasionally used in a poetical sense. In 1795 the seven provinces of the Netherlands united and assumed the name "Batavian Republic," which was in use until 1806, when the country became the "Kingdom of Holland," under Louis Bonaparte as king. (The town of Batavia in western New York State was laid out by an agent for the Holland Land Company.)

Bozzy

The libertine Scottish biographer and gossip James Boswell (1740–1795) made a career of associating with and writing about the great: Rousseau, Casanova, Voltaire, Burke, Garrick, Reynolds. During his lifetime and in later literature, he has sometimes been referred to with the diminutive "Bozzy." The first to use this name—with affection, but only once—was "Dr. " Samuel Johnson, the great lexicographer, whose biography (1791) by the vainglorious Boswell did more than any other work to establish Bozzy's fame. "You have but two subjects, yourself and me, and I'm sick of both," Johnson said to Boswell.

The Whiskey Rebellion

Farmers in western Pennsylvania refused to pay federal taxes on home-distilled spirits. In 1794, President George Washington, the first of only two US Presidents to take the field as commander in chief (the other was Lincoln), rode as far as Bedford, Pennsylvania, with Secretary of the Treasury Alexander Hamilton as 13,000 militiamen from four states, along with public opinion, suppressed "the Whiskey Rebellion" and vindicated the authority of the national government. The seven-year-old Constitution worked!

The Reign of Terror

The term "the Reign of Terror," also simply "the Terror," refers to the 420-day period of the French Revolution, between the fall of the Girondists (May 31, 1793) and the overthrow of Robespierre (July 27, 1794), that was characterized by anarchy, violence, and bloodshed. Among the more than one million victims, 18,603 were guillotined (1,278 noblemen, 750 noblewomen, 1,467 wives of laborers and artisans, 350 nuns, 1,135 priests, 13,623 common people); 18,748 women, 22,000 children, and 900,000 men were killed in La Vendée; 32,000 people were killed at Nantes (including 2,000 children, 764 women, and 760 priests); and the number of victims at Lyons was 31,000. The total of over one million does not include the massacres at Versailles and at the Abbaye, the Cannes, and other prisons, and the many uncounted victims at Avignon, Toulon, and Marseille, and at Bedouin, where the entire population perished. An epitaph proposed for Robespierre said: "Passer-by, lament not for Robespierre; for, were he living, thou wouldst be dead."

Damned Old Devil

Thomas Paine (1737–1809), several times a failure in England as a cobbler, staymaker, corsetmaker, and (briefly) privateer, sailed in 1774 to the colonies with both a letter of introduction from Benjamin Franklin, the colonists' agent, whom he had met by happenstance, and an abiding hatred of the rigidly structured English society. Paine's bold advocacy of the colonies' separation from England hastened the Declaration of Independence, and he coined the designation "The United States of America." His outspoken views on religion earned him the description "Damned Old Devil." He declared, "My own mind is my own church. All national institutions of churches . . . appear to me no other than human inventions, set up to terrify and enslave mankind, and monopolize power and profit. "His book *Common Sense* (1776) was the first bestseller in America. In *The Age of Reason*(1794–96), "Citizen Tom Paine" told his readers not to look for cheap, tawdry miracles when they themselves and the world they lived in were the greatest of all miracles.

L'Autrichienne. Madame Veto. Madame Deficit. The Baker's Wife. The Widow Capet

Austrian-born Josèphe Jeanne Marie Antoinette (1755–1793), wife of Louis XVI, remained unpopular with the French, who referred to her as "L'Autrichienne," which on the surface simply means "the Austrian," but which to the French ear sounds like *L'autre chienne*, meaning "the other female dog." "Madame Veto" alludes to the queen's supposedly great influence on her husband in legislating (although their marriage was not consummated for seven years); "Madame Deficit" refers to her extravagant spending habits; and "the Baker's Wife" stems from her husband's giving bread to starving people who came to Versailles in 1789. She became "the Widow Capet" (a surname of the kings of France since 987), until she herself was guillotined for treason by the Revolutionary Council. (There is no truth to the story that, on being informed that the country people had no bread, she replied, "Let them eat cake"—a slander started by Jean Jacques Rousseau.)

The Matterhorn of the Americas

Rocks on the flanks of Canada's glacier-gnawed Mount Assiniboine, in Alberta—"the Matterhorn of the Americas"—have revealed marine fossils at least 225 million years old, leftovers from an inland sea. (The Matterhorn, first climbed in 1865, is a 15,000-foot-high Alpine mountain on the Swiss-Italian border, forming a distinctive peak.)

The Circe of the Revolution

Jeanne Roland de la Platière (1754–1793) was one of the leaders of the Girondists in the French Revolution, and the "inspiring soul" of the party. When she died on the guillotine, her last words, according to popular reports, were: "Oh Liberty! What crimes are committed in thy name!" (Her sobriquet refers to Circe, the enchantress of Greek mythology.)

King Cotton

Cotton became the principal product of the American South with Eli Whitney's invention in 1793 of the hand-operated cotton gin. Because it could clean 50 pounds of cotton a day, the machine became a factor in bringing on the Civil War: More hands than ever were needed to pick the enormous amounts that gins could process, and so even more labor—slave labor—was needed. (Whitney [1765–1825] also invented a mass-production technique for muskets.)

The National Razor. The Blade of Eternity

Paris's guillotine during the Reign of Terror (1793–94) was seen as "the National Razor" and "the Blade of Eternity"—an "ingenious and gentle way" of spilling human blood. "The grandeur and elegance of the spectacle" enthralled the masses. The official executioner for seven years was Charles Henri Sanson (1740–1795), who beheaded Louis XVI. His son and colleague, Henri, guillotined Marie Antoinette.

Chrononhotonthologos

John Burgoyne (1722–1792), the lieutenant general who commanded the British army that invaded New York in 1777, was nicknamed "Chrononhotonthologos" for his pretentious behavior, especially for a pompous address he delivered to Native American tribes. Chrononhotonthologos is a self-important character in a burlesque tragedy of the same name by Henry Carey (first performed in 1734). Burgoyne himself was the author of several plays—all, of course, pompous.

The September Massacre

On September 2, 3, 4, and 5, 1792, an indiscriminate slaughter of Royalist prisoners in the Abbaye and other French prisons took place. It was instigated by the Swiss-born revolutionist Jean Paul Marat (1743–1793) when he was inflamed by the news that France's enemy, Prussia, had captured Verdun. Estimates of the number of victims range from 1,200 to 8,000.

The Pale

Catherine II (1729–1796) in 1791 established a zone, "the Pale," in Russia and eastern Poland for settlement by Jews and beyond which Jews were not permitted to travel. (A pale is defined as a district or territory within set bounds, restricting locality.) Before Cromwell's victories, "the English Pale" was the country around Dublin held by the English conquerors of Ireland. To go "beyond the pale" is to go beyond the limit of what is permitted or acceptable.

The National Adding Machine.
The National Snapshot

Mandated by the Constitution (Article 1, Section 2), the national census began in 1790 for a wholly fiscal and political purpose: to provide a fluid basis for taxation and for the composition of the House of Representatives. There were about three million whites, 50,000 free blacks, and 600,000 slaves in 1790 (about 5,300,000 persons 10 years later); the medium age was 16; and nearly everyone lived on farms. Today, "the National Adding Machine" is an integral part of the American economy of about 250 million people. Everyone uses census data, for purposes ranging from learning where marriageable persons of the opposite gender reside to where orthodontists can find a lot of teenagers in high-income households within 10 miles of an ocean beach, to reapportionment of the US House of Representatives.

The problem is that the "census" is merely an extrapolation based on a count that misses a full third, or much more, of the population: Millions of people are not approached for a count, and tens of millions are unwilling to respond. For this reason, and because of the Census Bureau's general inefficiency, it is now being proposed that this costly federal agency be abolished and that private demographic firms using professional sampling and statistical techniques be hired. Their acknowledged extrapolations may prove more reliable than a specious count. "The National Snapshot," as the census has been called, is underexposed.

The Compromise of 1790

Meeting in New York, the nation's first capital city, nearly a year after ratification of the Constitution by the states, the first Congress of the United States reached a great compromise, "the Compromise of 1790." The federal government would assume the 13 states' Revolutionary War debts (a decision favored by northern states), and in turn the capital would be moved to Philadelphia for 10 years, then to a permanent location on the Potomac River (a decision favored by southern states).

The Great Smoke. Dream Parlors

It was said that a Chinese coolie's life was not worth living without "the Great Smoke" that brought dreams: opium. There were thousands of illegal "Dream Parlors" throughout Shanghai alone. "Smoke lords" justified their profiteering on human misery by claiming that it was inhuman to deny the wretched their only consolation in life.

The Wisest American. America's First World Citizen. The American Socrates. The Busybody

The youngest son of the 17 children of a Boston candlemaker was a one-man phenomenon, a polymath, a genius, protean—Benjamin Franklin (1706–1790), "the Wisest American," "America's First World Citizen." At the end of his long life, he helped to direct the compromise that brought the Constitution of the United States into being (1787). "Our Constitution," he wrote a year before his death, "is in actual operation; everything appears to promise that it will last; but in this world nothing is certain but death and taxes." The sobriquet "the American Socrates" was first used by the Scottish philosopher Sir James Mackintosh (1765–1822) because Franklin bore a likeness to his Greek prototype in independence of thought and in preferring the useful over the merely beautiful. His ceaseless curiosity also earned him the name "the Busybody." The American poet William Carlos Williams (1883–1963) wrote, not without affection, "He is our wise prophet of chicanery, the great buffoon, the face on the penny stamp." Sixty-two years before his death, Franklin wrote this epitaph for himself: "The body of Benjamin Franklin, printer (like the cover of an old book, its contents torn out, and stripped of its lettering and gilding), lies here, food for worms; but the work shall not be lost, for it will (as he believed) appear once more in a new and more elegant edition, revised and corrected and amended by its Author."

Foggy Bottom

US State Department offices were built in Washington, DC, on land originally called Foggy Bottom. A fogginess of official language emanating from State eventually prompted application of "Foggy Bottom" to the institution itself.

The 1780s

July 14

By July 14, 1789, a massive structure with eight great towers and a moat—the Bastille, which means fortress in French—had become a hated symbol of tyranny. Lower-class Parisians spontaneously seized arms from the Invalides building and stormed the Bastille for its stores of ammunition, then razed the structure: the French Revolution was on fire. "Bastille Day" acquired symbolic significance and became the national holiday of republican France.

The Highest Bench

The Supreme Court of the United States—"the Highest Bench"—makes sure that the supreme law of the land, the Constitution, isn't tampered with. It has been a nine-justice court since President Ulysses Grant's administration (1869–87). (Franklin D. Roosevelt, in 1937, tried to add six justices, to "pack the Court.") The Court is a vital third branch of the federal government; it can find unconstitutional and unenforceable any law or action not in agreement with the Constitution.

The Columbia Patriot

The poet and historian Mercy Otis Warren (1728–1814), of Massachusetts, called herself "the Columbia Patriot." She was the only woman to take part in the public debate in 1788 over approval of the proposed Constitution for the United States, writing with great spirit against its ratification. She feared it would "draw blood from every pore by taxes, impositions, and illegal restrictions" and that it would endanger liberty. She saw it as a "many-headed monster," framed by men who did not have authority to establish institutions and laws.

An Assembly of Demigods.
An Assembly of the Well-Bred,
the Well-Fed, the Well-Read,
the Well-Wed

Thomas Jefferson was the first to describe as "an Assembly of Demigods" the 55 delegates from 12 states (Rhode Island was not represented) who struggled in almost total secrecy for four months at the Federal Convention in Philadelphia (1787) to create a charter for the United States that would work. (Jefferson himself was 3,000 miles away at the time, serving as US minister to Paris.) The "demigods," "the well-bred, the well-fed, the well-read, the well-wed," as they've also been termed, included George Washington, James Madison, James Wilson, Gouverneur Morris, Alexander Hamilton, Benjamin Franklin, and Charles Cotesworth Pinckney.

The Father of the Constitution

James Madison (1751–1836), indefatigable despite a weak physique, was the driving force behind the composition of the Constitution at the super-secret Federal Convention in Philadelphia in 1787, and he made the most extensive notes of any of the 55 delegates from the 12 states. He urged the assembly to recognize that the national government would be more stable, more durable, if it rested on the solid foundation of the people themselves. He was labeled "the Father of the Constitution," but he always renounced the title, emphasizing that the charter replacing the Articles of Confederation (1781) was the collective work of all of the delegates. Madison urged that no notes should be made public until the last delegate had died; it turned out to be Madison himself. Mrs. Madison (Dolley) then sold his ledgers to the government.

Three Fifths of a Person

Rufus King (1755–1827), a Massachusetts delegate to the 1787 Federal Convention, in Philadelphia, declared as a "necessary sacrifice to the establishment of the Constitution" the decision to count every slave as only "three fifths of a person" in determining representation. Women and Native Americans were not counted as persons at all. In 1787, there were about three million whites and 50,000 free blacks in the United States: "We the People." There were 600,000 slaves—or 360,000 "whole people."

Publius

In 1787, Founding Fathers Alexander Hamilton (1755–1804), James Madison (1751–1836), and John Jay (1745–1829) took the collective pseudonym "Publius" and under the title *The Federalist* composed 85 newspaper essays in a comprehensive, reasoned, and candid defense of the just-drawn Constitution for the United States. The Constitution became the law of the land in June 1788, with the ninth state's ratification, nine months after the charter had been circulated for approval.

The Elastic Clause

Eighteen paragraphs in Article 1 of the Constitution of the United States grant urgently needed power to Congress. The first 17 are called enumerated powers (for example, to establish post offices and post roads, to declare war, to coin money). The last paragraph, the 18th, is known as "the Elastic Clause"; it refers to implied powers: "to make all laws which shall be necessary and proper for carrying into execution the foregoing powers, and all other powers vested by this Constitution in the government of the United States, or in any department or officer thereof." "The Elastic Clause" was a sweeping grant of power, little noticed when enacted, to enable Congress to pass legislation giving effect to the specified powers.

The Treason Clause

The only crime defined in the Constitution of the United States (1787) is treason. Article 3, Section 3, reads: "Treason against the United States shall consist only in levying war against them, or in adhering to their enemies, giving them aid and comfort. No person shall be convicted of treason unless on the testimony of two witnesses to the same overt act, or on confession in open court. The Congress shall have power to declare the punishment of treason, but no attainder of treason shall work corruption of blood, or forfeiture except during the life of the person attainted."

The Inadmissible Amendment

More than 10,000 amendments to the Constitution of the United States have been proposed, but only one can never be proposed. Article 5 of the Constitution states that "no State, without its consent, shall be deprived of its equal suffrage in the Senate." The clause was adopted to head off Connecticut delegate Roger Sherman's (1721–1793) concern that "three-fourths of the states might be brought to do things fatal to particular states, such as abolishing them altogether or depriving them of their equality in the Senate."

Shays's Rebellion

The most famous and important debtors' insurrection during the quandary of the new Confederation of the United States (1781) was led in part by Daniel Shays (c.1747–1825), a former captain in the Continental Army. In 1786–87, western Massachusetts farmers took up stave, pitchfork, and musket against foreclosures and jail sentences. Clashes with militia resulted in many deaths. The legislature pardoned almost all of the rebels; Shays fled to Vermont. One consequence of rural insurrections was the calling of the Federal Convention (1787), which led to a strong national government capable of dealing with such uprisings. "Shays's Rebellion" also brought about specific reforms in taxation and judicial procedure.

Rogue Islanders

Only one of the 13 states—Rhode Island and Providence Plantations—was not represented in Philadelphia at the Federal Convention (1787) called "for the sole and express purpose of revising the Articles of Confederation and reporting to Congress and the several legislatures such alterations and

provisions therein." The littlest state's rural "leaden-headed legislators"—
"Rogue Islanders"—wanted no interference with their popular cheap-
money schemes, which other states viewed as the scourge of sound credit.
Until Rhode Island grudgingly ratified the Constitution, by two votes in
1790, it was treated like a foreign nation and even faced the threat of im-
port duties on its goods.

The Affair of the Diamond Necklace

The Paris jewelers Bohmer and Bassenger were tricked into believing that
Queen Marie Antoinette (1755–1793) wished to buy the necklace of 500
diamonds they had created for Madame Jeanne Du Barry (1743–1793). A
fraudulent pair—a high-class courtesan and her young accomplice and
lover—gained the necklace and sold individual diamonds. The 1785 affair
is one of French history's most celebrated scandals, gravely discrediting
and weakening the monarchy.

The End of the Beginning

In 1783, two years after British General Charles Cornwallis (1738–1805)
surrendered his forces at Yorktown, Virginia , and the world turned upside
down, the American War of Independence finally ended with the signing
of the Treaty of Paris and Britain's recognition that its 13 former colonies—
the United States—were free, sovereign, and independent. The British finally evacuated the principal city in the former colonies, New York. Several hours later, General George Washington made a triumphant ride
through the nation's first capital.

The National Bird

The Great Seal of the United States (1782) is illustrated with the American
eagle— "the National Bird"—but six years earlier Benjamin Franklin had
proposed that the seal show the Pharaoh engulfed by the waters of the Red
Sea while pursuing the children of Israel. The design was supported by
John Adams and Thomas Jefferson, but it was rejected by the Continental
Congress. When the eagle was selected, Franklin wrote that it is a "bird of
bad moral character," living by "sharping and robbing." He then proposed
that the turkey be the symbol.

Tar Heels

North Carolinians, "Tar Heels," have never been known as sticks-in-the-
mud. During the American Revolution, they imaginatively impeded the
retreat of British troops in the fateful Carolina campaign of 1781 by pouring tar into a stream: The Redcoats emerged with the dark, oily substance
sticking to their boots and couldn't get moving. On the heels of the Caro-

lina campaign came the Yorktown confrontation. The American triumph there sealed final victory in the war.

The 1770s

The Line Drawers

Devised originally to settle a boundary dispute between the Calvert-family proprietors of Maryland and the Penn-family proprietors of Pennsylvania, the Mason-Dixon line (39°, 43', 26.3" north latitude) became in 1779 the symbolic border between north and south, politically and socially, dividing the free states from the slave states. (Mason and Dixon were the English surveyors-astronomers Charles Mason [1730–1787] and Jeremiah Dixon, who died in 1777.)

The Great Commoner.
The British Cicero

The British statesman William Pitt (1708–1778) was known for his insistence on constitutional rights. During the American Revolution, he urged conciliation: "If I were an American, as I am an Englishman, while a foreign troop was landed in my country, I never would lay down my arms,— never— —never never. You cannot conquer America." He was also known as one of "the Wondrous Three," the other two being Edmund Burke and Charles James Fox. His son, William Pitt the Younger (1759–1806), became prime minister at the age of 24.

The Betsy Ross Myth

It is merely a myth that Betsy Ross (1752–1836) was involved in any way in designing the American flag. It was designed in 1777 by a lawyer, the first American-born composer, and a signatory to the Declaration of Independence—Francis Hopkinson (1737–1791). The Continental Congress's resolution of 1777 creating Old Glory called for 13 red and white stripes— for the 13 colonies—but whether they should run horizontally or vertically, or even both ways, was not indicated. (The name "Old Glory" was first used in 1831.)

The First Salute

Four and a half months after the Declaration of Independence had been proclaimed, in 1776, the first official salute to the United States of America occurred. A ship flying the red-and-white striped flag of the Continental

Congress fired a salute when it entered the foreign port of St. Eustatius in the West Indies, and the island's fort, adhering to custom, made a ritual response. This act of recognition acknowledged that the vessel and its banner represented a legitimate nation.

John Hancock

John Hancock (1737–1793), twice president of the Continental Congress, was the first revolutionist to sign the Declaration of Independence (on August 2, 1776). He did it with such a bold flourish (and with the remark "There, I guess King George can read that!") that a signature has come to be called a "John Hancock," especially one signed with authority.

The Philosopher

Vermont's Ethan Allen (1738–1789), known to his troops, the Green Mountain Boys, as "the Philosopher," stunned the British at Fort Ticonderoga (1775) on Lake Champlain during the Revolutionary War, then informed the Continental Congress that he had been fighting solely for the independence of Vermont: It was to be an independent nation, not just another state in the Union. When Allen was subsequently captured during a raid on Montreal, he schemed with the British to make Vermont a British province or to help Vermont secure independence. (Vermont joined the Union as the 14th state, in 1791.)

The Coat Roll

In the winter campaign against the Redcoats in 1775, when the American Continental Army was freezing to death, people throughout the colonies responded with 13,000 winter coats to an appeal by the Continental Congress. The names of the makers and givers of coats were listed in communities in a "coat roll."

The Shot Heard 'round the World

Five days after the Battle of Lexington (1775) had ignited the American Revolution—five days after "the Shot Heard 'round the World"—it was learned in the colonies that Parliament had voted to allow the colonies to tax themselves and to provide for their own civil administration and defense. It was too late.

The Protestant Pope

The derogatory name "the Protestant Pope" was given to Pope Clement XIV (1705–1774) because of a 1773 bull in which he ordered the supression of the Society of Jesus (the Jesuits) under pressure from nearly all Roman Catholic rulers of Europe. His act put the church wholly into the hands of the princes' secular power, giving great offense to the more devout among the Roman Catholics, who regarded the act as a concession to Protestantism. Clement was the founder of the Clementine Museum at the Vatican.

Old Bailey

The Central Criminal Court in London, erected in 1773, is popularly called "Old Bailey" because it is located at a street with the name Bailey. The way derives its name from the *ballium*, or open space, that existed in front of the old city wall, along which the street extended from Lud Gate to New Gate. (The famous Newgate Prison adjoins Old Bailey.)

Corporal John. The Silly Duke

John Churchill, first duke of Marlborough (1650–1722), remained "Corporal John" to his English troops because he had once held the rank of corporal. The name "the Silly Duke" is an allusion to his habit of answering all unwelcome questions with the words "Oh, silly! silly!" (Napoleon and Hitler also were referred to by their rank of corporal for the rest of their lives—"le Petit Caporal" and "der Gefreite," respectively.)

The Boston Massacre

In 1770, eight armed British soldiers, pelted by snowballs and taunted by a boisterous mob of Bostonians, lost their cool and fired their muskets. Three colonists were slain, eight were wounded. The royal government arrested the Redcoats and promised a fair trial. They were defended by Founding Father John Adams (1735–1826), who did not want a mob thirsty for vengeance satisfied—justice must be supreme over political expediency. Six soldiers were acquitted, three were branded on their thumbs and released.

Alexander the Corrector

Alexander Cruden (1700–1770) was an English bookseller and the compiler of the *Complete Concordance to the Holy Scriptures*. He imagined himself divinely commissioned as a corrector of morals. Besides attacking targets such as the notoriously dissolute John Wilkes (who authored an obscene parody of Pope's *Essay on Man*), Cruden carried a moistened sponge wherever he went, to wipe out any scrawls on walls and buildings that he found objectionable. He was several times confined to a lunatic asylum.

The 1760s

The River in the Ocean

The protean Benjamin Franklin was the first to chart systematically, in 1769, an ocean current—"the River in the Ocean"—the Gulf Stream in the Atlantic. He had noted that eastbound ships crossed the Atlantic in two weeks less time than westbound ships.

The Bloody Butcher.
The Butcher of Culloden

William Augustus, Duke of Cumberland (1721–1765), was called the names "the Bloody Butcher" and "the Butcher of Culloden," for the shocking and needless cruelties he inflicted on the inhabitants of Scotland after the battle of Culloden (1746). On his return to England, he was hailed as a savior, and a huge annual pension was settled on him and his heirs.

Sons of Liberty

In the British House of Commons, Major Isaac Barre (1726–1802) enthusiastically championed the American colonists, calling them "those sons of liberty," in 1765, and declaring roundly that Britain owed more to America than America did to Britain. American merchants, lawyers, journalists, and others who protested Parliament's Stamp Act—a tax on printed matter in the American colonies—became "Sons of Liberty," arguing that taxation without representation was tyranny. The Sons of Liberty were a powerful revolutionary force that included Paul Revere, Samuel Adams, and James Otis, and the Boston Tea Party (1773) was engineered by Beantown Sons.

The Gotha

Periodically published since 1763 (first in Gotha, Germany), "the Gotha" is an authoritative reference work, a Who's Who of the royal houses and the nobility of numerous countries—the *Gothaischer Hofkalender*, or the *Gotha Almanac*, or "the Gotha" in popular parlance.

The 1750s

Old Grog

The English Admiral Edward Vernon (1684–1757) was called "Old Grog" because of his habit of wearing a grogram coat (a kind of rough, stiffened material), not because he drank "grog." Grog, however, *is* derived from this very same nickname: Vernon ordered all sailors' rum to be diluted with water. (George Washington's older half-brother, Lawrence, named his Virginia estate Mount Vernon, for Admiral Vernon, under whom he had served.)

The Black Hole of Calcutta

In the mid-1750s, French and British interests supported local princes' rival claims for power in Calcutta, which had been founded about 1690 by the British East India Company. In 1756, the Indian governor, or nawab, of Benjal, Sirajuddaula, captured Calcutta, took 146 British prisoners, and had them stuffed into a small, suffocating prison. The next morning, only 23 were still alive. The reckless, rapacious British administrator, Robert Clive (1725–1774), governor of Fort St. David, near Madra, avenged the deaths of his countrymen and retook Calcutta.

The Great Cham of Literature. The Great Moralist. The Great Seer

"Dr." Samuel Johnson (1709–1784) is the author of the *Dictionary of the English Language*, which was published in 1755 and which has been called the single most extraordinary creation in English literature—Shakespeare notwithstanding. In the preface he wrote: "I am not so lost in lexicography as to forget that words are the daughters of earth, and that things are the sons of heaven." What "the Great Cham of Literature" ("Cham" is an older form of "Khan") wrote about John Dryden could be said about Johnson himself: "He delighted to tread upon the brink of meaning." (*See also* 1795: Bozzy.)

Albany Plan

Dissatisfied with white–Indian relations, in 1754, the British brought together in Albany, New York, representatives of several of their American colonies and of the Six Nations of the Iroquois Confederation. Pennsylvania delegate Benjamin Franklin was once again full of ideas. His "Albany Plan" proposed the creation of "one general government." It would "make peace or declare war with Indian Nations," regulate Indian trading, and otherwise control matters of common interest. The meeting and the proposal came to naught.

The Calendar Riots

When the Gregorian calendar was adopted in England, on September 3, 1752 (replacing the Julian calendar whose year of 365 days 6 hours was too long), September 3 became, just like that, September 14. People insisted they had been deprived of 11 days, and there was widespread rioting. The new calendar had been introduced by Pope Gregory XIII in 1583, but England, like other non-Catholic countries, was slow (169 years slow) in adopting it.

The Encyclopedists

Denis Diderot (1713–1784), Voltaire (1694–1778), Jean Jacques Rousseau (1712–1778), Montesquieu (1689–1755), and other French philosophers—"the Encyclopedists"—wrote the *Encyclopédie ou dictionnaire raisonné des sciences, des arts et des métiers,* whose 28 volumes were published between 1751 and 1772. This landmark of Western culture championed the skepticism and rationalism of the Enlightenment and paved the intellectual road to the French Revolution. The Encyclopedists attacked legal, judicial, and religious abuses and stressed scientific determinism. (Among the few items on which they blundered was the perpetuation of the old literary theme of the *droit du seigneur* or *ius primae noctis*—the "virginal tribute" or "right of the first night"—the traditional but mistaken belief that feudal lords in certain countries had "the right of the lord" to "deflower" the bride of a serf during the first night after marriage.)

Bushido

Japan's medieval Samurai class lived and died by the code that became known in the 18th century as Bushido: To die in war is the greatest honor; to be taken prisoner is the ultimate disgrace; to commit suicide under certain circumstances is a glorious act of true valor.

The Anandrynes

"The Anandrynes" were a lesbian secret society in Paris in the 18th century, with chapters in London and other European cities. The society, founded by a Madame de Fleury, included members in the highest aristocratic circles. ("Anandrynes" comes from the Greek words *anandre,* "sexless," and *gynandre,* "female-male.")

1749–1700

The War of Jenkins's Ear

The 1739–41 war in the West Indies between England and Spain got its name from an incident in 1731: English shipmaster Robert Jenkins displayed before the House of Commons in London, in 1738, an ear pickled in brine, which he identified as his own, charging that a Spanish patrol had cut it off while he was sailing in the West Indies. Appalled, the British declared war on Spain—"the War of Jenkins's Ear," which expanded into the larger King George's War (1740–48), also known as the War of Austrian Succession.

The Paper King

John Law (1671–1729), the originator of the infamous Mississippi Scheme, or Mississippi Bubble, became known as "the Paper King." The Scottish financier pretended belief in the efficacy of a paper currency that is issued greatly in excess of the specie available to cover it. As a young man, he had been condemned to death in London for killing "Beau" (Edward) Wilson in a duel but escaped to continental Europe, where he led the life of a gambler and financial adventurer, eventually becoming involved in the politics of the New World.

La Belle Indienne

Françoise d'Aubigné, Madame (Marquise) de Maintenon (1635–1719), mistress and second wife of King Louis XV of France, was called "la Belle Indienne" (the beautiful Indian). Although she was a native of France, she spent much of her early life in the West Indies, on the island of Martinique.

Clio

The English essayist, poet, and statesman Joseph Addison (1672–1719) was nicknamed "Clio" in allusion to the muse of history. He was very quotable: "Books are the legacies that a great genius leaves to mankind, which are delivered down from generation to generation, as presents to the posterity of those who are yet unborn." "A man should always consider how much he has more than he wants, and how much more unhappy he might be than he really is." "Mirth is like a flash of lightning, that breaks through a gloom of clouds, and glitters for a moment; cheerfulness keeps up a kind of daylight in the mind."

The Big Easy. The Party Town. The Crescent City

New Orleans (founded in 1718)—relaxed, laid back—has been called "the Big Easy" and "the Party Town" and "the Crescent City" and . . .

The Madman of the North. The Alexander of the North. The Brilliant Madman

Charles XII of Sweden (1682–1718), king at age 15, dead at 36, had an extremely active life. Besides his impetuous love of war, he was so eccentric in his personal conduct that Voltaire, his biographer, regarded him as an old Norse Sea-King, born 10 centuries after his time. He may have been the most peculiar personage of the 18th century. At his coronation, he omitted the usual oath and crowned himself. He was killed invading Norway, and Sweden presently lost its rank as a great power.

Old Eli

A collegiate school chartered in Connecticut in 1701 moved to a permanent location in New Haven in 1716 and changed its name to Yale College, "Old Eli," in honor of Elihu Yale, a major contributor. In 1887, the expanding college was renamed Yale University.

Le Roi Soleil. The Sun King. Louis the Great. Le Grand Monarque. Dieu-Donné

Louis XIV (1638–1715) became king of France at age five. He was the most powerful European sovereign all through his 72-year reign, which coincided with the greatest flowering of French civilization and political importance. "Louis was the center of all; mythological or classical shows displayed his fine figure and handsome face, as a hero or a god; he delighted to appear as an Apollo, God of the Sun, of cultures, of the arts, dispensing vivifying smiles and warmth of life" (Kitchin, *History of France*). His lavish patronage of art, literature, and women was balanced by wars, conquests, and extravagances that left France near bankruptcy. As a child he was known as "Dieu-Donné" (God-given) because his mother (Anne of Austria, daughter of Phillip III of Spain) had been barren for 23 years of her marriage. In 1709, when Louis heard of the defeat of his army at Malplaquet by the allied English, Dutch, and Austrian forces (with a loss of about 14,000 French and 20,000 enemy soldiers—one of Louis's rare failures), he was reported to have exclaimed, "Has God forgotten all I have done for him?"

The Sin-On Bible

In an edition of the Bible that was first printed in Ireland in 1716, John 5:14 reads "Sin on more" instead of "Sin no more." The mistake went undiscovered until the printings of "the Sin-On Bible" had reached 8,000 copies, a considerable number at that time.

Brandy Nan

Anne (1665–1714), queen of Great Britain and Ireland (1702–14) and wife of Prince George of Denmark, was the daughter of James II of England and Anne Hyde. Under her reign the War of the Spanish Succession and the union of England and Ireland took place, but most of her "rule" was under the influence of the Duke and Duchess of Marlborough and, later, of Mrs. Abigail Masham. She consoled herself with drinking strong spirits, which earned her the name "Brandy Nan." Nevertheless, her given name, Anne, became associated with a graceful 18th-century style of interior decoration.

The Athens of America. Beantown. Trimountain

Boston became "the Athens of America" when The Old Corner Book Store was built there in 1712. It later attracted such literary lights as Henry Wadsworth Longfellow, Ralph Waldo Emerson, Henry David Thoreau, Oliver Wendell Holmes, and Harriet Beecher Stowe. The city is "Beantown" in casual reference. Its original name, when founded in 1630, was "Trimountain." (The eminent architect Frank Lloyd Wright, 1869–1959, said about Boston: "Clear out eight hundred thousand people and preserve it as a museum piece.")

The Man in the Iron Mask

For more than four decades, an unnamed prisoner known as "the Man in the Iron Mask" was held in isolation by the French King Louis XIV. He died in the Bastille in 1703, his identity never disclosed. Among historians' many theories is that the man was Count Girolamo Mattioli, minister to the Duke of Mantua, who had signed a treaty to give up to Louis the fortress of Casale—the key gateway to Italy—but then reneged; Mattioli could have been lured to French soil, then captured and imprisoned. But neither this nor other speculations would explain why it was so important that not even the jailers knew the man's identity, so important that the man himself feared to be identified, cooperating with the king in wearing, decade after decade, the "iron mask"—which was made of velvet.

The Window on the West

The reformer Czar Peter the Great (1672–1725), who had traveled in western Europe and wanted to develop imperial Russia, founded in 1703 a new city, St. Petersburg, and made it his capital instead of Moscow. (Contruction at the swampy area in northwest Russia, which had been conquered from Sweden, proceeded at tremendous human and material cost.) St. Petersburg became known as "the Window on the West": It provided a Russian outlet to the sea and a port for trade through the Baltic. In 1914 its name was changed to Petrograd; in 1924 it became Leningrad.

The French Devil

The French naval hero Jean Bart (1651–1702) was a terror to England in the wars between Louis XIV and William III, and a privateer at the outbreak of the Dutch War (1672). He was indeed "the French Devil."

The Printers' Bible

In a 1702 edition of the Bible, the word "princes" was mistakenly set as "printers," so that David complains, in Psalms 119:161, that "printers have persecuted me without a cause." Among collectors it is still known as "the Printers' Bible."

The War Started by Water

The War of the Spanish Succession (1701–14) was given the name "the War Started by Water" because it is said to have been triggered by a glass of water that one Mrs. Mashaur of England accidentally spilled on the French Marquis de Torey. According to the report, the nobleman's indignation over this incident escalated, eventually stirring up enmity between the courts of England and France. The war was the last of the general European wars caused by the efforts of King Louis XIV to extend French power.

1699-1650

Father Goose

The rhymes of Mother Goose originated with Mother Goose Tales, which in a roundabout way were derived from the *Contes de ma mère l'oye* by Charles Perrault (1628–1703)—"Father Goose"—which Perrault published in 1697 under the name of his 10-year-old son (gosling?), Perrault d'Armancourt. They seem to have first been told a century earlier, in an Italian collection. In this century, Walt Disney's (1901–1966) animated cartoons for children earned him the sobriquet "Father Goose."

The Wizard

King John III of Poland (John Sobieski, 1624–1696, crowned 1674) was dubbed "the Wizard" by the much larger Turkish army after his troops' extraordinary victories. John checked the Turks' siege of Vienna, and in 1684 he made a Holy League with the Pope, the Holy Roman Emperor, and Venice.

The Old Lady of Threadneedle Street

The Bank of England, established 1694, has been referred to as "the Old Lady of Threadneedle Street" because of its location. Threadneedle Street was originally Thridenal Street, meaning the third street from Cheapside (*thriddle* meaning "third" in Anglo-Saxon).

The Upholsterer of Notre Dame

The name "the Upholsterer of Notre Dame" was given to François Henri de Montmorency-Bouteville, Duke of Luxembourg (1628–1695), because of the large number of flags that he had captured from the Prince of Waldeck in the battle of Fleurus (1690) and which he then sent to Paris to decorate the cathedral of Notre Dame in celebration of the victory.

The Universal Genius

Sir William Petty (1623–1687) was a physician and a founder of the English Royal Society, but he is best known for being the foremost political economist of his time. "The Universal Genius" disapproved of the ban on bullion export, he favored an Irish–British union—he was the first to make a detailed map of Ireland—and he contended that labor determines price.

The Son of the Last Man

The Parliamentary party referred to Charles I (born 1600) as "the Last Man," namely, the last who should ever sit on an English throne—he was beheaded in 1649. When his son Charles II (1630–1685), after much turmoil, nevertheless succeeded as king in 1651, he became, naturally, "the Son of the Last Man." He is popularly remembered for his pleasure-loving life and for his favorite mistress, the actress Nell Gwynn (1650–1687). (*See also* 1649: The Last Man.)

The Mad Cavalier

Prince Rupert of Bavaria (1619–1682), nephew of Charles I of England, represented an enigma as commander of Charles's forces during a part of the (English) Civil War: On the one hand, he displayed efficiency and courage in battle; on the other hand, his disregard of authority and his impatience resulted in several defeats, and he was eventually removed as commander—he was considered too "mad" to lead the Royalist army: "the Mad Cavalier."

Blue-Books. Yellow-Books. Red-Books. White-Books. Green-Books

"Blue-Books" was the popular name given to reports and proceedings printed and bound in blue by the British Parliament, beginning in 1681. As of 1836, these printings were sold to the public, at a low price. (The corresponding official publications of other governments also became known by the color of their covers: the "Yellow-Books" of France, the "White-Books" of Germany, the "Red-Books" of Spain, the "Green-Books" of Italy, the "White-Books" of Portugal.) In the United States, the "Blue-Book" came to mean a volume that listed all persons holding public office, both civilian and military, with their dates and places of birth, their salaries, and the like (corresponding to the "Red-Books" of Great Britain and Canada—and of the Chinese Empire, with its 14,000 officials).

Bacon's Rebellion

Virginia frontier farmer Nathaniel Bacon (1647–1676), thwarted by Governor William Berkeley in his plan to drive friendly Indians off wanted lands, clashed with the administrator's army in 1676 and captured and burned Jamestown. Bacon died of dysentery, the revolt was crushed, 23 rebels were executed in defiance of a royal pardon, and a discredited Berkeley (1606–1677) was removed from office by King Charles II.

The Cabal Ministry

The unprincipled and intrigue-plagued ministry that existed under Charles II in England from 1667 to 1674 was called "the Cabal Ministry" because the initials of the names of its main five members formed the word "cabal": Clifford, Ashley, Buckingham, Arlington, and Lauderdale. Originally, the word meant simply a council or committee, but since those days it has assumed the sinister sense of a secret, plotting, dangerous political group.

Cleopatra's Nose

"Cleopatra's nose, had it been shorter, the whole face of the world would have been changed," wrote the French mathematician and philosopher Blaise Pascal (1623–1662) in his *Pensées*, published posthumously in 1670. In our logical approach to things, we often forget seemingly insignificant factors that make all the difference—Cleopatra's romantic appeal to Julius Caesar, for example. What factor or event would have made the Confederates win the American Civil War, or Hitler win World War II? Equivalents of the shape of Cleopatra's nose!

The Shakespeare of Divines

Jeremy Taylor (1613–1667), bishop of Down in England, was famous for his rich, clear, imaginative style and his fervid eloquence. His principal works include *The Golden Grove*, a devotional manual (1655), *The Liberty of Prophesying*, a work on religious tolerance (1647), and *Ductor Dubitantium, or The Rule of Conscience* (1600). Among the intellectuals who sang "the Shakespeare of Divines"'s praise was the Transcendentalist Ralph Waldo Emerson.

Annus Mirabilis

"Annus Mirabilis," Latin for "the wonderful year," is 1666—the year of the Great Fire of London (the year after the Great Plague) and of English victories over the Dutch. The Great Fire (September 2–7) took only eight lives but destroyed 13,200 houses, 88 churches, 4 city gates, 4 stone bridges, the Guildhall, the Royal Exchange, and Sion College—396 acres of devastation. (In the Great Plague of London a year earlier, nearly 100,000 people had perished: one-fifth of the population.) John Dryden commemorated 1666 in the poem "Annus Mirabilis."

The Hugh Williams Coincidence

On December 5, 1664, a series of coincidental events began at the Menai Strait, off North Wales, when a ship sank and the only survivor, out of 81 passengers, was a Hugh Williams. On the same date in 1785, a ship with

60 passengers sank at Menai, and again the only survivor was a Hugh Williams. On the same date in 1860, another ship sank at Menai, with 25 aboard; the only survivor was, of course, a man named Hugh Williams. (Lesson: Do not go by ship through Menai Strait on a December 5 unless your name is Hugh Williams.)

The Indian Bible.
The Apostle of the Indians

A Bible in the Algonquin language, by John Eliot (1604–1690), was the first Bible printed in the New World, in 1663, and for nearly a century it remained the only Bible issued in the colonies. Eliot, "the Apostle of the Indians," believed that the Native Americans were the descendants of "the long-lost Ten Tribes of Israel."

Blue-Skins

After the Restoration, in 1660, of the English monarchy, under Charles II (1630–1685), the Presbyterians were referred to as "Blue-Skins" because of their serious and grave demeanor. Generally, anything of the dreary days of the Commonwealth, the period that preceded the Restoration, was ridiculed as being "blue."

Queen Dick. King Dick.
Tumbledown Dick

Richard Cromwell (1626–1712), son of Oliver Cromwell, succeeded his father as England's Lord Protector in 1658 but had to resign the following year. His brief rule was characterized by timidity and incapacity—hence "Queen Dick," as well as the also derisive term "King Dick." As he was a tottering wall at best, he was also called "Tumbledown Dick," an expression that has come to mean anything that will not stand firmly.

Pilgrims

The Pilgrims landed on Cape Cod in the New World in 1620, but they weren't known as "Pilgrims" until Plymouth governor William Bradford (c.1590–1657) wrote in his *History of Plimmoth Plantation*, "They knew they were pilgrims."

The French Bedlam

An institution for aged and insane women, the Salpêtrière—"the French Bedlam"—was founded in Paris by Louis XIV in 1656. At one time, it contained nearly 10,000 people, and the treatment was proverbially brutal. In the 1890s, it became the center for Jean Martin Charcot's school of psychopathology, which was based on the use of hypnosis. (The name stems from the fact that the ground had once been occupied by a saltpeter factory.)

Ussher's Notation

Dr. James Ussher (1581–1656), archbishop of Armagh, in Ireland, calculated in 1654 that the universe had been created in the year 4004 BC. Among the many odd uses that have been made of this "fact" was the Freemasons' dating their official documents from this *Annus Lucis*, this "year of light."(Too bad he forgot to note the month, the day, the hour.)

The Father of Angling

The English writer Izaak Walton (1593–1683) remains famous as the author of *The Compleat Angler, or the Contemplative Man's Recreation* of 1653, dialogs on the joys of fishing, with many quotations and anecdotes and other delightful digressions. He is also known as biographer of the English poets John Donne, George Herbert, and Richard Hooker. "The Father of Angling" wrote in *The Compleat Angler*: "I have laid aside business, and gone a-fishing. . . . Doubt not but angling will prove to be so pleasant that it will prove to be . . . a reward to itself." "Thus use your frog . . . Put your hook through his mouth, and out at his gills; . . . and then with a fine needle and silk sew the upper part of his legs, with only one stitch, to the arming-wire of your hook; or tie the frog's leg, above the upper joint, to the armed-wire; and in so doing use him as though you loved him."

The Protector. King Oliver. The Almighty Nose. The Sagest of Usurpers. Old Noll

The English revolutionary leader Oliver Cromwell (1599–1658) was proclaimed Lord Protector of the Realm in 1653, replacing monarchy with dictatorial rule. The names he was given were not all laudatory. "King Oliver" was used in derision, as were "Old Noll" and "the Almighty Nose" (the latter in the journal *Mercurius Pragmaticus* by Marchamont Needham), while "the Sagest of Usurpers" is fulsome praise (resumed by Lord Byron in his *Childe Harold*). After the Restoration of the monarchy, Cromwell's remains were dug up, cut in pieces, and displayed in public. But Thomas Carlyle wrote: "Nay, Old Noll, whose bones were dug up and hung in chains here at home, had not he, too, got to be a very respectable grim bronze figure, of whom England seems proud rather than otherwise?"

1649–1600

The White King. Man of Blood.
The Royal Martyr. The Last Man

Charles I of England (born 1600, crowned 1625, beheaded 1649) wore a
white state robe instead of the traditional purple. The Puritans called him
"Man of Blood" because of the war he waged against Parliament. He became "the Royal Martyr" when he was executed under the charge of treason (the judges condemning him became known as the "regicides"). The
Parliamentary party called him "the Last Man," that is, the last man who
should ever sit on an English throne. (*See also* 1685: The Son of the Last
Man.)

The Exalted of the Palace

It was to his favorite wife, Mumtaz Mahal, "the Exalted of the Palace,"
who had died in childbirth in 1629, that the stricken Shah Jahan built
(1630–48) the memorial monument to love that is said to be one of the
world's most beautiful buildings. The Taj Mahal, in Agra, India, speaks a
language of its own to the soul when seen by moonlight.

The Devil's Bible

A Bible manuscript, inscribed on the skins of 300 donkeys, was brought to
Stockholm at the end of the Thirty Years' War (1648). Legend has it that a
monk who was condemned to death would be spared if he could copy the
entire Bible on asses' skins in a single night, which he accomplished in a
pact with the devil.

The Seven Days' King

An Italian fisherman named Tommaso Aniello (1622–1647) led a successful insurrection against the viceroy of Naples in 1647, forcing him to abol-
ish a tax on provisions. Aniello "ruled" the city for seven days—"the
Seven Days' King." But his friends and supporters became alienated by his
despotic acts; they betrayed him and permitted his assassination by the
viceroy's adherents. His body was flung into a ditch, but on the following
day it was interred with great pomp and ceremony. Daniel Auber's opera
La Muette de Portici (1828), which treats the subject, appealed to the revolutionary sentiments of the time and was instrumental in triggering the
Brussels uprising of 1830, which drove the Dutch out of Belgium. ("Tommaso Aniello" is often corrupted to "Masaniello," as in Auber's opera.)

The Witchfinder-General

The cruel fanatic Matthew Hopkins (1600–1647), who traveled through England in search of witches, sent many women to the stake, some 60 in 1644 alone. Eventually accused of witchcraft himself, "the Witchfinder-General" was declared to be a "wizard" and put to death. Witchfinders were cruel fiends in 17th-century England. They showed up when anyone was thought to be a witch and forced the victim to confess by means of "examination" and torture.

The Whore of Babylon

The epithet "the Whore of Babylon" for the Roman Catholic Church was used by early Puritans and some of their descendants. In the New Testament (Revelations 17–19), Babylon is the city of the Antichrist.

Blue Laws

When Theophilus Eaton (1590–1658) became the first governor of the colony of New Haven, in 1639, he and the clergyman John Davenport (1597–1670) implemented a set of Puritan rules that became known, derisively, as "Blue Laws," for the color of the paper on which they were printed or for the epithet "blue," which had been applied to the Puritans in England after the Restoration. This strict legal code imposed the death penalty for offenses such as (a) worshipping any God but the God of the Bible, (b) speaking disrespectfully of sacred things, and (c) witchcraft, adultery, theft, perjury, and disobedience to one's parents. Lesser penalties than death were imposed for offenses such as wearing fancy clothes or baking the wrong kind of cakes.

Green Hell

Some of Brazil's junglelike forests, *silvas*, are still unexplored—the boa, the jaguar, and piranhas have given the region the reputation of being a "Green Hell."

The Father of Spanish Drama. A Prodigy of Nature

Felix Lope de Vega (1562–1635) has been Spain's most prolific playwright. In Cervantes's words, he was "a Prodigy of Nature." Lope wrote at least 1,800 plays and many pieces that can be accompanied by song. His historical plays based on national events are the most important and most representative of his works. The phrase *Es de Lope* became a synonym for perfection.

The Wicked Bible.
The Adulterous Bible

In a 1632 Bible the word "not" was omitted in Exodus 20:14, so that the seventh commandment reads, "Thou shalt commit adultery." Dr. James Ussher, the Irish archbishop who is still remembered for "figuring out" that the universe was created in the year 4004 BC, was so outraged by this error that a fine of £2,000 or £3,000 was imposed on Robert Barker and Martin Lucas, the "Wicked Bible"'s London printers.

The Golden Door. New Amsterdam.
Vanderheyden's Ferry.
New Orange. The Big Apple

New York City was "the Golden Door" to freedom and opportunity through which passed millions of immigrants, mainly around the turn of the century. (Emma Lazarus's sonnet on the bronze plaque on the pedestal of the Statue of Liberty, of 1884, reads: "Send these, the homeless, tempest-tossed, to me: / I lift my lamp beside the golden door.") New York has been called many names, ever since Peter Minuit or Minnewit (1580–1638) bought what is now Manhattan, for $24, in 1626. They include "New Amsterdam" (its original name after the purchase), "Vanderheyden's Ferry" (another early name), "New York" (named by the British), "New Orange" (named by the Dutch when they took it back for a while), "New York" (renamed when the British got it back), and "the Big Apple," its most popular name today. (*See also* 1807: Gotham.)

The English Solomon. The Solomon
of England. The British Solomon.
The Wisest Fool in Christendom

James I of England (1566–1625, crowned 1603) was well-read and the author of several scholarly books. "The English Solomon" wrote a treatise with the title *Counterblast to Tobacco*, of which the last paragraph follows: "It is a custom loathsome to the eye, hateful to the nose, harmful to the brain, dangerous to the lungs, and in the black . . . fume thereof, nearest resembling the horrible Stygian pit that is bottomless" (that is, hell). (*See also* 1485: The English Solomon.)

Democritus Junior

The English writer and clergyman Robert Burton (1577–1640) is best remembered as the author of a work that is the embodiment of the late-Renaissance spirit in England and that has had a lasting influence on much of later English writing: *The Anatomy of Melancholy* (1621). Some biographers see significance in the fact that he died on the day that he had astrologically predicted (January 25, 1640), but such timing could easily stem from the effect of mounting apprehension as the date came nearer—a self-fulfilling prophecy. ("Democritus Junior" alludes to the Greek philosopher Democritus, c.400 BC.)

Defenestration

Europe's bewildering Thirty Years' War (1618–48), fought mainly in German states, was prompted when Protestant members of the Bohemian Diet, or national council, "defenestrated" two Roman Catholic royal officers, that is, threw them out of the window of Hradshin Castle in Prague (without, however, hurting them). The war was fought in fits and starts amid shifting alliances and local peace treaties. The Holy Roman Empire was in disarray, German states could not get their act together, and other European powers wanted their own window on the world.

Napier's Bones

The first new calculating device since the ancient abacus was a useful invention by the Scottish mathematician Sir John Napier (1550–1617) that promptly became known as "Napier's Bones." It consisted of a set of flat rods (the "bones") on which digits and their multiples were arranged in a manner that facilitated multiplication and division. Napier is best known as the inventor of logarithms.

The White Devil

Vittoria Corombona, a notorious Italian murderess, was called "the White Devil." The English dramatist John Webster (1580–1625) put her story on the stage in 1611 with this title. "White devils" was also a contemporary slang term for prostitutes; Webster wrote, "I saw him now going the way of all flesh."

The Dark Lady of the Sonnets

Shakespeare's sonnets 127–154 are dominated by "the Dark Lady," who is for a time the mistress of the fair young man, the poet's dear friend and patron, who dominates sonnets 1–126. The Dark Lady appears momentarily in the first series, stealing the affection of the friend. Several names have been identified with the men in the sonnets (1609), but the Dark Lady has never been identified. She may have been common, no beauty, "yet, by heaven, I think my love as rare / As any she beli'd with false compare." Some Shakespeare scholars say she was a man, in literary disguise.

The Noblest Bay in the Universe

Chesapeake Bay, the largest bay in the United States, with about 6,000 miles of shoreline, has been called "the Noblest Bay in the Universe." The Atlantic arm is the largest inland body of water on the East Coast: 3,237 square miles; the deepest point only 156 feet; 195 miles long; 22 miles at its widest; 3 miles at its narrowest; 48 principal tributaries; a drainage area about the combined area of the six New England states. A modern boatman has written, "No cruising waters in the United States have more to offer the boatman than Chesapeake Bay."

New Holland. Land of Inverted Order. Down Under

Australia was discovered by Dutch mariners in 1606, and in 1664 the Dutch government named the continent "New Holland." In 1770 Captain James Cook made a claim for England, and the Latin name "Australia"—meaning the "southern land"—was adopted in 1817, 29 years after Britain had established a penal colony there. The once popular description "Land of Inverted Order" came about through the strange "inversions" of nature seen in its flora and fauna. A more current nickname for Australia is "Down Under," which may also include New Zealand: down under the equator, at the other end of the world—at least to people in the Northern Hemisphere. There are more people in New York State than there are in all "Down Under," which is almost as large as the continental United States. Australia is the only nation that is a continent.

The Beast with Two Backs

In the tragedy *Othello,* which Shakespeare wrote about 1604, Iago says to Brabantio (I, 1, line 117): "I am one, sir, that comes to tell you your daughter and the Moor are making the beast with two backs"—that is, having face-to-face sexual intercourse. The French version, too, is cited in literary English-speaking circles: *Faire la bête à deux dos.*

The King's Chambers

King James I (1566–1625), claiming most of the waters surrounding Great Britain, cozily called them "the King's Chambers." By 1604, 16 years after defeating the Spanish Armada, England had become the world's leading sea power, and it would continue its reign for centuries. Britannia indeed ruled the waves.

1599–1550

Beautiful Parricide

The name "Beautiful Parricide" was given to Beatrice Cenci (born 1577), a Roman lady of great beauty and high birth, who was beheaded in 1599 for the murder of her father—he had raped her. She protested her innocence to the last. Shelley's powerful drama *The Cenci* is devoted to this subject. The famous *Portrait of Beatrice Cenci* by Guido Reni, in the Barberini Palace in Rome, was said—no doubt wrongly—to have been painted on the night before her execution; the American novelist Nathaniel Hawthorne called it "the very saddest picture ever painted or conceived; it involves an unfathomable depth of sorrow."

The Wooden O

London's circular Globe Theatre, built in 1598, was referred to by Shakespeare and others as "the Wooden O." In *Henry V,* the chorus asks in the prologue, "Can this cockpit hold / The vasty fields of France? Or may we cram / Within this wooden O the very casques / That did affright the air at Agincourt?" The theater burned down in 1613, was rebuilt in 1614, and was destroyed by the entertainment-opposed Puritans in 1644.

The Prince of Music.
Princeps Musicae

The title "Princeps Musicae" was held for several centuries by the Italian composer Giovanni Pierluigi da Palestrina (c. 1524–1594). He was the first who united the art with the science of music, and he set the standard for ecclesiastical composition. His multifaceted work includes about 100 masses.

The White Queen

Mary Stuart, or Mary Queen of Scots (born 1542, beheaded 1587), wore white instead of black mourning when her husband (and cousin), Henry Stewart, Lord Darnley, was murdered. She became "the White Queen" or, to French-speaking Europeans, "la Reine Blanche."

The Admirable Crichton

James Crichton (1560–c.1583), a Scottish adventurer and scholar, reputedly spoke 12 languages and displayed amazing erudition and powers of memory in public disputations. Extravagant praise from the Italian printer and scholar Aldus Manutius (1547–1597) led to the sobriquet "the Admirable Crichton."

The Apollo of Portugal. The Homer of Portugal

Luiz Vaz de Camões, or Camoëns (c.1524–1580), the most celebrated Portuguese poet, author of the epic *Lusiads,* was referred to with the names "Apollo of Portugal" and "Homer of Portugal" in allusion to the charm and stateliness of his verse. *Lusiads* is about the Portuguese navigator Vasco da Gama's historic voyage around Africa to India at the turn of the 15th century. Camões was a soldier in Morocco, India, and China, and he lost an eye in battle; his ship was wrecked in the East, but he managed to save his manuscript of the *Lusiads.*

The Madman

Sebastian (1554–1578), crowned king of Portugal at age three, had the wild desire to emulate the warlike, world-conquering deeds of Alexander the Great 19 centuries earlier. He was slain in battle with the Moors in North Africa at age 24. His people refused to believe the report of his death and declared that he would return and restore Portugal to power and glory.

The Bloody Wedding

The description "Bloody Wedding" is applied to the Catholic wedding of Henry of Navarre (1553–1610)—afterward King Henry IV of France, Henry the Great—and Marguerite of Valois, daughter of King Henry II. The chief Protestant nobles were invited, but on the eve of the wedding—St. Bartholomew, August 24, 1572—Protestants were slaughtered throughout Paris, and the next day throughout the country. The victims, both male and female, were reported to number between 30,000 and 70,000. The butchery—also known as "the St. Bartholomew Massacre"—was ordered by Catherine de Medici, the mother of the bride.

The Cain of America

The epithet "Cain of America" became attached to Nicolas Durand, Chevalier de Villegaignon or Villegagnon (1510–1571), the French vice admiral who was sent to Brazil to found a French colony as a refuge for Protestants. But it included Catholics, quarrels arose, and Villegaignon went to France for reinforcement in 1559; he never returned with the promised help, and the colony was destroyed by the Portuguese eight years later.

The Five Nations

Around 1570, the Mohawk, Oneida, Onondaga, Cayuga, and Seneca Indians formed "the Five Nations"—the "Iroquois Confederacy" or "Iroquois League," which the Tuscarora later joined. About 5,500 Native Americans lived in long houses in New York State, from the Hudson River to the St. Lawrence River, and west to the Genesee River. The confederacy was formed to eliminate incessant intertribal warfare and to end cannibalism.

The First New England

Sir Francis Drake (c.1540–1596) claimed a slice of California for Queen Elizabeth I and dubbed it "New England," in the 1570s. (Decades before the Pilgrims set foot in New England on the East Coast, Spain had explored the southwestern United States.)

The Casket Letters

Did Mary Queen of Scots write the eight letters and the series of poems to James, Earl of Bothwell, that were found in a casket by the Earl of Morton? If she indeed did, she was properly charged by rebelling Scottish lords with complicity with Bothwell in the murder of her husband, Henry, Lord Darnley. The authenticity of "the Casket Letters" (1567) is still a matter of dispute, more than four centuries later.

Mother Shipton

The semilegendary English prophetess Ursula Southiel (1488–c.1559) was said to be the child of Agatha Shipton and the devil, and the author of *Mother Shipton's Prophecies*. In people's minds, her prophecies were so accurate that she was supposed to have predicted the London fire of 1666 and the fate of many members of the royal family. Much of rural England was upset as the year 1881 loomed because that was the year she was supposed to have predicted as marking the end of the world.

Bloody Mary

Mary I, or Mary Tudor (1516–1558), queen of England from 1553 to 1558, earned the name "Bloody Mary" through her sanguinary persecutions of Protestants when she tried to restore the Roman Catholic religion in England. During her five-year reign, nearly 300 people were burned at the stake, and others were punished in different ways. Her persecutions were fully equaled by those inflicted on Catholics by her Protestant successor, Elizabeth (1533–1603).

The Scourge of Princes

The Italian poet and playwright-satirist Pietro Aretino (1492–1556) wrote fearlessly about the high and mighty; he is often called the father of journalism. His pen was so feared that the gifts of those who sought either to buy him or buy him off made him a very rich man. "The Scourge of Princes" was also known as a pornographer, and he is said to have blackmailed Michelangelo for his homosexuality. Aretino was a friend of Titian's, who portrayed him many times. His last words, after receiving the Extreme Unction, were, "Keep the rats away now that I'm all greased up."

The Black Pope

"The Black Pope" is the title conferred upon the head (the "general") of the Society of Jesus (the Jesuits), the largest religious order in the Roman Catholic Church. It may stem partly from the black vestments of the order and partly from the power of the Society, which at various times practically equaled that of the Pope himself. In use to this day, the name was first applied to the founder of the highly disciplined Jesuit order, (Saint) Ignatius of Loyala (1491–1556), originally named Iñigo López de Recalde or Iñigo de Oñez y Loyola.

The Maiden. The Widow

Popular names for a beheading instrument that was introduced into Scotland in the middle of the 16th century and in use until about 1700 were "the Maiden" and "the Widow." Except for details, it was constructed like the device that later became known as the French guillotine. One of its last victims, the Earl of Argyle, quipped near the ultimate moment that "the Maiden" was the sweetest maiden he had ever kissed. (*See also* 1520: Scavenger's Daughter; 1460: The Iron Maiden of Nuremberg; 1447: The Duke of Exeter's Daughter; 550 BC: The Brazen Bull.)

1549–1500

Sigismund Grammar

Sigismund Augustus II (1520–1572), king of Poland from 1548 to his death 24 years later, made Lithuania and the Ukraine part of Poland. He was called "Sigismund Grammar" because he considered his own use of language above any grammatical rule: "Ego sum Imperator Romanorum, et supra grammaticam" (I am emperor of Rome and [therefore] above grammar). (Three centuries later, an American President, Andrew Jackson, would say, in defense of his poor spelling, that he had no respect for anyone who knew only one way to spell a word.)

The Antichrist. The Devil's Sow

The German leader of the Protestant Reformation, Martin Luther (1483–1546), commonly used the terms "the Antichrist" and "the Devil's Sow" to refer to the Pope (any Pope), whom he considered the embodiment of all evil (and no doubt vice versa, from the Pope's perspective). In his *Table Talk*, Luther wrote: "The spirit or soul of the Antichrist is the Pope, his flesh or body is the Turk." The label "Antichrist" also has been variously conferred upon Nero, Muhammad, Napoleon, and others, and it is the title of a book by Nietzsche. Luther's "Devil's Sow" seems to have been reserved for the Pope alone. (The earthy Luther also said, "If I were Christ, and the world had done to me what it has done to Him, I'd kick the beastly thing to pieces!")

The Sea of Cortes. The Vermilion Sea

The Gulf of California is the 700-mile-long arm of the Pacific Ocean separating the Lower (Baja) California peninsula and the Mexican mainland in part of a depression in the Earth's surface that extends inland to the Coachella Valley in southern California. It was once called "the Sea of Cortes," for the Spanish conquistador, and conqueror of Mexico, Hernando Cortes, Marquis del Valle de Oaxaca (1485–1547). It was also called "the Vermilion Sea."

The Maid of Kent. The Holy Maid of Kent. The Nun of Kent

Elizabeth Barton (c.1506–1536) became an influential figure in England through her prophecies concerning political matters, which included a denouncement of the opponents of the Catholic Church. She inveighed in vain against Henry VIII's marriage to Anne Boleyn, and when she did not cease her railing against Henry's decision, he had her beheaded, along with a priest and others, for "treasonable conspiracy." Although she had been clever enough to deceive even Sir Thomas More and Cardinal Wolsey, she said on the scaffold that she was just "a poor wench without learning," who had been led astray by praise and flattery for her prophetic gifts.

The Bug Bible

The Coverdale Bible of 1535 (also the Matthew's Bible of 1561) became known as "the Bug Bible" because Psalms 91:5 says, "Thou shalt not nede to be afrayed for eny bugges by nighte, nor for the arrow that flyeth by day." "Bug" was originally identical with "bogie," or "terror." "Terror" is the term that appears in the Authorized Version.

The New Jerusalem. The Kingdom of Zion

In 1534, the Anabaptist Johann von Leiden (né Jan Bockelson, 1509– 1536) took over the Hanseatic League city of Münster and declared it "the New Jerusalem" or "the Kingdom of Zion." He ruled over an anarchic death cult that is said to make Jonestown seem like a church picnic. After two years, Münster was conquered, and Johann was executed, at age 27. (*See also* 1856: A New Jerusalem.)

The Last of the Incas

Atahualpa (or Atahuallpa, Atabalipa) was born about 1502 and succeeded to the throne as Inca chief of Peru in 1525. Seven years later, his land was invaded by the Spanish conquistador Francisco Pizarro (c.1471–1541), who treacherously made him prisoner when he refused to convert to Christianity and who finally had the trusting Inca strangled, on August 29, 1533. (Atahualpa's offer of a room filled with gold in exchange for his free- dom had not been accepted.) In his *History of the Conquest of Peru* (1847), William Hickling Prescott wrote: "The blood-stained annals of the con- quest afford no such example of cold-hearted and systematic persecution, not of an enemy, but of one whose whole deportment had been that of a friend and benefactor."

The Mohacks Abatoir

In 1526, a Turkish army, led by Sultan Suleiman the Magnificent (c.1494– 1566), slaughtered a poorly equipped, badly organized Hungarian-Bohe- mian force of 28,000 soldiers led by Louis II (1506–1526)—there may not have been a survivor. When confronted with a current catastrophe, it may be said that "more was lost at Mohacks Field."

People with Big Feet

During his historic circumnavigating feat (1519–22), Ferdinand Magellan (c.1480–1521) dubbed the natives at the tip of South America "Patagones"—"people with big feet"—so the land came to be called Pata- gonia. Jorge Luis Borges (1899–1986), the blind Argentine novelist, has said, "There is nothing in Patagonia. It's not the Sahara, but it's as close as you can get to it in Argentina. No, there is nothing in Patagonia."

Scavenger's Daughter. Skeffington's Daughter

An instrument of torture that was invented around 1520 was given these names for its designer, a Sir Leonard (or William) Skeffington (or Skevington), who was lieutenant of the Tower of London under Henry VIII. ("Scavenger" is a distortion of the inventor's name.) The device was a spiked iron frame that compressed the victim's body by bringing the head to the knees, forcing blood out of the nose, the ears, and often the hands. (See also 1550: The Maiden; 1460: The Iron Maiden of Nuremberg; 1447: The Duke of Exeter's Daughter; 550 BC: The Brazen Bull.)

The 95-Theses Myth

Nearly every textbook and every reference work tells us that the German religious reformer and Bible translator Martin Luther (1483–1546) "published" 95 antipapal theses by nailing them on the door of the church at Wittenberg castle, on October 31, 1517. He did no such thing. (He did write the theses, and they were of crucial importance, starting theological arguments that persist to this day, but he merely made them known to a bishop, privately at first.) The church-door scene makes a good story, though, and many an illustration shows the defiant Luther in the act of swinging the hammer.

But truth is truth. Duns Scotus was no "dunce." There was never a "droit du seigneur," a feudal lord's right to deflower the bride of a serf. No "chastity belts" were ever worn; they are a hoax, perpetuated in museums and for the tourist visiting old castles. Columbus did not have to persuade anyone that the world was round; that was well known by his day, only its exact size was in doubt. Prince Grigory Potemkin did not build "Potemkin villages" to deceive Catherine the Great. Washington did not chop down that cherry tree. Betsy Ross had nothing to do with designing the American flag. Abner Doubleday did not invent baseball. There is no proof that Peary ever was at the North Pole. The "Great Wall" in China that is passed off to tourists as the great wall that Ch'in Shih-huang is said to have built more than 2,000 years ago is actually a smaller and more recent wall, only 400 years old, built by the Ming dynasty. But truth never stands in the way of a good story.

The Great Captain

"El Gran Capitán," the Spanish General Hernández Gonzalo de Córdoba (1453–1515), was a soldier all of his life, mainly against the Portuguese, the Moors, and the French. He helped to conquer Granada (1492), ending the Moors' occupation of Spain (setting the stage for the expulsion of the Jews and for Columbus's first voyage to the west), and he was governor of Naples for a time. Ferdinand II named him Duke of Sant-Angelo.

Bluff King Hal. Burly King Harry.
Stout Harry. Defender of the Faith

Many, many names have been applied to the supreme egotist Henry VIII (1491–1547), king of England from 1509 to his death 38 years later. The name he was said to like best was "Bluff King Hal," an allusion to his curt and hearty manner.

The Mountain of the Cold Devils

Africa's highest mountain—Kilimanjaro, in northeast Tanzania—is an extinct volcano rising in two snow-capped peaks. One peak, Kibo, is the highest point on the continent (19,340 feet) and always covered with snow and ice about 200 feet deep. "The Mountain of the Cold Devils" is the shorter peak, Mawenzi (17,564 feet), which doesn't have glaciers. (It has been suggested that the leopard that Ernest Hemingway encountered at the top of Kilimanjaro might have fallen out of a passing airplane.)

La Gioconda

Mona Lisa—*La Gioconda*—the Renaissance-type portrait par excellence, the world's most famous, was probably the portrait of Lisa Gherardini, who at 16 was married to the rich, twice-widowed Florentine merchant Francesco del Giocondo, who had commissioned Leonardo da Vinci (1452–1519) to paint the portrait after Lisa, at 24, had suffered the loss of her only child. Late in the day for three years (until 1506), when the soft light "gives most grace to faces," Lisa sat amid musicians and readers providing melody and poetry and further inspiration. For two years in this century (1911–13), *La Gioconda* lay hidden under a bed in Italy, having been stolen from the Louvre.

The Lake of the Clouds

The world's highest lake, Lake Titicaca, is 12,500 feet above sea level in the Andes, at the Bolivia–Peru border in South America. "The Lake of the Clouds" is 110 miles long and 900 feet deep, covering about 3,200 square miles. (A ferry boat was hauled up the mountains to the lake—piece by piece on the backs of mules—and reassembled at the shore.)

The 15th Century

The White Rose of England

The 15th-century pretender to the English crown, Perkin Warbeck (born about 1474, executed 1499)—"the White Rose of England"—was probably born in Flanders, but he claimed to be Richard, Duke of York, son of Edward IV. After several attempts to seize the English throne, he was captured and put to death. His fate became the subject of a number of plays throughout the centuries, including *King Henry VII, or the Popish Impostor* by Charles Macklin and *The Pretender* by Joseph Elderton.

The Great Bonfire of the Vanities

In the 1490s, the classic works of Ovid, Propertius, Boccaccio, Dante, and others were burned by "the Unarmed Prophet," the "exceptionally ugly" monk Girolamo Savonarola (born 1452, executed 1498) in Florence's "Great Bonfire of the Vanities"—antedating by almost four and a half centuries Hitler's burning of "degenerate" books: the great writers of *our* time.

The Nuremberg Chronicle

The most comprehensive illustrated encyclopedia of the 15th century, *The Nuremberg Chronicle*, was published in 1493, too early to record Columbus's historic discovery the previous year. The three volumes, published by Anton Koberger's press, include about 2,000 woodcuts by Albrecht Dürer's teacher, Michael Wolgemuth (1434–1519), and Wilhelm Pleydenwurff (c.1462–1494). The first edition was in Latin, the second in German. The German title is *Schedelsche Weltchronik*, for the work's lone author, Hartmann Schedel (1440–1514), a Nuremberg physician and historian with a passion for collecting books and manuscripts.

The Columbian Exchange

The interaction of the Old World and the New World in the wake of Columbus's four historic voyages (1492, 1493, 1498, 1502) across the Great Ocean Sea—the way that microbes, plants, and animals moved from one hemisphere to the other and how these "exchanges" affected life on both sides of the Atlantic—is studied as "the Columbian Exchange."

The Admiral of the Great Ocean Sea. The Chosen Person

Cristóbal Colón (1451–1506)—Latin: Christoforus Columbus; Italian: Cristoforo Colombo; English: Christopher Columbus—sailed west across the Atlantic Ocean, "the Great Ocean Sea," to the New World four times. On the 71st day of the first voyage from Spain, in 1492—and 33 days out of the Canaries—land was spotted the day before Columbus would have turned back. The commander of the three-ship fleet believed he had reached some part of Japan ("Cipango") and gave thanks that God had guided him to "the Indies." He named what was a Bahamian island (oddly, we are not absolutely sure which one) San Salvador, meaning "the Holy Savior." The inhabitants, "the color of Canary Islanders, neither black nor white," wore only paint and swam out to offer gifts. "The Admiral of the Great Ocean Sea" promptly made plans to enslave them.

As a lad, Columbus could quote the Jewish prophets and mystics, and his early exercise books (as well as his later letters) displayed a style of writing much influenced by the Old Testament. In his last letters to his son, he used *beit-hay*, the Hebrew symbol "Praised be the Lord," and his will adhered to Jewish traditions in disposing of worldly goods. It has been inferred that when Columbus reached Spain from his birthplace in Italy, he became a *converso*, a convert to Christianity, as were so many Jews in that antisemitic land. In 1492 he postponed setting sail from Palos in Andalusia for a whole day beyond the scheduled embarkation, though he had dreamt of getting underway for a decade: Was it because the original sailing date coincided with Tishah B'ab, the Jewish holy day of fasting and mourning to commemorate the destruction of the First and Second Temples of Jerusalem? As the admiral finally unfurled his sails, he saw on the wharf Jews (non*conversos*) being expelled from Spain.

The Expulsion

Persuaded by the churchman and chief inquisitor Tomás de Torquemada (1420–1498), Spain's monarchs, Isabella I and Ferdinand II, in 1492, expelled Spain's several hundred thousand Jews, many of whom were luminaries in the nation's cultural life. About 100,000 found sanctuary in Portugal but eventually were expelled from there as well. Thousands went to Italy and to North African cities; some trekked as far east as Turkey and Poland.

Morton's Fork

The English prelate and statesman John Morton (1420–1500) was principal counselor to King Henry VII and was made archbishop of Canterbury (1486–1500), lord chancellor, and a cardinal. With "Morton's Fork" (1485), sumptuously attired bishops and monks were taxed with a surcharge because their fine attire attested to their well-being; poorly dressed prelates were taxed with a surcharge because their humble attire attested to prudence and therefore to surplus savings.

Beefeaters

The popular name for the Yeomen of the Guard, organized for his protection by King Henry VII on the day of his coronation in 1485, was "the Beefeaters." The term may stem from their well-fed look. "Beefeaters" is the popular name today for the warders of the Tower of London.

The English Solomon.
The Solomon of England

Henry VII of England (1457–1509, crowned 1485), also called Henry Tudor, became famous for his skill in uniting the rival houses of York and Lancaster and for his peaceful reign, which was favorable to the industrial development of the nation. (*See also* 1625: The English Solomon.)

The Universal Spider

Louis XI of France (1423–1483, crowned 1461) was given the epithet "the Universal Spider" in allusion to his crafty and cruel nature. He spent the last years of his life withdrawn, in constant fear of assassination, and surrounded by quacks and astrologers.

The Bear. The Brave Bear.
The Kingmaker

The Earl of Warwick (Richard Neville, Earl of Salisbury and Earl of Warwick, 1428–1471), English politician and military leader, had a multifaceted career. Near the end of his life, he returned to England from exile, drove Edward IV—whom he had made king 10 years earlier—out of the country, and restored Henry VI to the throne in 1470. Warwick's emblem was a bear and a ragged staff.

The White Devil of Wallachia

The Albanian national hero Scanderbeg, or Skanderbeg (1403–1468), had been sent as a hostage to the Turkish court when he was very young; there he became a Muslim and rose to important administrative positions. In 1444 he returned to Albania, declared himself a Christian, and led his people successfully against the Turks—who henceforth called him, not without respect, "the White Devil of Wallachia." (His name is a shortened form of Iskander Bey, meaning Prince Alexander; the name he was given at birth was George Castrioto.)

The Bastard of Orleans

The honorable title "the Bastard of Orleans" was conferred upon Jean Dunois (1402–1468), who was the natural son of Louis, Duke of Orleans, and a nephew of King Charles VI of France. For his brilliant victories in the Hundred Years' War, he was made by Charles VII a "Prince of the Blood" under the title Count of Orleans. It was he who was in charge of the defense of Orleans when it was relieved, in 1429, by Joan of Arc; he joined her in subsequent campaigns, including the capture of Paris (1436).

The Iron Maiden of Nuremberg. The Iron Virgin

An instrument of torture, introduced around 1460, was a hollow wooden case shaped like a maiden—ergo, "the Iron Maiden of Nuremberg" and "the Iron Virgin." It was studded with sharp iron spikes in the interior and equipped with a hinge between the two halves. The victim was forced in, and the halves were slowly closed, piercing him or her through and through. It was an agonizing and usually lingering death. (*See also* 1550: The Maiden; 1520: Scavenger's Daughter; 1447: The Duke of Exeter's Daughter; 550 BC: The Brazen Bull.)

The Duke of Exeter's Daughter

The people gave the name "the Duke of Exeter's Daughter" to the torture rack in the Tower of London; when it was introduced into England, in 1447, the Duke of Exeter was high constable of the Tower. (*See also* 1550: The Maiden; 1520: Scavenger's Daughter; 1460: The Iron Maiden of Nuremberg; 550 BC: The Brazen Bull.)

The Great Sow

Queen Isabella "of Bavaria" (1371–1435), regent-wife of the demented French King Charles VI, was known to lead a debauched life and consequently entered history as "the Great Sow." In 1420 she signed the Treaty of Troyes, recognizing as heir to the French crown King Henry V instead of her own son Charles, who was exiled but who eventually succeeded as Charles VII.

Forehanded and Backhanded Margot

A female tennis champion in 1427 was "Forehanded and Backhanded Margot," who, according to contemporaries, "played both forehanded and backhanded very powerfully, very cunningly, and very cleverly, as any man could, and there were few men whom she did not beat except the very best players." The reference to forehanded and backhanded shows that she used a racket, evidence that rackets were introduced into the ancient game of tennis at least by 1427.

The 14th Century

The Devil's Picture Book

There are many conflicting stories about the origin of playing cards, but it seems certain that they were manufactured as early as 1392 in France (before 1425 in Italy, before 1463 in England). They were often referred to as "the Devil's Picture Book," a term that became widely used by the Puritans in the 17th century. It is not certain whether the early cards were similar to ours or had features that can still be found in the 22-card tarot decks.

The Morning Star of the Reformation. The Gospel Doctor. The Evangelic Doctor

The English religious reformer John Wycliffe (or Wickliffe or Wyclif or Wiclif, c.1324–1384) was the first major pre-Reformation personality who argued against the doctrines and practices of the Roman Catholic Church.

The Green Count

Amadeus VI, count of Savoy (1334–1383), was the son of Amadeus V, the ancestor of the House of Savoy. During his 40-year reign (from age nine to his death at 49), he acquired large territories in Piedmont and elsewhere, usually fertile land, which earned him the name "the Green Count."

The Prince of Storytellers. The Father of Italian Prose

The Italian poet, storyteller, and humanist Giovanni Boccaccio (1313–1375) has often been referred to by the names "Prince of Storytellers" and "Father of Italian Prose." He is one of the "Triumvirate of Italian Poets," the other two being Dante Alighieri (1265–1321) and Petrarch, or Francesco Petrarca (1304–1374). Boccaccio's *Decameron*, a secular classic, is an assembly of 100 witty and occasionally licentious tales set against the somber background of the Black Death. His satire *Corbaccio* was a vicious attack on the female gender.

The Kensington Stone

In November 1898, Olof Ohman and his son Edward, Swedish immigrant farmers, found a large flat stone under the tap roots of a tree on their farm near Kensington, Minnesota. According to the runic inscription on the stone, it had been left behind in 1362 by a Viking expedition. The stone was long thought to be a forgery, but its authenticity is now considered proven: This part of America—so far inland!—*was* visited by Europeans, 130 years before Columbus. The inscription reads, in close translation: "Eight Goths and 22 Norwegians on [this] discovery-voyage from Vinland over [the] west we had camp by 2 skerries one day's journey north from this stone we were and fish[ed] one day after we came home found 10 men red with blood and dead AV[e] M[aria] preserve from evil have 10 men by the sea to see after our ship[s] 14 day-journeys from this island year 1362."

Buridan's Ass

The French philosopher Jean Buridan (c.1295–1356) declared that the freedom a person possesses is the power to suspend choice and reconsider motives for action. A hypothetical donkey that stands between two identical bundles of hay starves to death through indecision because there are no reasons for choosing one stack or the other. To this day, the dilemma is called "Buridan's Ass," although Buridan merely quoted Aristotle's example.

The Last of the Romans.
The Last of the Tribunes

The Italian patriot and tribune Cola di Rienzi (1313–1354) championed the cause of the people in their struggle against the oppression of the nobles. After overthrowing the aristocracy and reforming the government, he himself became arrogant and alienated the people. He was expelled from Rome. When he returned, he provoked a riot, in which he was killed. Richard Wagner composed an opera in five acts, *Rienzi, the Last of the Tribunes* (1842), which was based on a novel (1835) of the same name by Bulwer-Lytton (Edward George Earle Lytton).

The Black Death

Up to 70 percent of Europe, or about 60 million people, were wiped out by the Black Death in less than 20 years in the 14th century. Plague and smallpox entered the continent through trade with the East. Venice became the first state to pass sanitary regulations for protection against the introduction of "quarantinable" disease.

The Mellifluous Doctor. Oracle of the Church. The Last of the Fathers

There were at least three epithets for St. Bernard (1091–1153), the ecclesiastic whose writings have been called "a river of Paradise." ("Fathers" means church Fathers, that is, the early Christian writers who are considered authorities on the teachings of the church.) He wrote, "You will find something more in woods than in books. Trees and stones will teach you that which you can never learn from masters." And he probably wrote, "Hell is full of good intentions or desires."

The Great Captain

Byzantine Emperor Manuel I Comnenus (c.1120–1180) was "the Great Captain," who tried to reunite the western and eastern empires and to heal the schism between the western and the eastern churches. He ruled from 1143 to his death 37 years later. Comnenus (or Komnenos, the Comneni) was the family name of six Byzantine emperors between 1057 and 1185 and of many statesmen, generals, and authors. The Comnenus emperors revived Hellenism and on the whole were able rulers.

The Conceptualist Reconciler

Pierre (Peter) Abelard (Abaelard, Abailard, Abeilard, or Petrus Abelardus [1079–1142]) was an eminent French logician, philosopher, and theologian. In the fight of the medieval doctrines of nominalism and realism, he was famous for his espousal of a middle doctrine called conceptualism. But he may be best remembered for his star-crossed love affair with his 17-year-old pupil Héloïse. They fled, married secretly, and had a son. Héloïse's powerful uncle had Abelard castrated by hired thugs (1118) and put away in a monastery, and Héloïse was forced to become a nun. Their correspondence, maintained over several decades, is among the most famous love letters of all time. "The name wife may seem more sacred or more binding, but sweeter for me will always be the word mistress, or, if you will permit me, that of concubine or even whore. . . . To her master or, rather, her father, husband or, rather, brother; [from his] handmaid or, rather, his daughter, wife or, rather, sister; to Abelard, [signed] Héloïse."

The 11th Century

The Domesday Book. The Doomsday Book. The King's Book. The Winchester Roll

When William the Conqueror (c.1027–1087) wanted to know how much English land he had, what cattle was in the several counties, and how much revenue he should yearly receive from each, he ordered a survey of nearly all of England. The result, in 1086, was a book of two volumes in vellum: a large folio of 382 pages and a quarto of 450 pages. It was used for many years for taxation and general governmental reference. It became also known as "the King's Book" and "the Winchester Roll." It was called "the Domesday Book" because it was said to assess all people without bias, like the Last Judgment.

Canossa

"Canossa" is a code word for doing the most abject kind of penance or for humiliating oneself abjectly, as in German Chancellor Bismarck's "We shall not go to Canossa" during his controversy with the Roman Catholics around 1875. The expression alludes to the humiliation of the German Emperor Henry IV who, after excommunication by Pope Gregory VII, was forced to do penance by standing for three entire days (January 25–28, 1077) outside Canossa Castle in northern Italy, shivering, bareheaded, and barefoot in the open, until the arrogant pontiff granted him absolution.

The Year of the Conquest

One of history's fateful years was 1066. William (c.1027–1087), Duke of Normandy and bastard son of Robert the Devil, secured the support of the Pope, led an army of 5,000 men across the English Channel, slew King Harold II (born c.1022) in a momentous clash on October 14, established Norman rule of England, and henceforth was known as William the Conqueror.

The Boy Pope

Benedict IX became Pope in 1032 at the age of 10 or 11 and was ousted at the age of 21. Twice thereafter, in 1045 and 1047, he briefly seized the papal throne. He was dissolute, tyrannical, and extravagant during and outside his papacy, but he seems to have repented later. He died in 1056, at the ripe age of 35. (For another very young Pope, *see* 955: The Boy Pope.)

Slayer of Bulgarians. Bulgaroktonos

Basil (Basilius) II (c.958–1015), Byzantine emperor from 976 to his death 49 years later, had waged war against the Bulgarians for several decades, and in 1014, to break their spirit, he blinded nearly 15,000 Bulgarians whom he had taken prisoner. One hundred fifty were blinded in one eye only, so that each of these "lucky" ones could lead a contingent of 100 all-blind men back to Ohrid, the Bulgarian capital, whose ruler, Samuel, suffered a fatal stroke at the sight of these sightless thousands. Basil became known as "Bulgaroktonos," "Slayer of Bulgarians."

The 10th to the 6th Century AD

The Boy Pope

John XII became Pope in 955 AD at the age of 18 and occupied the pontifical chair to his death at age 26, in 964. He greatly influenced the power structure of Europe. He also led a dissolute life. One of his mistresses, named Joan, exercised much authority during his pontificate, and these circumstances may have given rise to the story of "Pope Joan," the imaginary female who is said to have concealed her gender and to have succeeded to the papacy as John VII in 855—a story almost universally believed until the 17th century. (For the better-known juvenile Pope, *see* 1032: The Boy Pope.)

Cathay. The Celestial Empire. The Sleeping Giant

Cathay is the medieval—and now poetic—name for China (937 AD). It is derived from the Khitai, a seminomadic people of southern Manchuria whose rule under the Liao dynasty extended to northern China. The name was popularized by Marco Polo (c.1254–1324) and usually applied only to China north of the Yangtze River (southern China was sometimes called Mangi). In 1842, Tennyson wrote: "Better fifty years of Europe than a cycle of Cathay." Napoleon was among those who saw China as "the Sleeping Giant": "Let China sleep. When she awakes, the world will be sorry."

The Dom-Boc. The Doom-Book

This book of "dooms," or sentences, was a compilation in 890 AD of English laws and customs prepared by authority of Alfred the Great (849–899 AD), king of Wessex from 871 AD to his death 28 years later. It was based on the West Saxon collection of Ina, the Kentish collection of Ethelbert, and the Mercian laws of Offa; it is a combination of the Ten Commandments, the part of the Mosaic law that relates to criminal offenses, parts of the New Testament, the Golden Rule, and ecclesiastic and civil laws. Alfred made few, if any, original laws.

The Abode of Peace

Its many gardens and scholarly retreats justified Baghdad's claim to be the "Abode of Peace." The greatness of the Iraqi capital was reflected in the series of anonymous stories in Arabic, *A Thousand and One Nights* (c.809 AD), a literary classic.

Bell, Book, and Candle

One of the forms of Roman Catholic excommunication, known as "Bell, Book, and Candle," originated in the eighth century. After the excommunication formula is read, the bell is rung, the book is closed, and the candle is extinguished, meaning that the excommunicated is now excluded from the society of the faithful and from divine worship. The closing words of the formula are "Cursed be they from the crown of the head to the sole of the foot. Out be they taken from the book of life, and as this candle is cast from the sight of men, so be their souls cast from the sight of God into the deepest pit of hell. Amen."

The Kaifeng Jews

Five centuries before the Polos set foot in China, Jews from Persia and India had settled in Kaifeng, c.750 AD, at the invitation of Chinese emperors. China's textile industry was suffering from a shortage of silk, and the immigrants were skilled in manufacturing and dyeing cotton fabrics. Kaifeng, northwest of Shanghai, was the eastern capital of China; with as many as a million residents, it may have been the largest city in the world.

Martel. Charles Martel. Karl Martell. The Hammer

Charles (c.689–741 AD), illegitimate son of Pepin of Héristal and grandfather of Charlemagne, is best remembered for his defeat of the Saracens in the pivotal battle of Poitiers and Tours in 732 AD. The name "Martel" may be read as meaning "the hammer," for his pounding the enemy so effectively, but some historians say it is merely the ancient Frank word *Martel*, an abbreviation of Martellus, or Martin.

The Last of the Goths

Roderick (Roderic, Rodrigo), king of the Visigoths in Spain, was slain by the Moors under Tarik in 711 AD. He was the 34th, and last, of the Visigothic line of kings, who reigned in Spain from 414 to Roderick's death. The story of "the Last of the Goths" has been retold by several English-language writers, including Robert Southey, Washington Irving, and Walter Savage Landor.

The Keys of Knowledge

In the Koran (635 AD)—the world's most important book besides the Bible—"the Keys to Knowledge" are five things known to God alone. They are (1) the time of the day of judgment, (2) the time of rain, (3) the sex of an animal before it is born, (4) what will happen tomorrow, and (5) the place where any person will die.

The White Prince

The Byzantine General Belisarius (c.505–565)—called "the White Prince" in many languages—was probably the greatest soldier of the Eastern Roman Empire. He excelled especially in the war against the Vandals in North Africa in 534. (His name, Belisarius, comes from the term *Beli-tzar*, Slavonic for "white prince.")

The 5th to the 1st Century AD

Scourge of God. Terror of the World

Short, swarthy, broad-chested, and snub-nosed, Attila (c.406–453) led the Huns out of Asia on their ponies. They rode roughshod through the lower Volga Valley and over the Ostrogoths, the Visigoths, and the Eastern Roman Empire, vandalizing, brutalizing, sodomizing, ravaging, looting, plundering, pillaging, savaging, slaughtering. "The Scourge of God" set up his palace in Hungary and received in tribute the territories that now constitute much of Poland, Germany, and European Russia. ("Attila" means "daddy" in Gothic baby talk.)

The Dark Ages

The Middle Ages (5th–15th centuries) used to be referred to as "the Dark Ages," but historians have found out that there was much more learning, more sensual enjoyment, more humanity, more "light" than had been thought. If the term is still used, it is now generally reserved for the first four medieval centuries, from the fall of the Roman empire to Charlemagne.

The City in Two Continents

Istanbul—Constantinople to 1930, Byzantium before 330 AD—is the only city in the world that is situated in two continents: Europe and Asia. It sits on both sides of the Bosporus at its entrance into the Sea of Marmara. The northwest Turkish city has been linked since 1973 by the Bosporus Bridge, a 3,524-foot suspension bridge.

The Emperor-Philosopher.
The Philosopher

Marcus Aurelius Antoninus, or Marcus Annius Verus (121–180 AD), was both a Stoic philosopher and, for the last 19 of his 59 years, the emperor of Rome: "the Emperor-Philosopher" or, to many historians, just "the Philosopher," because of his wisdom, learning, and virtue. His main, Greek-written book, *The Meditations of Marcus Antoninus*, is one of the finest works in the history of philosophy. "Think of the totality of all Being, and what a mite of it is yours; think of all Time, and the brief fleeting instant of it that is allotted to yourself; think of Destiny, and how puny a part of it you are." "The universe is change; our life is what our thoughts make of it." "Don't be careless in your deeds, or confused in your words, or rambling in your thoughts." "The one who lives the longest and the one who lives the shortest, when it comes to dying lose one and the same thing." "See how fleeting and trifling is the condition of humans; yesterday an embryo, to-morrow a mummy or ashes. So for the tiny sliver of time that you are given, live rationally, and depart from life cheerfully, the way the ripe olive falls, praising the season that brought it forth and the tree that nurtured it." Marcus Aurelius lived what he taught.

The Son of a Star

The leader of the Jewish insurrection of 132–135 AD against the Romans, Bar Cocheba, claimed to be the "star" predicted by Balaam (Numbers 24:17), and many did believe him to be the Messiah. He was proclaimed king; he held out against Emperor Hadrian (76–138 AD) for two years but was overthrown amid the slaughter of more than half a million of his people and the destruction of 985 villages and 50 fortresses in Palestine. He himself was killed near Caesarea in 135 AD. (Other spellings of his name include Bar Cochba, Barcochabas, Bar Kokba, and Bar Coziba; he was also called Simon.)

Loaded Ship

The old Roman expression "loaded ship" refers to the practice of having sexual intercourse during pregnancy, especially between a wife and her lover to avoid an unwanted pregnancy. The phrase became notorious when Caligula's sister Agrippina (c.15–59 AD) bragged that, despite her uncountable lovers, all of her children were her three husbands' "because only as a loaded ship do I carry passengers." (With her first husband, the tribune Domitius Ahenobarbus, she was the mother of the future Emperor Nero. Her third husband was Emperor Claudius, her uncle. She poisoned him, in 54 AD, and she herself was killed, five years later, by Nero.)

Amor

Rome has also been known as "Amor"—"Roma" spelled backward. The pun—perhaps from the first century AD—is on anal intercourse, which enjoyed great popularity in ancient Rome.

The Messalina Complex

"The Messalina complex," in psychology, is an approximate synonym of nymphomania, named for the Roman Empress Valeria Messalina, who was well known for her indiscriminate sexual appetite. She was the third wife of Claudius. After she had caused the death of many persons who tried to cross her, she herself was executed, in 48 AD, by order of the emperor.

The Augustan Age

The 41 years of the reign of Emperor Augustus (Gaius Octavius, Caius Julius Caesar Octavianus, born 63 BC), from 27 BC to his death in 14 AD, stand out for their splendid achievements in arms and arts, and especially in literature: Horace, Virgil, Ovid, Livy, Lucretius, Sallust, Catullus. Of his achievements in architecture, Augustus said he had found a city of bricks and would leave it a city of marble.

The 1st to the 3rd Century BC

The Most Learned of Romans

An honorary title was conferred upon Marcus Terentius Varro (116–27 BC), the eminent Roman author, "the Most Learned of Romans." His practically universal erudition is said to have been reflected in the 490 books he wrote, few of which have survived.

The Veni Vidi Vici Battle

The forces of Julius Caesar (100–44 BC) fought those of Pharnaces, king of Pontus and son of Mithridates, in the battle at Zela, in northern Asia Minor, in 47 BC. The battle was desperate, but the Romans prevailed, and Caesar penned perhaps (according to Plutarch) the most laconic military dispatch of all time: He supposedly announced his victory to the Roman senate with the words *Veni, vidi, vici*—"I came, I saw, I conquered."

Our Sea.
The Sea Between the Lands

The chief existing fragment of the Tethys Sea, which once girdled the Eastern Hemisphere, is the world's largest sea—"Our Sea" (*Mare Nostrum*), as the Romans called it: the Mediterranean. It is approximately 2,500 miles long and averages about 500 miles in width, "the Sea Between the Lands," a cradle of Western civilization.

Caesar's Wife

To indicate that a person in an official position, and his or her immediate family and associates, must avoid even the impression of wrongdoing, one may invoke "Caesar's wife," in allusion to an incident in 62 BC: Julius Caesar (100–44 BC) divorced his second wife, Pompeia, when she seemed to be involved in a scandal concerning the violation of the secret rites of Bona Dea, the ancient fertility goddess worshipped only by women; he said that "Caesar's wife must be above suspicion."

Caledonia

The conquering Romans gave the name Caledonia to the part of Britain north of the firths of Clyde and Forth. Today, Caledonia is Scotland, or the

Scottish Highlands. The name first occurred in the works of Lucan, in the first century, about the time that a Roman general named Agricola marched against the Caledonians, or Picts. The natives were seen as little more than savages, naked, wild, their bows and arrows and small shields finally bowing before the metal-clad invaders; when night fell after one battle, 10,000 Caledonians lay dead on the field.

The Prince of Grammarians.
Grammaticorum Princeps

Apollonius, son of Mnesitheus (Dyscolus), who lived in the second century BC, in Alexandria, wrote some 20 books on Greek grammar, the most important works on the subject of all time, but little is known about his life, except that he once made a brief visit to Rome. The scholarship of "the Prince of Grammarians" was essential to all later Latin and Greek grammarians.

The Last of the Greeks

Philopœmen (c.252 BC–183 BC), as commander in chief of the Achaen League, tried to smooth out the domestic troubles in Greece and so protect his country against the aggressions of Rome. He did not succeed, largely because of his countrymen's indecisiveness. Within 50 years after his death, Greece became a Roman province, under the name of Achaia. Philopœmen has gone down in history as "the Last of the Greeks."

The Illustrious. Epiphanes

Ptolemy V (c.210 BC–181 BC) became king of Egypt in 205 BC, at age five, and remained on the throne until his death 24 years later. The Rosetta Stone commemorates his reaching maturity in 196 BC. He is known in history as "the Illustrious" or by a Greek name with the same meaning, "Epiphanes."

The 4th Century BC

Ultima Thule

"Ultima Thule" was the name the Greeks, and then others, gave to the northernmost region of the world. It was said to be an island discovered by the Greek navigator and astronomer Pytheas (fourth century BC), some of whose works survive: the source of our earliest firsthand information on northwestern Europe. What Pytheas discovered has variously been identified as Iceland, Norway, and the Shetland Islands. The phrase "Ultima Thule" is used figuratively to denote the most distant goal of human endeavor or a land remote beyond all reckoning. "Thule" (no doubt with the "Ultima" implied) is the name of an Eskimo settlement with a population of 1,000 and a US air base, on the northwest coast of Greenland.

The First Westerners

Greeks earned (retroactively) the title of "the First Westerners" by breaking with the traditional and intellectual systems of the ancient Near East. Their achievements in science, art, philosophy, mathematics, and other forms of knowledge were unprecedented in the world.

The Stagirite.
The Pope of Philosophy

Aristotle (384–322 BC), student of Plato and teacher of Alexander the Great, divided philosophy into physics, logic, ethics, and metaphysics, including psychology under physics. His "categories," that is, classes or genera of thought and being, are (1) substance, (2) quantity, (3) quality, (4) relation, (5) action, (6) passion, (7) the where, (8) the when, (9) position in space, and (10) possession. No other system of philosophy has exercised such a vast influence over the minds of humans, for over 2,000 years. After it had gone into decline with the fall of the Roman Empire, it was revived through the works of Arab and Jewish scholars of the Middle Ages. The appellation "the Pope of Philosophy" refers to the almost despotic influence that his philosophy had for a long time on the thought of Europe. He is "the Stagirite" because he was born in Stagira in Thrace, north of Greece. Alexander Pope wrote (in *The Temple of Fame*, 1715): "There, in a shrine, that cast a dazzling light, / Sat, fixed in thought, the mighty Stagirite."

The Prince of Orators.
The Demosthenes Complex

The reputation of Demosthenes (384–322 BC) as the greatest of Greek orators stems mainly from about 10 major "orations," in which he argued for or against social and political causes and leaders. According to tradition, he became an orator because he stammered; putting pebbles in his mouth, he forced himself to speak slowly and clearly. His style in oratory was simple, pithy, and effective. As a result of political vicissitudes, he ended his life by taking poison to avoid capture by Antipater (c.398–319 BC), the regent of Macedonia. (In psychology, a "Demosthenes complex" is a form of neurotic behavior that is marked by an impulse to overcome feelings of inferiority through the use of the spoken word.)

The Dog. The Diogenes Syndrome

The Greek philosopher Diogenes of Sinope (c.412–323 BC) was called *Kyon*, "Dog," on account of what was considered his "shamelessness," that is, his primitivist philosophy: Happiness means "living according to nature," satisfying our simplest "natural" wants in the simplest manner. His disciples were called the "cynics," the "doglike," and his philosophy became known as "cynicism" (a word that is used in a different sense today).

Diogenes was an eccentric. He lived in a tub or barrel, almost nude. When Alexander the Great came to pay him homage and asked him whether there was anything he could do for him, "the Dog" replied, "Yes, there is. Don't stand between me and the Sun." To condemn contemporary corruption, Diogenes would walk through the streets with a lighted lamp in broad daylight, in search—as he would tell anyone who asked him—of "an honest person." Alexander the Great, despite that snub, admired him so much that he said, "If I were not Alexander, I would wish to be Diogenes." (In psychology, the "Diogenes syndrome" is the neglect of one's home or personal environment sometimes found among the elderly. Also called "senile neglect," it is often accompanied by the irrational accumulation of otherwise insignificant objects, such as old magazines or rags.)

Macedonia's Madman. The Son of Jupiter Ammon

Widely different appellations reflect the negative ("Macedonia's Madman") and positive ("the Son of Jupiter Ammon") opinions of Alexander the Great, king of Macedonia, who was born in 356 BC and died of a fever in 323 BC, at the age of 33, after conquering much of the then-known world. One of the most powerful personalities of antiquity, Alexander (meaning the "helper and defender of humankind") influenced the spread of Hellenism and stimulated major changes in the history of the world.

God of All Philosophers. Deus Philosophorum. Prince of Philosophers. The Athenean Bee. The Bee-Mouthed. Plato

The Greek sage Aristocles (c.427–347 BC) was first called "Prince of Philosophers" and "God of All Philosophers" by Marcus Tullius Cicero (106–43 BC); in his lifetime, he was nicknamed "the Athenean Bee" or "the Bee-Mouthed" because it was said that a swarm of bees alighted on his mouth while he was asleep as an infant, foretelling that sweet words of wisdom would flow from his lips. The nickname that is best remembered, however, is "Plato," from the Greek word *platus*, meaning "broad," for his broad shoulders. Aristocles, or Plato, who was the student of Socrates and the teacher of Aristotle, wrote mainly "Dialogues," including *Phaedrus, Symposium, Timaeus, Apology, Parmenides, Republic, Gorgias,* and the *Laws,* in which he dealt with nearly every philosophical problem that would occupy humankind in the subsequent 23 centuries. He was the founder of "Platonism."

At the height of his fame, he was once captured at sea and offered for sale in the slave market at Aegina, Greece; a former student purchased him and, of course (of course?), set him free. Yet, in Plato's concept of the ideal society, he would keep slaves—and expel poets. He can sound timeless, though: "What is happening to our young people? They disrespect their elders, they disobey their parents. They ignore the laws. They riot in the streets, inflamed with wild notions. Their morals are decaying. What is to become of them?" He also wrote: "An unexamined life is not worth living." "We can easily forgive a child who is afraid of the dark; the real tragedy of life is when adults are afraid of the light." "The time to say good-bye has come, and we each go our way—I to die, you to live. Only the gods know which is better."

The Laughing Philosopher.
The Abderite

The Greek philosopher Democritus was born at Abdera, in Thrace, about 460 BC, and died about 357 BC. For many years, he expounded the fifth-century Greek philosopher Leucippus's atomistic theory: All is atoms, even our souls, even the gods. Democritus is said to have put out his eyes so that he would be less distracted by outward matters in his thinking. He was of cheerful disposition, laughing at the follies of his contemporaries. (*See also* 475 BC: The Weeping Philosopher.)

The Think-Horses Axiom

Medical students in Greece were exhorted to think horses, not zebras, when they heard hoofbeats. In other words, they should consider the simple solution first.

The Father of Medicine

The Greek physician Hippocrates (c.460–c.377 BC) founded the foremost school of medicine in antiquity and is said to have written more than 80 books. He tried to separate the study of physical and mental illnesses from religious mysticism, centuries before others did. For example, he did not think that epilepsy was "the divine illness." He believed that "healing is a matter of time, but it is sometimes also a matter of opportunity." The Hippocratic Oath (symbolically perpetuated to this day) begins with the words, "I swear by Apollo Physician, by Asclepius, by Health, by Panacea, and by all the gods and goddesses, making them my witnesses."

The 5th and 6th Centuries BC

The Father of Comedy

Mixing political, social, and literary satire, the Athenian poet Aristophanes (c.448–388 BC) was the greatest of the ancient writers of comedy. Eleven of his plays survive, including *The Clouds*, a satire on the sophists and on Socrates; *The Wasps*, a satire on the Athenian passion for litigation; *The Birds*, an escape into an imaginary kingdom; and *Lysistrata*, in which Athenian women boycott their husbands sexually to end a war. He observed that "under every stone lurks a politician." Some joke.

The Wisest Man in Greece

Others professed knowledge without realizing their ignorance. "The Wisest Man in Greece," Socrates (469–399 BC), said he at least was aware of his own ignorance. The Socratic method, the dialectic, tends to expose ignorance by showing that many things people assume to be true are false. Socrates lived by his principles and died by them. Clear knowledge of the truth, he said, "is essential for the conduct of life. Action equals knowledge." "Rulers should be men who know how to rule, not necessarily those who have been elected."

The Father of Greek Prose. The Father of History. The Father of Lies

The Greek historian Herodotus (c.484–c.424 BC) was given the name "the Father of History" by Cicero, and he was, in a way, "the Father of Greek Prose," but he also deserves a less flattering epithet that historians bestowed on him: "the Father of Lies." Herodotus turned out to be a rich but unreliable source; nearly all of his statements have to be taken with a grain of salt.

The Father of Tragedy

Aeschylus (524–456 BC), whose resolve was not to seem but to be the best, was the first of the three great writers of Greek tragedy; the others were Sophocles (c.496–406 BC) and Euripides (fifth century BC). He is not only credited with the invention of tragedy, but he made it an artistic and intellectual creation. Aeschylus composed perhaps 90 plays; seven survive in full, including *The Seven against Thebes* (467 BC). His poetry is also among the greatest ever written. "Destiny waits alike for the free man as well as for him enslaved by another's might." "God's mouth knows not how to speak falsehood, but he brings to pass every word."

The Final Solution

Mass extermination of Jews was not an original program with Germany's Third Reich. In the Old Testament book of Esther, about 475 BC, Haman proposed a "final solution" to Persia's King Ahasuerus. Esther 3:5-6: "And when Haman saw that Mordecai bowed not, nor did him reverence, then was Haman full of wrath. And he thought scorn to lay hands on Mordecai alone: for they had shewed him the people of Mordecai: wherefore Haman sought to destroy all the Jews that were throughout the whole kingdom of Ahasuerus, even the people of Mordecai."

The Weeping Philosopher. The Dark Philosopher

The Greek philosopher Heraclitus (c.535–c.475 BC) was born and died in Ephesus, Asia Minor. As one of the earliest metaphysical Greek thinkers, he taught that everything is relative and nothing absolute, that we are, and everything else in the world is, constantly changing, and that virtue consists in becoming part of this whole by denying one's individuality. Because of both the profundity of his thought and his misanthropy, he became known as "the Weeping Philosopher," also "the Dark Philosopher." (*See also* 357 BC: The Laughing Philosopher.)

The Philosopher of China

Confucius (c.551–478 BC) urged a philosophical system that would preserve peace and afford the Chinese people the stable, just government that he said they required, but he was never able to introduce his reforms. Confucianism is a moral and religious system of ethical precepts for the proper management of society. It envisages humans as essentially social creatures who are bound to their fellow humans by sympathy or human-heartedness: "Hold faithfulness and sincerity as first principles." "Good government obtains when those who are near are made happy, and those who are far off are attracted." "Without knowing the force of words, it is impossible to know humans."

The Buddha

The epithet "the Buddha," meaning "the Enlightened One," was given the Indian Prince Siddhartha Gautama (c.563–c.483 BC), the founder of Buddhism. He taught that life is suffering and that the way to end suffering is through enlightenment, leading to disappearance in the All, or "nirvana." The self is central yet must be given up as an illusion—a self that does not want to suffer but also does not want to love; a self that wholly respects others so as not to add to the total suffering in the world; a self that does not want to act and is ready to forgo what non-Buddhists see as the joy of struggling and creating; a self that wants peace and stillness and the absence of wishing. The true Buddhist is virtuous and compassionate from within , that is, without believing in a Supreme Being or a hereafter where he or she would be rewarded or punished.

The Brazen Bull

An instrument of torture that was devised by Perillus, in Athens, for the tyrant Phalaris in Sicily, around 550 BC, became known as "the Brazen Bull." The victims were placed in the interior, and a fire, burning underneath, roasted them to death. The inventor is said to have been the first to meet this fate—which Phalaris, after a revolt, eventually shared himself. (*See also* 1550: The Maiden; 1520: Scavenger's Daughter; 1460: The Iron Maiden of Nuremburg; 1447: The Duke of Exeter's Daughter.)

Solon's Happiness

The phrase "Solon's Happiness" came to mean death, in allusion to Solon's maxim, "Count no man happy till he is dead." The great Athenian statesman and lawgiver lived from about 639 to about 559 BC.

The Oldest Datable Event

When, in 585 BC, the armies of Lydia (on the west coast of Asia Minor) and Media (in the Iranian highland) were preparing for battle, in Asia Minor, a solar eclipse occurred. It sobered the two nations and made them settle their differences with a peace treaty instead of the sword. Astronomers in modern times have been able to fix the date of that eclipse at May 28, 585 BC—making it "the Oldest Datable Event" in human history.

Before the 6th Century BC

The Philosophers' Stone. The Elixir. The Grand Magistry

Alchemy sought to transform base metals (lead, for example) into gold and silver. The *lapis philosophorum*, "the Philosophers' Stone"—at times also called "the Elixir" and "the Grand Magistry"—was an imaginary substance thought to be capable both of transmuting the less noble metals and of restoring youth to the aged. Chemistry got its start in alchemy, which became popular in the seventh century BC.

A.U.C.

According to tradition, Rome was founded on April 21, 753 BC, by its first king, Romulus. (Romulus and his twin brother, Remus, were said to be sons of the god Mars; when they were abandoned at birth, they survived by being suckled by a female wolf. Romulus later was worshipped as a god under the name Quirinus.) Years were counted "A.U.C.," *ab urbe condita*, "from the founding of Rome"; a specific year could also be referred to as "A.U.C.," *anno urbis conditae*, "in the year [. . .] from the founding of Rome." This book, for example, was published A.U.C. 2743 (that is, 1990 AD).

The Draconian Code

The Athenian legislator Draco (seventh century BC) codified the laws of Athens, replacing individual revenge with public justice. The death penalty was prescribed for several crimes, and debtors could be claimed as slaves. The severity of the code gave rise to the word "draconian."

Boustrophedon

Boustrophedon is a Greek word that means literally "turning like oxen in plowing." It designates a system of writing, used in Greek, Hittite, and other ancient languages, in which the lines go alternately from left to right and from right to left, like the course of the plow in successive furrows. After many centuries of being used by scholars only, the term suddenly gained new currency with the invention of the high-speed boustrophedon computer printer, which works precisely in this manner. (David P. Stern, in *Science*: "Strange new words I relish / Like nectar or tonic. / I now know my line printer / Is boustrophedonic.")

The Cadmean Letters

In the old Greek alphabet, 16 letters were called "the Cadmean letters" because, according to mythology, they originated with Cadmus, king of Tyre, when he brought writing to Greece—that is, the "Phoenician," or North, Semitic alphabet. These letters are α, β, γ, δ, ε, ι, κ, λ, μ, ν, ο, π, ρ, σ, τ, and υ. The additional eight letters—ζ, η, θ, ξ, φ, χ, ψ, ω—were called Ionic letters.

The Pillars of Hercules

In mythology, the eastern entrance to the Strait of Gibraltar was flanked by "the Pillars of Hercules"—the Rock of Gibraltar in Europe and Mount Acha at Ceuta in Africa. The Jebel Musa, west of Ceuta, was probably a Pillar as well.

Hammurabi's Code

Hammurabi (or Khammurabi), king of the first dynasty at Babylon in the 18th century BC and founder of the Babylonian empire, reigned for more than 50 years, great in war and peace alike. (He is often identified with the biblical Amraphel.) Foremost among his creations is the most remarkable of ancient sets of law, known as Hammurabi's Code. The code is carved on a diorite (igneous-rock) column, in 3,600 lines of cuneiform characters. It was found at Susa in 1901, and is now in Paris. The laws are generally humanitarian, but they include the principle of retributive punishment, the *lex taliones*, which follows "an eye for an eye" literally. Hammurabi's Code is of immense importance as a historical document.

The Shepherd Kings

According to the Egyptian historian Manetho (c.250 BC), invaders from the East conquered Egypt without a battle about 2214 BC, destroying the temples and slaying or enslaving the people, and making one of their number king. The Egyptians called these intruders the "Hyksos," or "Shepherd Kings." They ruled for about 511 years, forming the 15th, 16th, and 17th dynasties. Among the rulers was Apophis, who some think raised the biblical Joseph to great power.

Ussher's Creation

According to Dr. James Ussher's calculation of 1654 AD, the year in which God created the world was 4004 BC. (*See also* 1654: Ussher's Notation.)

Ussher's is the only "precise" dating of the *beginning*. The *end* has been set "precisely" many dozens of times, from the exact year to the exact day, to the exact moment. They all came and went: the end of the fifth century, as predicted by early prophets of evil; January 1, 1000, when Christ was supposed to reappear and people committed suicide in large numbers; the year 1533, predicted by the German astronomer Stoeffler; the years 1654 and 1679, when Europeans again held their breath; March 14, 1844, expected by the American religious fanatic William Miller (1781–1849) and his "Millerites" or "Millerians" (who, *mirabile dictu*, were millenerians, or millenerists); the year 1881, "Mother Shipton"'s prediction; January 1, 1900, a worldwide frenzy; October 1908, according to the York, Pennsylvania, grocer Lee T. Spangler; and many other dates before and after and in between. (*See also* 1559: Mother Shipton.)

The Cradle of Civilization

Mesopotamia, literally "between rivers"—namely, the Tigris and the Euphrates—had land-cultivating settlements as early as 5000 BC and soon thereafter had city-states such as Erech and Ur. Its first empire, Arcad, emerged about 2340 BC, followed by Babylonia and Assyria. Mesopotamia (Aram Naharaim in Hebrew) became "the Cradle of Civilization" or, more soberly put, the cradle of Western civilization.

GRS

GRS stands for the Great Red Spot in the southern hemisphere of the largest planet of the solar system, Jupiter, whose volume is more than 1,300 times greater than Earth's. The GRS is about 30,000 miles long and about 10,000 miles wide; six Earths could be tucked into it. The Spot may be a prodigious storm system.

The Goldilocks Paradox

The planets Earth, Venus, and Mars were formed at the same time from the same cosmic dust. Venus has become too hot for life: Lead would melt there at noon. Mars has become too cold for life: Polar bears would freeze there at midnight. Only Earth is "just right"—usually. Space scientists (in the 1990s) refer to this as "the Goldilocks Paradox," in reference to the nursery tale of Goldilocks and the three bears, whose respective porridge Goldilocks found too cold, too hot, and just right.

Earth. Moon. Sun. Space. Time.

The Great Mother. Magna Mater. Cybele. A Meadow in the Sky. A Blue Marble. The Third Planet. The Green Planet. Terra. Spaceship Earth

The third planet from the Sun is a meadow in the sky, a blue marble. "One generation passeth away, and another generation cometh: but the Earth abideth for ever."

That Big Chunk of Green Cheese

The Moon weighs 81,000,000,000,000,000,000 tons and is Earth's only natural satellite. In the racial memory, the Moon is bad news, and the lunatic is simply a fellow who happens to remember better. Five hundred million years ago, the Moon summoned life out of its home, the sea, and led it onto the empty land: "The fortune of us that are but moon's men doth ebb and flow like the sea."

The Big Furnace

"Finally, we shall place the Sun himself at the center of the Universe. All this is suggested by the systematic procession of events and the harmony of the whole Universe, if only we face the facts, as they say, 'with both eyes open.'" At the center of the Sun, the temperature is between 10 million and 20 million degrees centigrade. The pressure there, about 700 million tons per square inch, is enough to smash atoms, expose the inner nuclei, and allow them to smash into one another, interact, and produce the radiation that gives off light and warmth. It takes about 8 minutes, 20 seconds for sunlight to reach Earth.

The Big Void

Father Time

Subtle thief of youth, a maniac scattering dust, the mercy of eternity, a bloody tyrant, a lovely gift, the soul of the world, a winged chariot, that aged nurse, the fourth dimension, an illusion perpetrated by the manufacturers of space, a mental device to give order to events by identifying them as coexisting or successive, the great conundrum—time—Father Time—the music of our being.

Index

This index lists verbal shortcuts and related terms. Where a term appears on more than one page, the more important references often are listed first, separated from the others by a semicolon.